Fleet Street
exposures

Published in 2021 by ArtCircus Books
an imprint of YouCaxton Publications

ISBN 978-1-914424-16-8

www.stephenmarkeson.com

FLEET STREET EXPOSURES

DIARY OF A PHOTOJOURNALIST

BY

STEPHEN MARKESON

ARTCIRCUS
BOOKS

FOREWORD

The career of a Fleet Street photographer can be made or stalled in an instant…the millisecond it takes for the camera shutter to capture an iconic image that speaks a thousand words or just yet another frame destined to be discarded on the darkroom floor.

A Fleet Street reporter's job is to find out what's happened and then build a picture for readers by quoting eye witnesses, giving colourful description and detail…answering the questions who? what? where? why? when? and how?

The photographer has either got '*the picture*'…or they haven't.

As this wonderful diary shows Stephen Markeson demonstrates both areas of expertise and has produced an elegant, fascinating and surprising record of his career in pictures.

The great 20th century American photographer, Ansel Adams, once said 'There are always two people in every picture: the photographer and the viewer.'

I think he meant that, like beauty, many images may only find their greatness in the eye of the beholder. I suspect that while many of the images in this impressive book will move, intrigue, fascinate, amuse and startle, many will also remain with most of us…as often as we choose to dip into the world of such an accomplished photojournalist.

Stephen allows the photographs to speak for themselves but brilliantly lets us in on some of the circumstances, opportunities and fortune that framed the story behind the story.

For most of my Fleet Street life, pictures could only be printed in black and white and there is something more compelling, artistic and engaging in monochrome. And boy did this book bring back memories.

Charles Wilson
Editor of The Times 1985-1990

Stephen Markeson FRPS

Fellow of the Royal Photographic Society: Visual Journalism
Fellow of the Royal Photographic Society: Portraiture

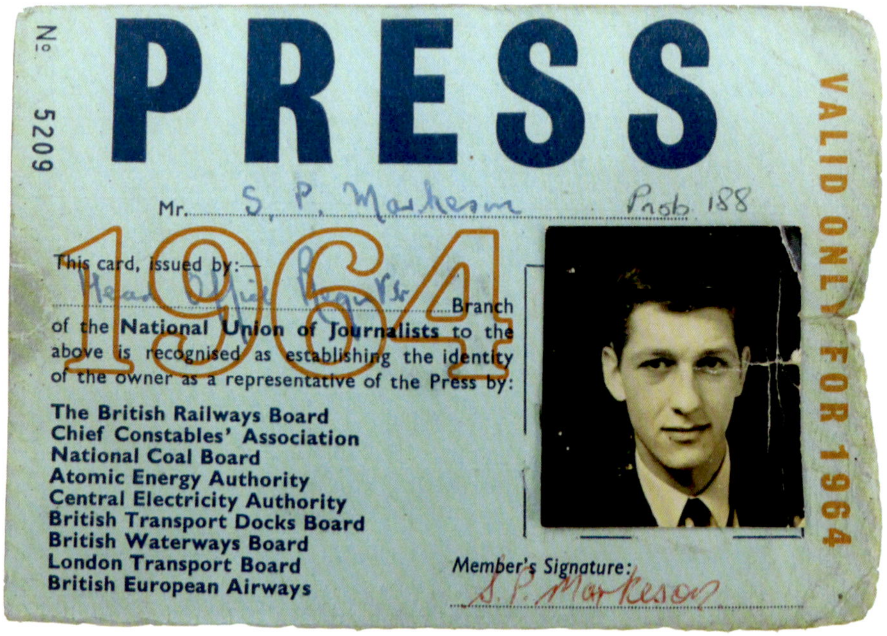

INTRODUCTION

FLEET STREET

The words 'Fleet Street' are still synonymous with newpapers - even though much of that industry moved out in the 1980s after Rupert Murdoch's News International, owner of *The Times* and *The Sun*, set up premises in Wapping.

The history of printing in Fleet Street goes back more than 500 years to when the first presses were introduced into London by William Caxton. After Caxton's death, his apprentice, Wynkyn de Worde set up a printing shop in Fleet Street at the 'Sign of the Sun' at the heart of Tudor London. The printing industry flourished here and became the centre for printers, booksellers and writers.

Two hundred years later in 1702, the first daily newspaper, *The Daily Courant*, was printed and by 1735, there were 31 newspapers being produced from Fleet Street with a total circualtion of around 100,000 copies when the population of London was only 650,000. The demand for news was insatiable and the estimated readership at that time was 250,000 including the papers that were read in bars and cafes. Foreign visitors to London were astonished by the extent to which even the illiterate Londoners were so well informed about the news.

At this time, newspapers had the freedom to criticise the government and the church and it's not surprising that they started to split along party lines. Fleet Street was on the main road from the City of London to Westminster and the bars, cafes and brothels along the street made a perfect environment for journalists to collect information and gossip.

By the 1930s, Fleet Street was lined with the headquarters buildings of all of the major newspapers including the huge art-deco *Telegraph* and *Express* buildings and still retains some of the oldest pubs in London.

HOW IT ALL STARTED

Determination, tenacity and a lot of luck all played a part on my route into photojournalism. The learning curve was steep and I served my time with local papers and agencies before progressing to some of the most widely read newspapers in the country, starting from the lowly position of messenger to that of Senior Staff Photojournalist for *The Times*, one of the most respected newspapers in the world.

I was never very clever at school although I did win the school prize for French. My father had his heart set on me becoming an architect, but I left school at fifteen with only one ambition. I've no idea what inspired me, but I wanted to be a photographer. In hindsight I can see that architecture had no appeal for me as it would be years before anything that I designed would be realized, but photography appealed both to the creative side of my nature and the impetuosity of youth. Art with instant results - what could be more perfect?

I had been saving up cash from birthdays, pocket money and a paper round and had about £100.00 (almost £2,500 today). It was just enough to buy a second-hand Rolleiflex - my first camera, which I still have today.

So I had the camera but little idea of how to use it. My hard-pressed parents encouraged me to look for a job. Time passed and I knew that I was a financial drain on them. Dad tried to persuade me to get a 'temporary' job in a mens' outfitter on the High Street. I was horrified at the thought!

It must have been towards the end of 1959, I hadn't quite reached 16 when, out of the blue, my mother said to me: 'Come on, I think I've found a job for you'. 'What on earth do you mean?' I asked. Unbeknownst to me, she had contacted *The Times* newspaper. In those days it was owned by Lord Astor and sited in Printing House Square in Blackfriars, London. I was spruced up and Mum took me to the newspaper. She had arranged an interview for me to be a messenger. I was less than enthusiastic, but I knew how important it was for me to earn some money to help ease the strain on the household budget. Time for me to swallow my pride.

I got the job. I think my first wage was about £1.00 a week, but it helped. My duties as a messenger required me to take post to the different departments. It wasn't long before I made friends with the photography department, grandly called the 'Art Department'. I wasn't supposed to spend time chatting, my job was just to deliver the post. But my passion to become a photographer was burning inside me and I spent every minute

I could asking questions. I was always in trouble with the head messenger for taking so long to do my rounds.
The picture editor was Norman Jeffries, a really very nice man. He could see how keen I was and let me spend as long as I liked in his department. Eventually I was transferred to be the 'art department messenger', huge progress and a step in the right direction. One day, when I proudly showed him my camera, he gave me my very first 'assignment'. You can have no idea how thrilled I was. He explained that *The Times* building was gradually being demolished, and that it was important to have a record in the library. He asked me to photograph the demolition progress. My very first pictures for *The Times*!
Next came a 'house' job. Michael Roffey, who worked in the art library, was getting married. The department had a whip round to buy him a present of some saucepans and I was asked to take pictures of him with his pots and pans for the house magazine. Bingo! My first publication.
In 1960, my parents decided to sell their London flat, which led to another turning point in my life. One evening a couple came to view the property. I was listening to the conversation they were having with my parents, when I heard the man say that he was a photographer... well my heart skipped a beat and I butted in straight away 'That's what I want to be!'
He chatted to me for a bit after my parents had successfully negotiated to sell him the flat and he offered me a job as his assistant. Of course, I had no idea who he was. His name was Dezo Hoffman, and he turned out to be one of the countries leading show business photographers. Wow, what luck! My enthusiastic interjection had earned me an incredible opportunity, working with many of the celebrities of the day. And so began my professional life behind the camera. I handed my notice in at *The Times*, where I will be eternally grateful to Norman Jeffries the art editor who had been so encouraging. Little was I to know then what my future would be back with that newspaper.

Cutting My Teeth

Dezo had a studio in Soho, where we photographed rising stars of the music industry for their album covers including the Beatles, the Rolling Stones, Cliff Richard and Adam Faith. In addition, I was given the opportunity to cover stories and concerts for the *Record Mirror*, including many occasions

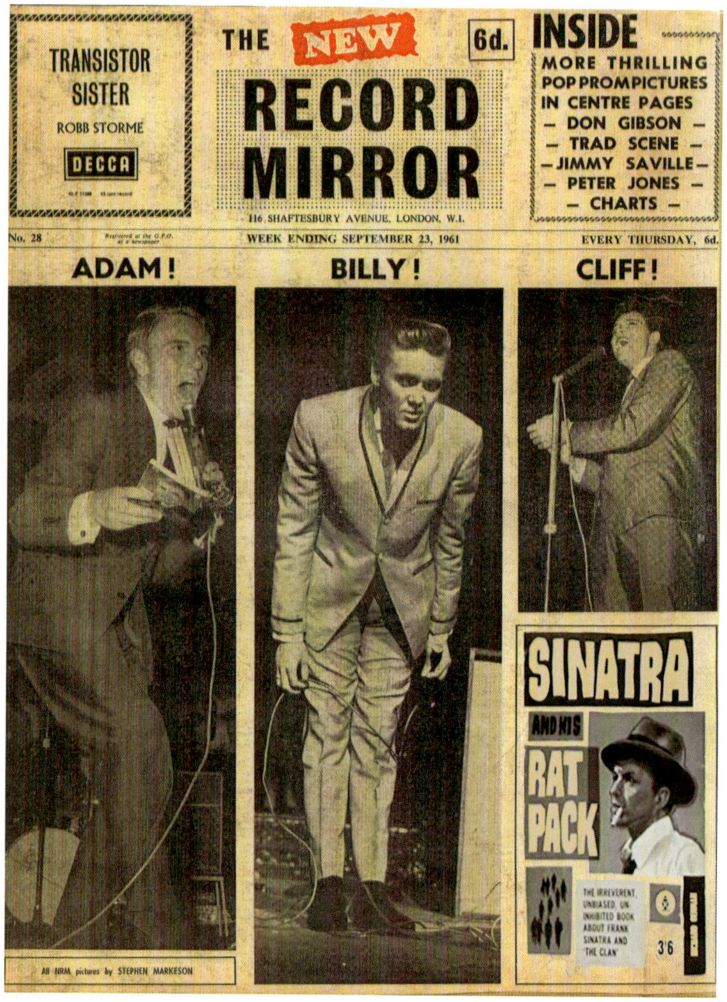

when I was sent to the EMI studios in Abbey Road where the Beatles and other big names were recording. Dezo not only had contracts with all major record companies but also undertook freelance work. I was learning a lot from Dezo and would sometimes stand in for him and this is where I really started to cut my teeth. I remember a very emotional visit to a school for blind children in North London where we were shooting a brochure. A totally blind three-year old girl asked if she could feel my face to 'see' what I looked like. As she ran her fingers over my face, I could feel my tears welling up. I'm still overcome by the same emotion whenever I think about it.
Another time, I was sent to a club in Wardour Street in Soho to get some pictures for the Swedish newspaper *Expressen* who believed that a Swedish au pair had been abducted into the 'White Slave Trade'. She was last seen at that club.
I climbed up the steep stairs and found myself in a strip club

1964, Harold Wilson on the campaign trail

(That's me standing third from left with my camera)

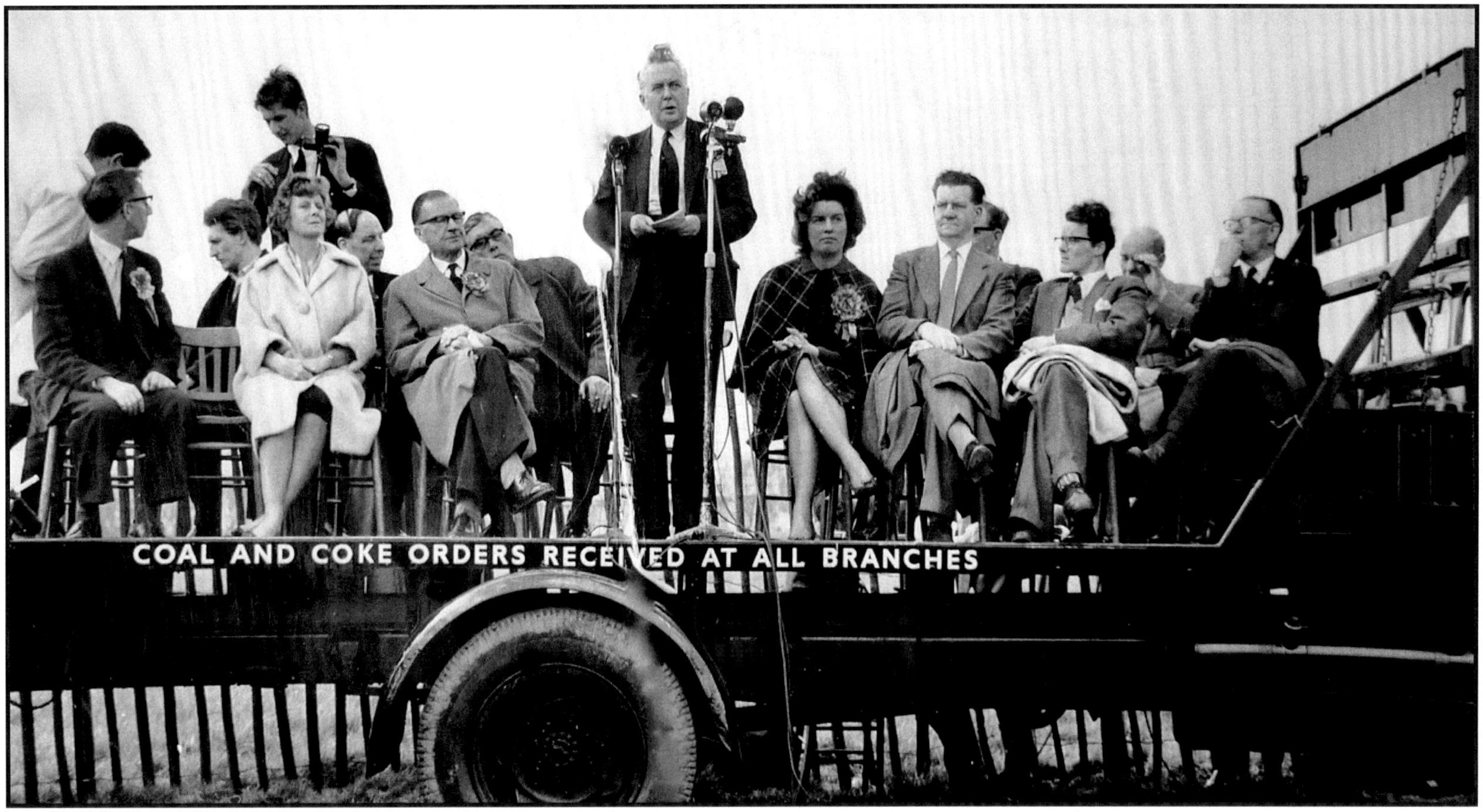

with beds around the room leaving nothing to the imagination. I bought a drink and waited for a suitable moment to take pictures with my camera which was hidden under my coat. I was using infra-red film and flash which wouldn't be visible. I left as quietly as I could. But I'd been seen and was followed down the stairs by a swarthy looking man who produced a flick-knife and chased me through the alleyways until I managed to get back into the studio and bolted myself inside where I stayed until Dezo arrived in the morning.

Expressen ran my picture and story 'Centre of the White Slave Trade in Soho'. The picture would never have been allowed in an English paper!

There were still big gaps in my technical knowledge and Dezo kindly sent me on a day release course at the London College of Printing & Graphic Arts. Part of the course was a module on the history of printing which included learning about Ancient Egyptian hieroglyphics and the Rosetta Stone.

Even though I had little interest in that part of the course, I did very well in the exams and later that morning I was called to the principal's office where he told me that I was the first student ever to write a perfect paper and that he had contacted both Oxford and Cambridge about my success, and that both had agreed to meet me. The principal was more excited than me. I told him that I wasn't at all interested in the idea of going to university and just wanted to be a photographer.

I was fortunate to have worked in Fleet Street during the glory days when daily papers were at the forefront of breaking news, with seemingly limitless budgets. My career path in national

daily newspapers started with the now defunct *Daily Herald*, a left wing paper renowned for its picture content.
At my interview with the picture editor Len Hickman, my work seemed to impress him but I was too young to be a member of the NUJ (National Union of Journalists). He was very keen to employ me and asked for a meeting with the FOC (Father of Chapel) - a term for the trade union representative in the office. The FOC was told all about me and how the management wanted me to work for the paper. He was being asked if there was any way this could happen. Newspapers were heavily controlled by the trade unions and as the *Herald* was part owned by the TUC, the rules were normally strictly adhered to.
An Extraordinary General Meeting of the Central London Branch of the NUJ had to be called and a deal of pressure was applied by the picture editor, and indeed the editor. It was put to the vote and agreed that I would be given a union card when I reached twenty - a year before it was normally allowed. Meanwhile, I was still only nineteen, but again a special dispensation was given for me to work and I was the youngest photographer ever to work in Fleet Street. Next came the broadsheet *Sun* (owned by IPC, publishers of the *Daily Mirror*), which was sold to Rupert Murdoch's News International in 1969 and converted to the familiar tabloid.
I then transferred within News International to *The Times*.
The need to get photographs swiftly back to the paper in time to meet deadlines involved solutions that would be unimaginable today. Sometimes a despatch rider was used, or the film might be put on a train to London via a parcel system called the 'Red Star' service, being collected by a messenger at the other end. On foreign assignments I was accompanied by a darkroom technician who had a specialist black-out tent and a mini-enlarger, plus dishes and chemicals to process my film on location. Another member of the team was the 'wire man'. He would strap the photograph produced by the printer onto a transmitter and using a special telephone line, would send the image to a picture receiver at the newspaper where the transmitted information was projected onto a sheet of photographic paper in a light-proof capsule. This would be taken to the darkroom to be developed.
Nowadays, of course, things are very different. It is now possible to take a high resolution picture on a mobile phone and transmit it anywhere in the world in an instant. How times have changed!
In 1990 I submitted two portfolios of my work to The Royal Photographic Society and was honoured to be awarded Fellowships in both Visual Journalism and Portraiture. A number of those images feature in this book, as do others taken from the various Fleet Street publications that I worked for. Some are accompanied by stories or, hopefully amusing, anecdotes and some are included just because I like them!

Stephen Markeson FRPS

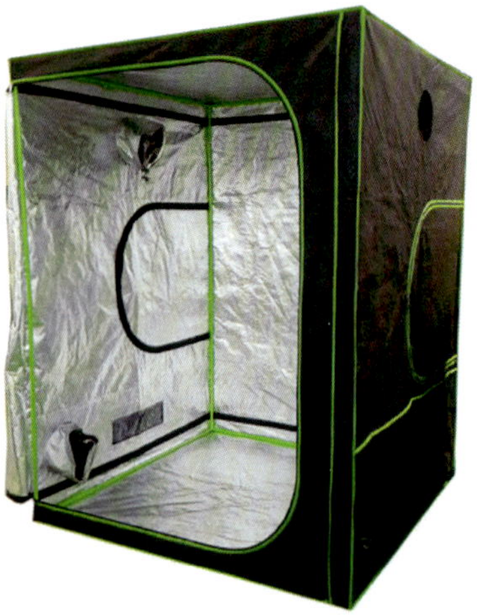

Black-out tent - Portable darkroom

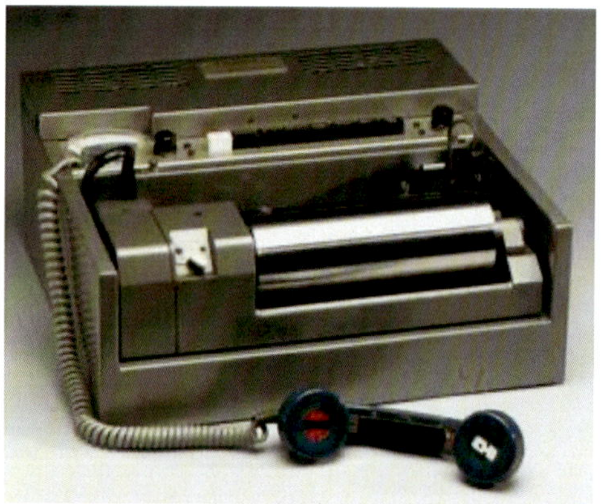

Muirhead 'Wire Machine'
to transmit photographs from
anywhere in the world

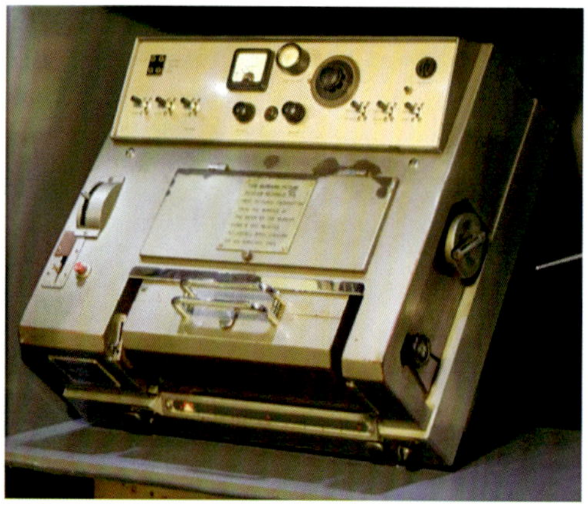

Wire Picture receiver
in London Office

1966, Photo-call at the finals of Miss World

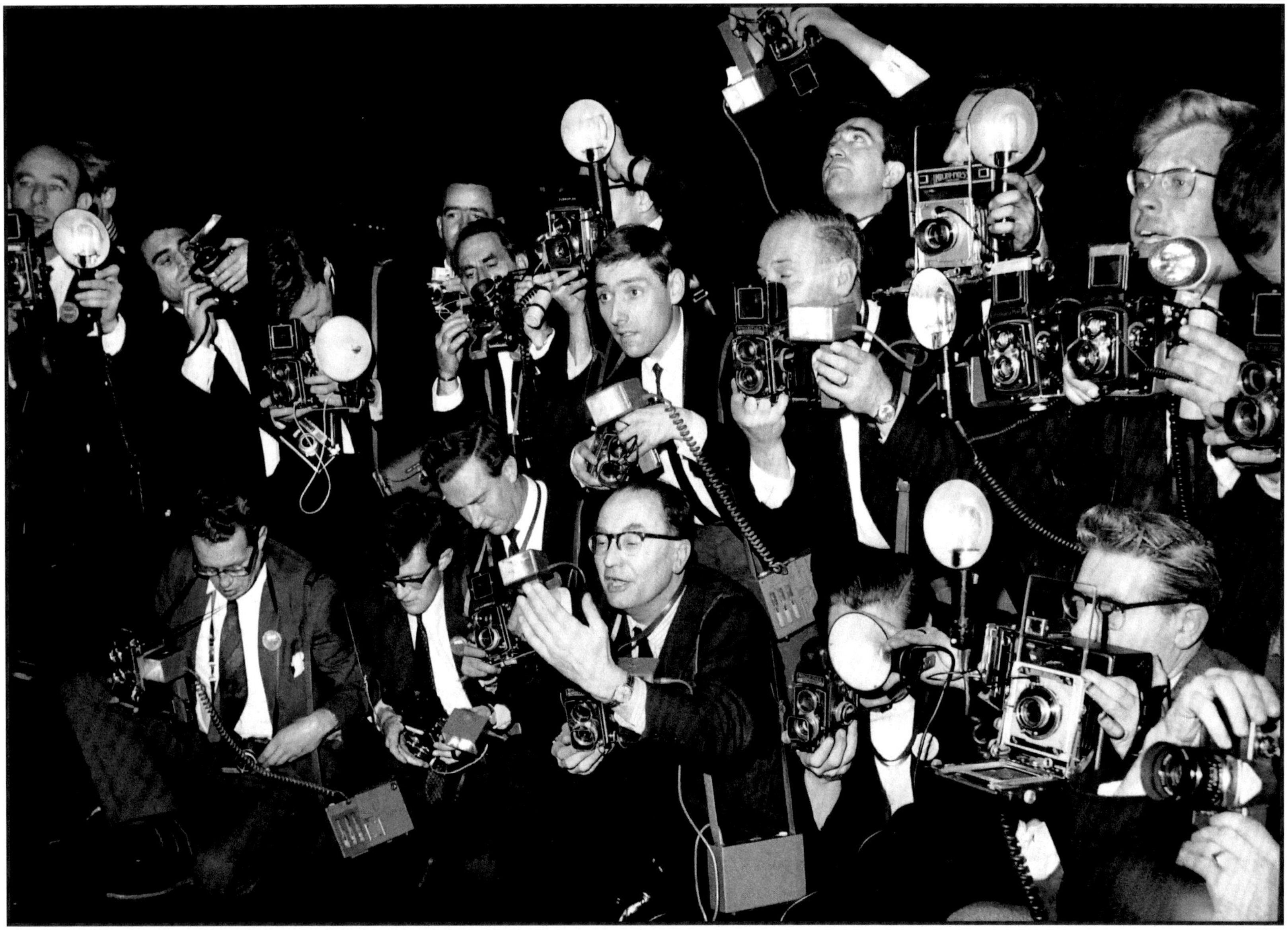

Newspapers and picture agencies trade elbows at the Miss World Finals held at the Lyceum Ballroom in London. Digital technology had not yet arrived and this picture illustrates the variety of film cameras, some 6cms x 6cms, some 35mm and even 5inch x 4inch plate cameras, all with large flashguns, that were the order of the day.

Today, all of that cumbersome equipment has been replaced by high resolution digital cameras including mobile phones that fit in your shirt pocket, which produce superb results.

(You can spot me, back row, third from the left)

Contents

Part 1
Lifestyle

The 60s and 70s were exciting times with new and more relaxed boundaries. Creative fashion designers, flower power and hippies added to the picture opportunities, followed by the groundbreaking introduction of the Page Three Girls in the 1980s.

1.
Policeman with a Pram
1964, Kings Road

One morning, driving from my flat in Chelsea to Fleet Street, I saw the most extraordinary thing. A policeman in uniform pushing a little girl in a pram. Once in the office, I called the local police station. It transpired that, thinking that she had been abandoned, the over-zealous constable was taking her to his police station. A short while after, a hysterical mother arrived screaming that someone had kidnapped her child. She had just popped in to a friend's house for a minute!
Red faced police all round...

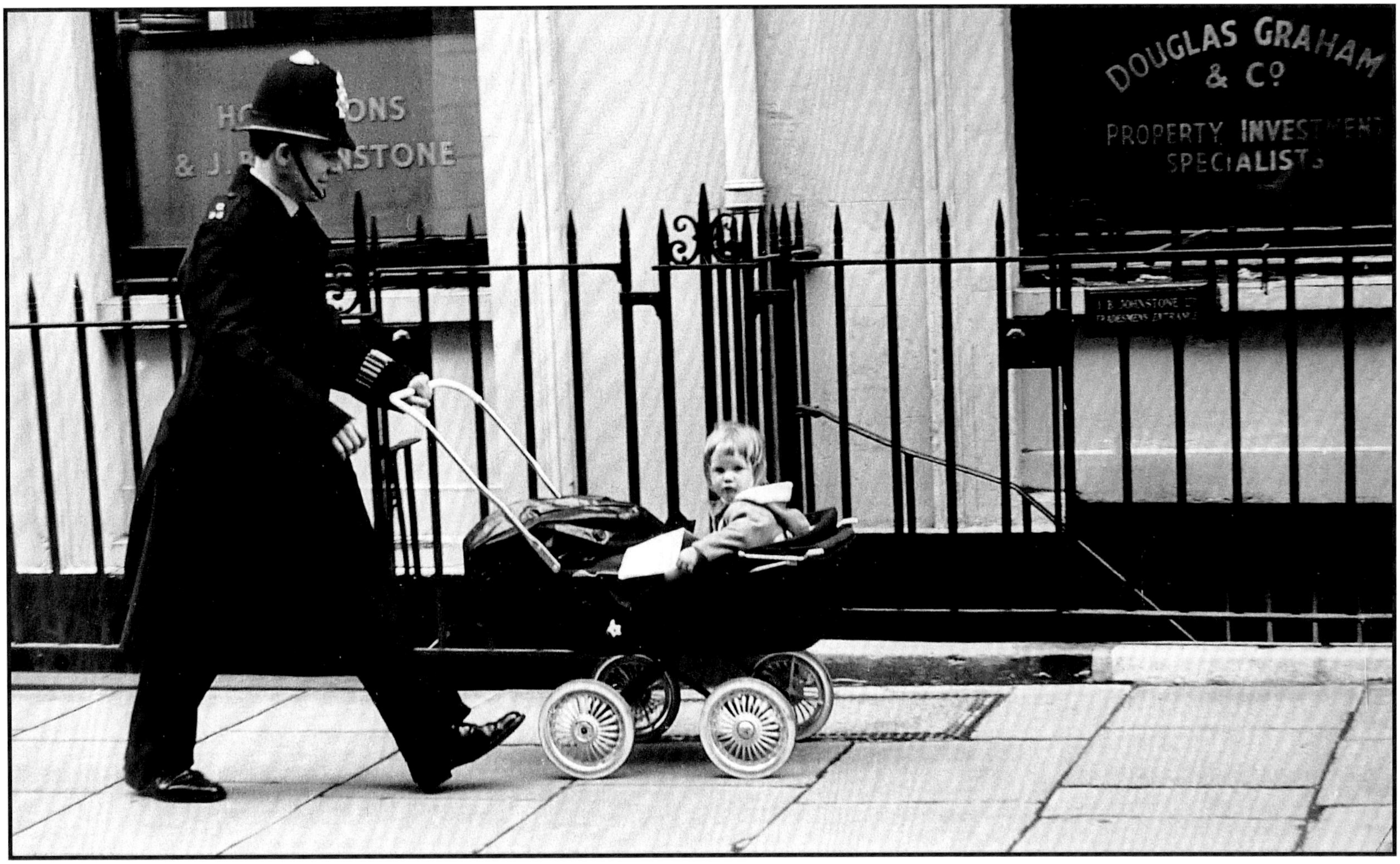
DOUGLAS GRAHAM
& Co
PROPERTY
SPECIALISTS

2.

Policeman Dancing

1966, Notting Hill

In terms of good community relations, this picture represents a great P.R. moment. I took lots of pictures of carnival floats and excited people in extravagant costumes, but my picture of a policeman joining in the fun was the real winner.

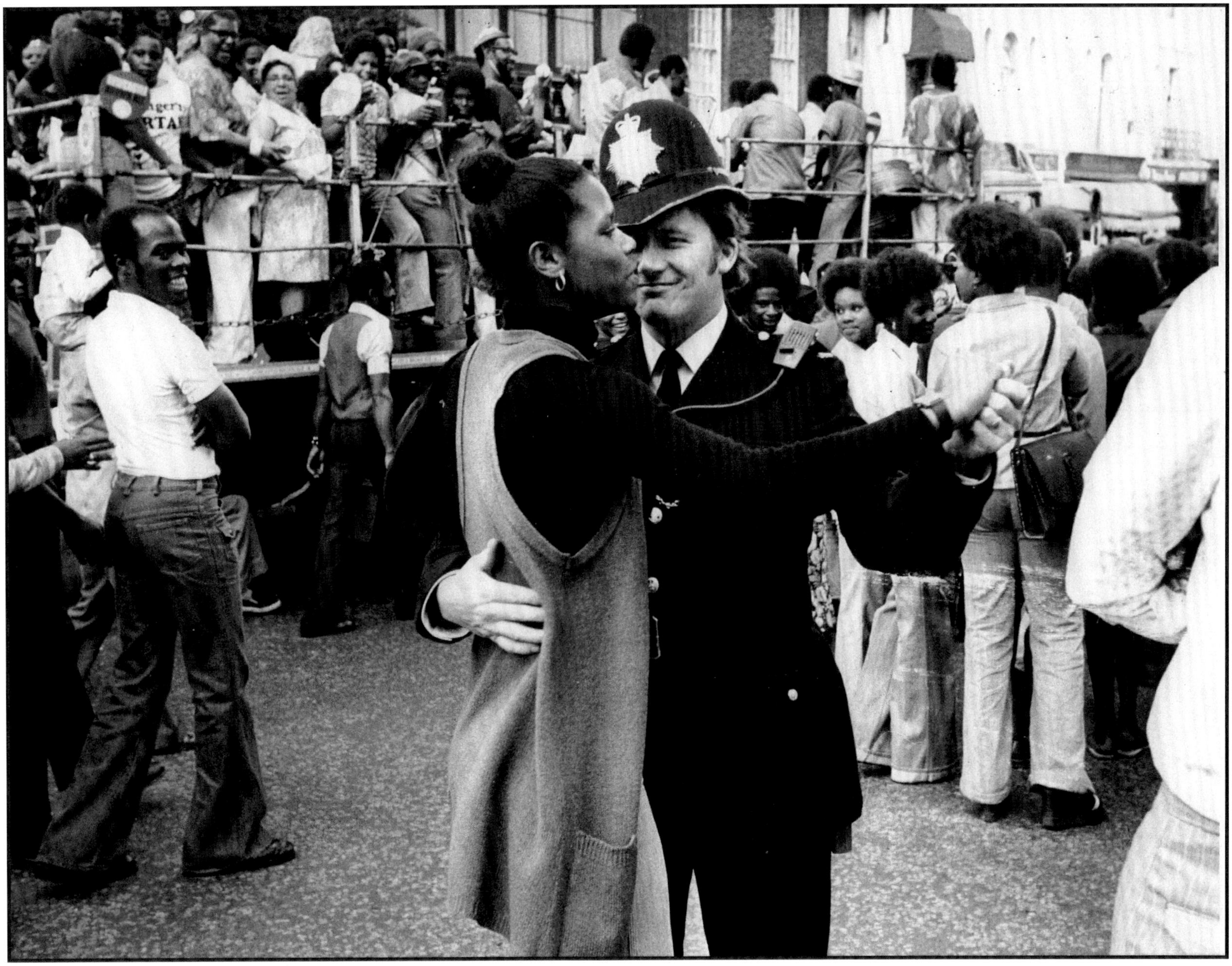

3.

Fashion & Bikers

1966, Chelsea Bridge

French fashion designer, Yves St.Laurent, launched a collection inspired by motor cycle jackets, so I took this model to the 'bikers' rendezvous on Chelsea Bridge.
They joined in the fashion shoot with enthusiasm!

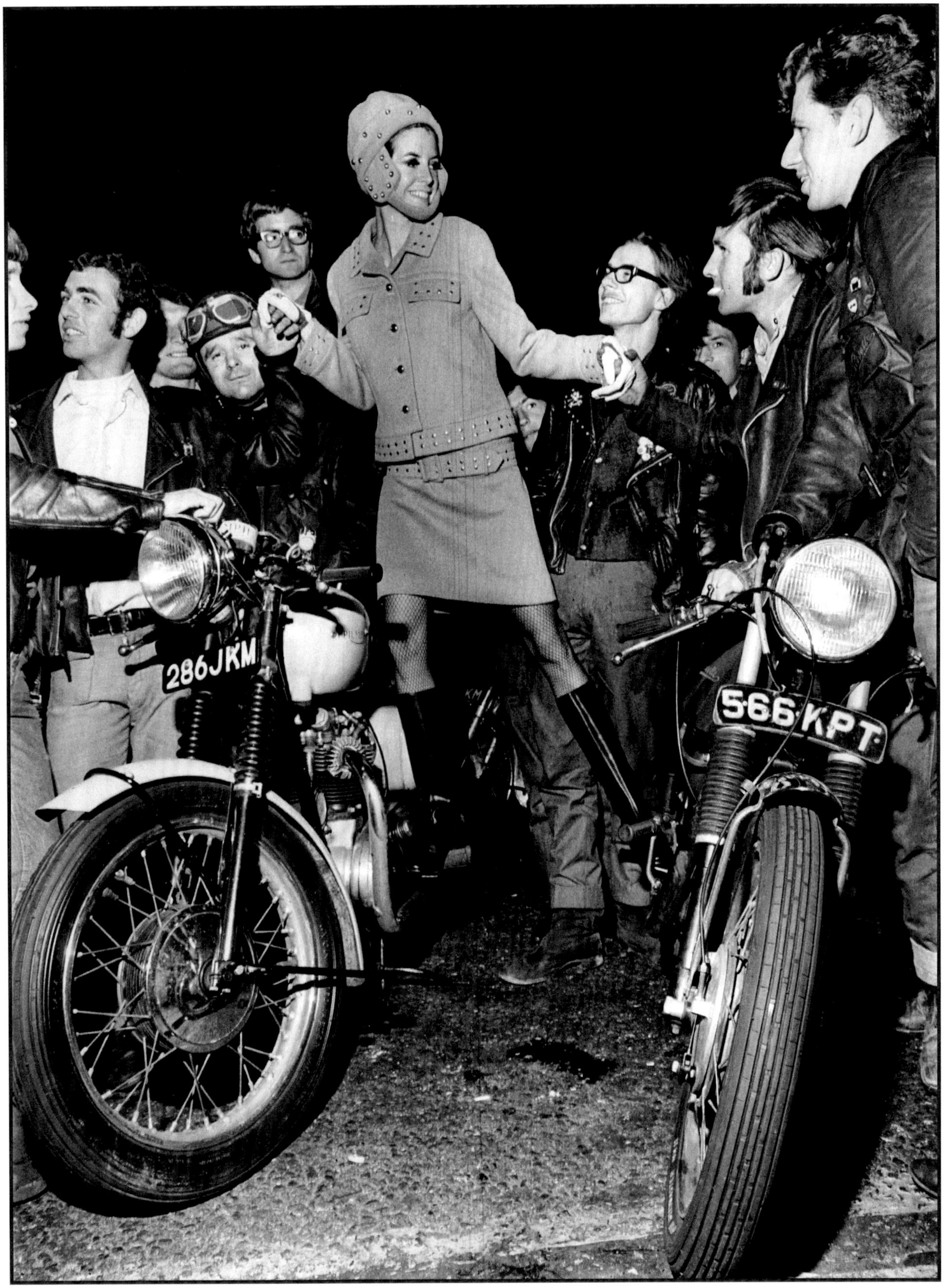
286JKM
566 KPT

4.

Policeman & Rose

1967, Flower Power at the Chelsea Flower Show

If I worked for Gardeners World then covering the annual Chelsea Flower Show would be easy. However, a national daily newspaper has a much wider audience and it was necessary to 'think outside the box'. Fortunately, this wonderful policeman was happy to help!

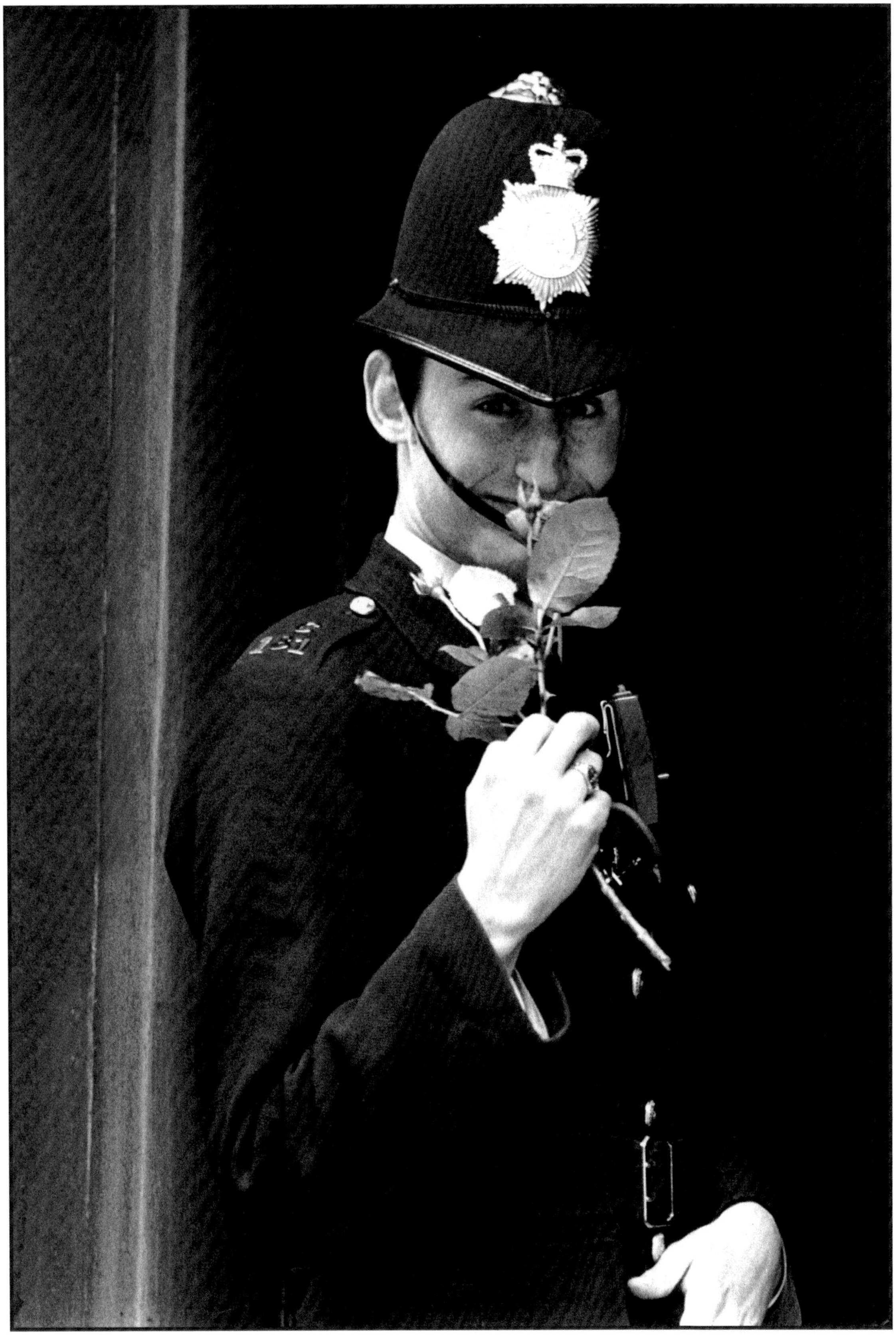

5.

Susannah York

1967, World's End

Actress Susannah York in World's End, Chelsea where she lived in the mid-60s.

She campaigned endlessly to save the area from development and I was briefed to photograph her as the paper wanted to publicise her efforts. We arranged to meet in a cafe near to where she lived, so that I could get to know her and discuss our picture session. A straightforward portrait would not attract the reader's attention as much as a more dynamic shot. Susannah and I chatted for ages and she was more than happy to help create this carefree image to highlight her campaign.

Her appearances in films of the 1960s, including *Tom Jones* (1963) and *They Shoot Horses, Don't They?* (1969), formed the basis of her international reputation.

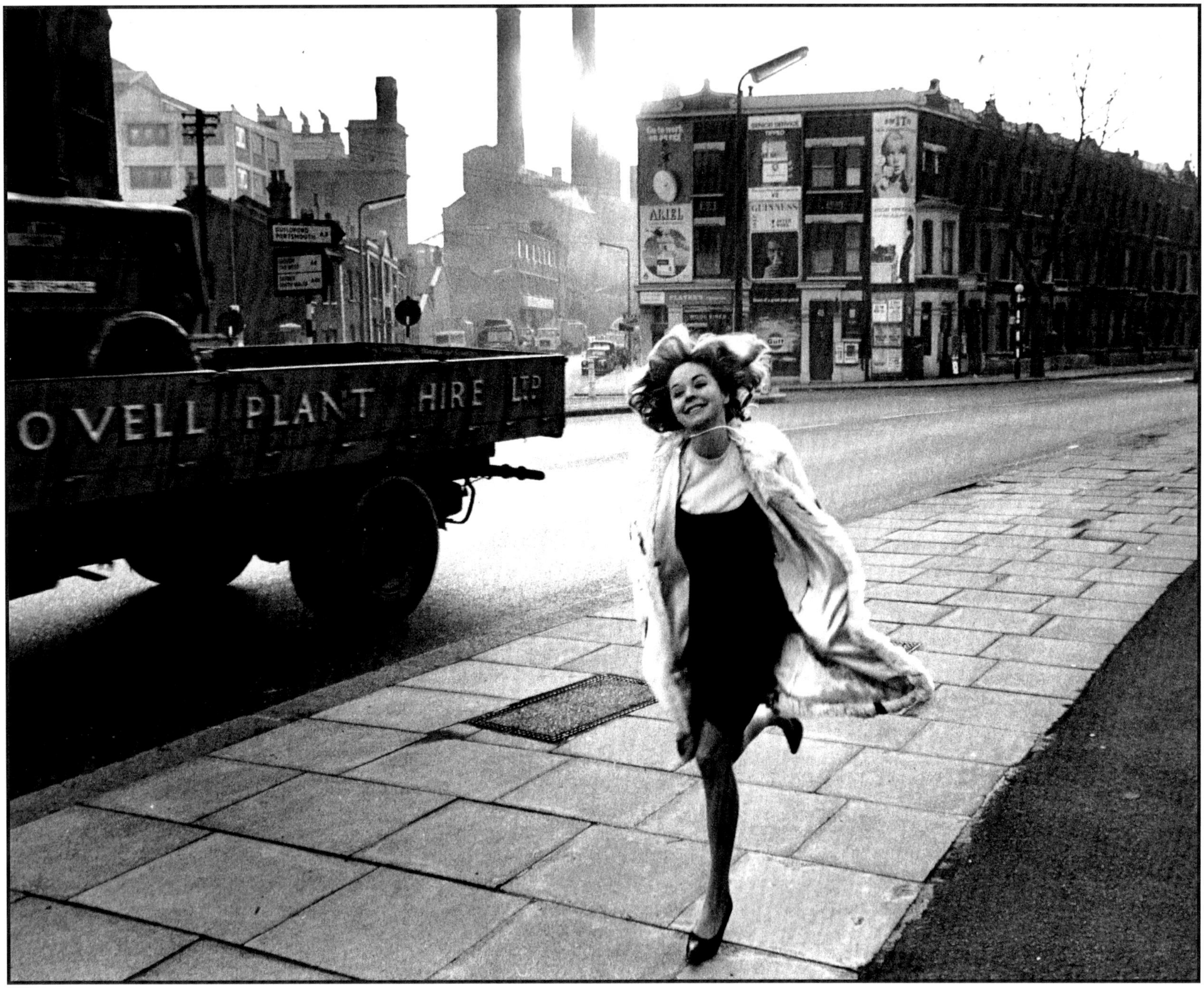
OVELL PLANT HIRE LTD
ARIEL
GUINNESS

6.
Hippy Wedding
1968 - Victoria

Bride & Groom 'Hippy' Style, the Hippy King of the Underground, Hoppy Hopkins, weds Suzy Creamcheese at Caxton Hall in Victoria, London.

The sixties was a great time for photographers. Colourful characters arrived on the scene all the time, and after taking this picture I was invited to join in the celebrations in true sixties style...

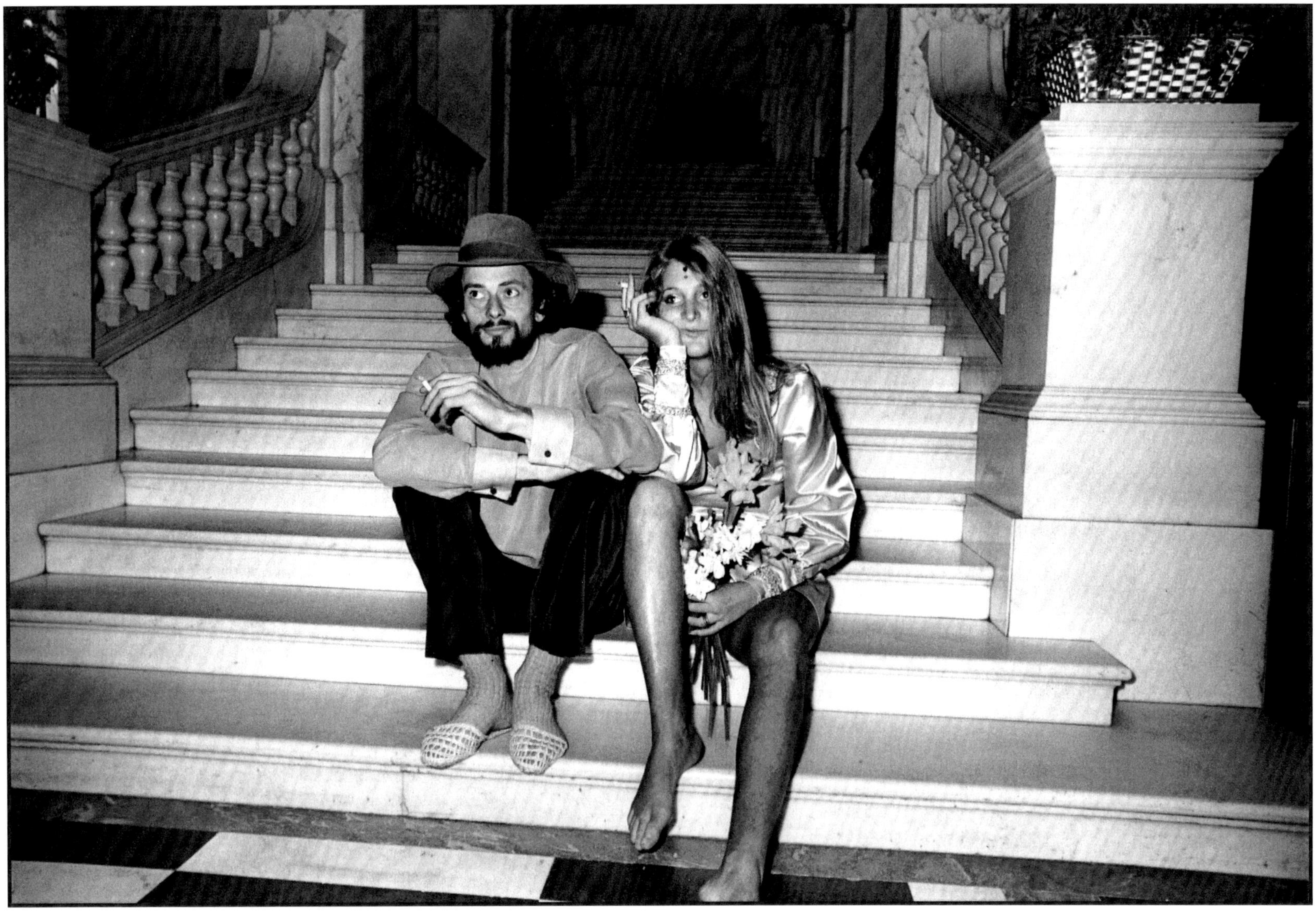

7.

Building Site Fashion

1969, Ludgate Hill

Sixties fashion shoot on a building site with a willing accomplice.
Not sure what 'Health & Safety' would have to say nowadays!
The costs associated with this type of picture were high.
I booked half a dozen models for two hours from the London agency *Top Models*, which was expensive, but in those days budgets seemed unlimited.

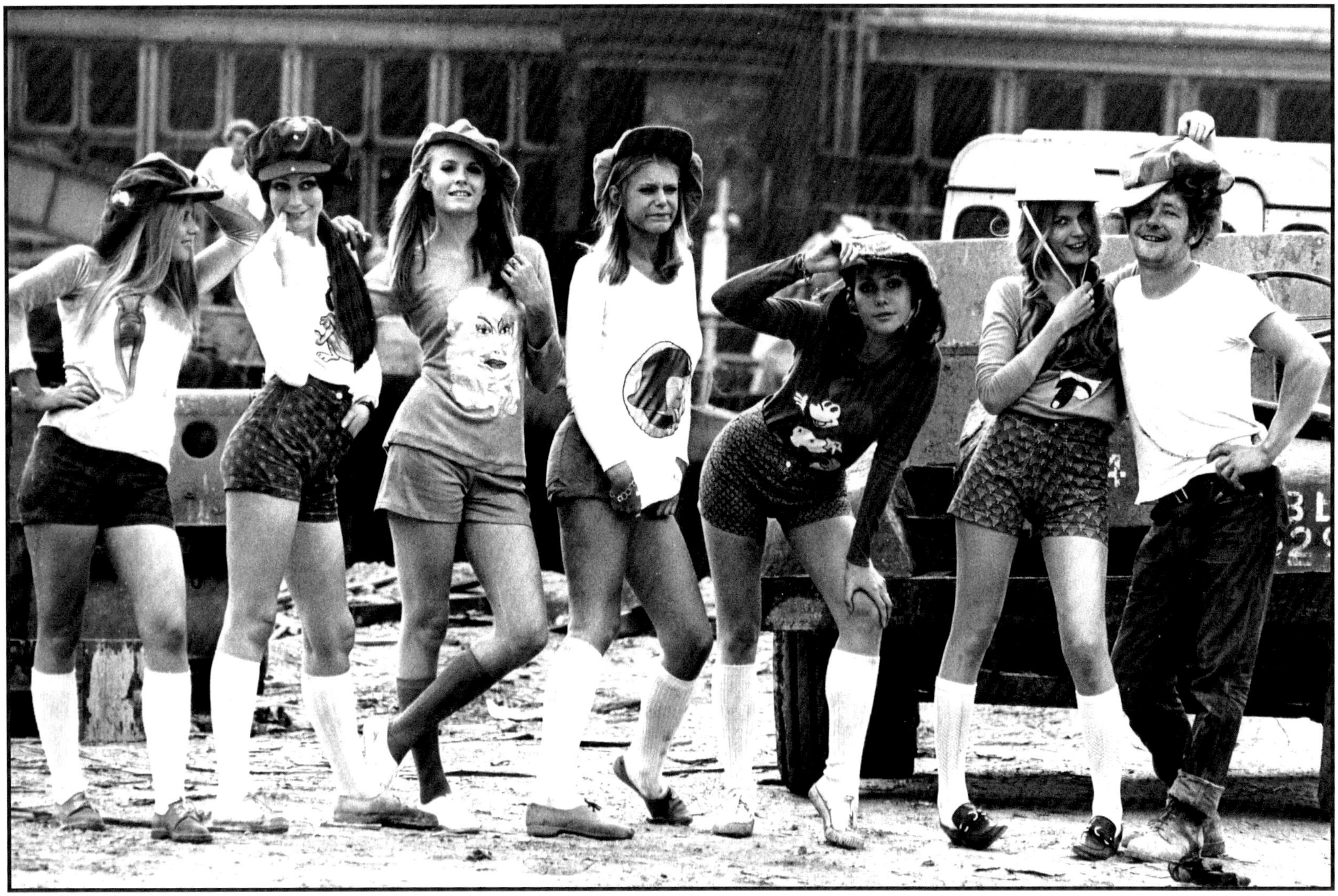

8.

Jilly Johnson

1970, Fleet Street Studio

The allure of working for a newspaper was that every day was different, with assignments varying from hard news to fashion and everything in-between.

The Sun tabloid's early success was no doubt boosted by the hitherto unknown feature of a picture of a topless girl. It appeared every day on 'Page 3' and quickly became the mainstay of the paper.

The sensational nature of *The Sun* was not really my style, as I was more interested in hard news and features. Mind you, I never really complained when I had to shoot the occasional Page 3 girl, as in this image of Jilly Johnson posing for a Christmas edition.

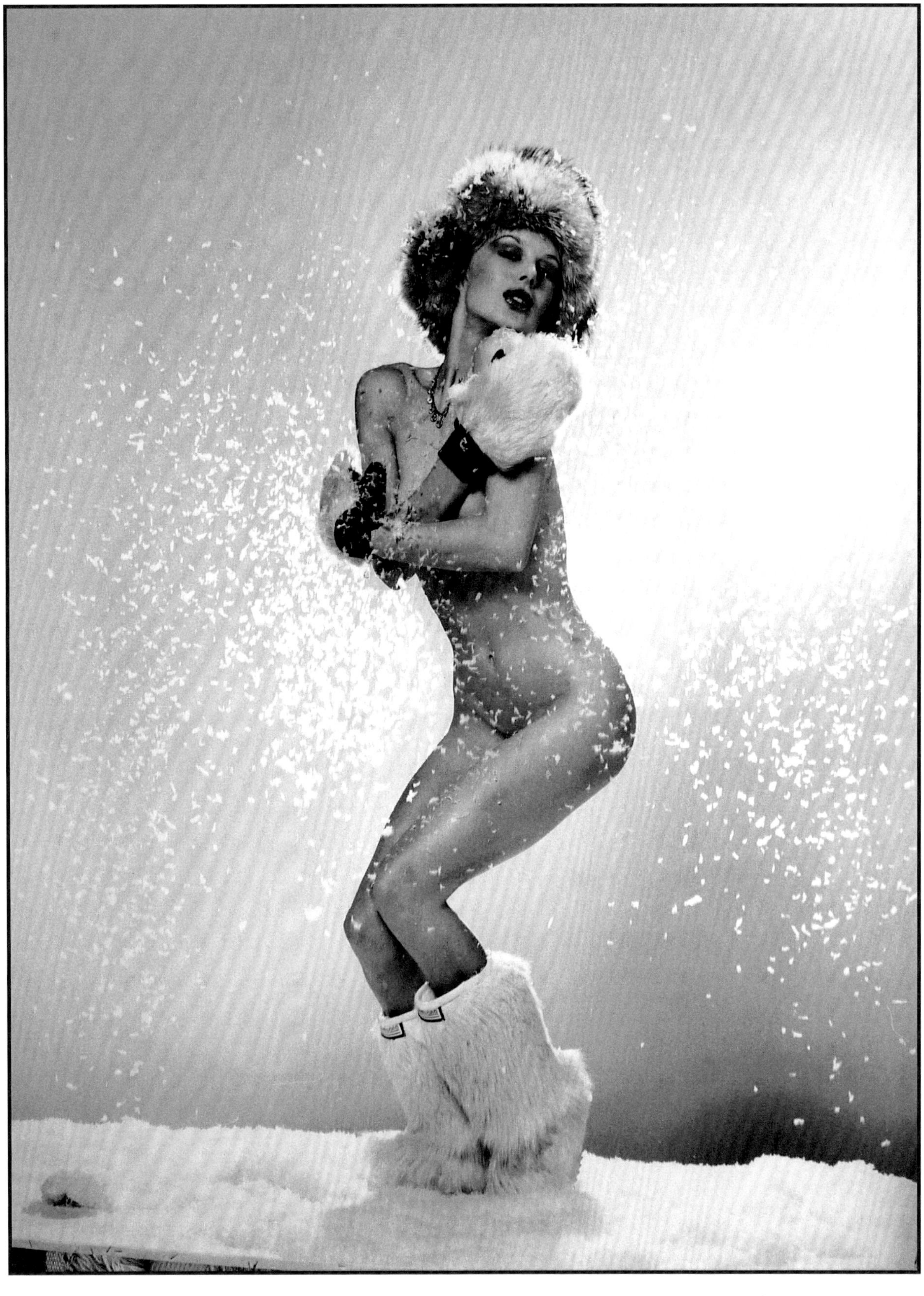

9.

Bumster Jeans

1970, Fleet Street Studio

Jane Maudsley modelling Mr.Freedom 'Bumster' jeans.
They never did catch on!
I took Jane for a glass of wine after the shoot but insisted she wore different jeans.

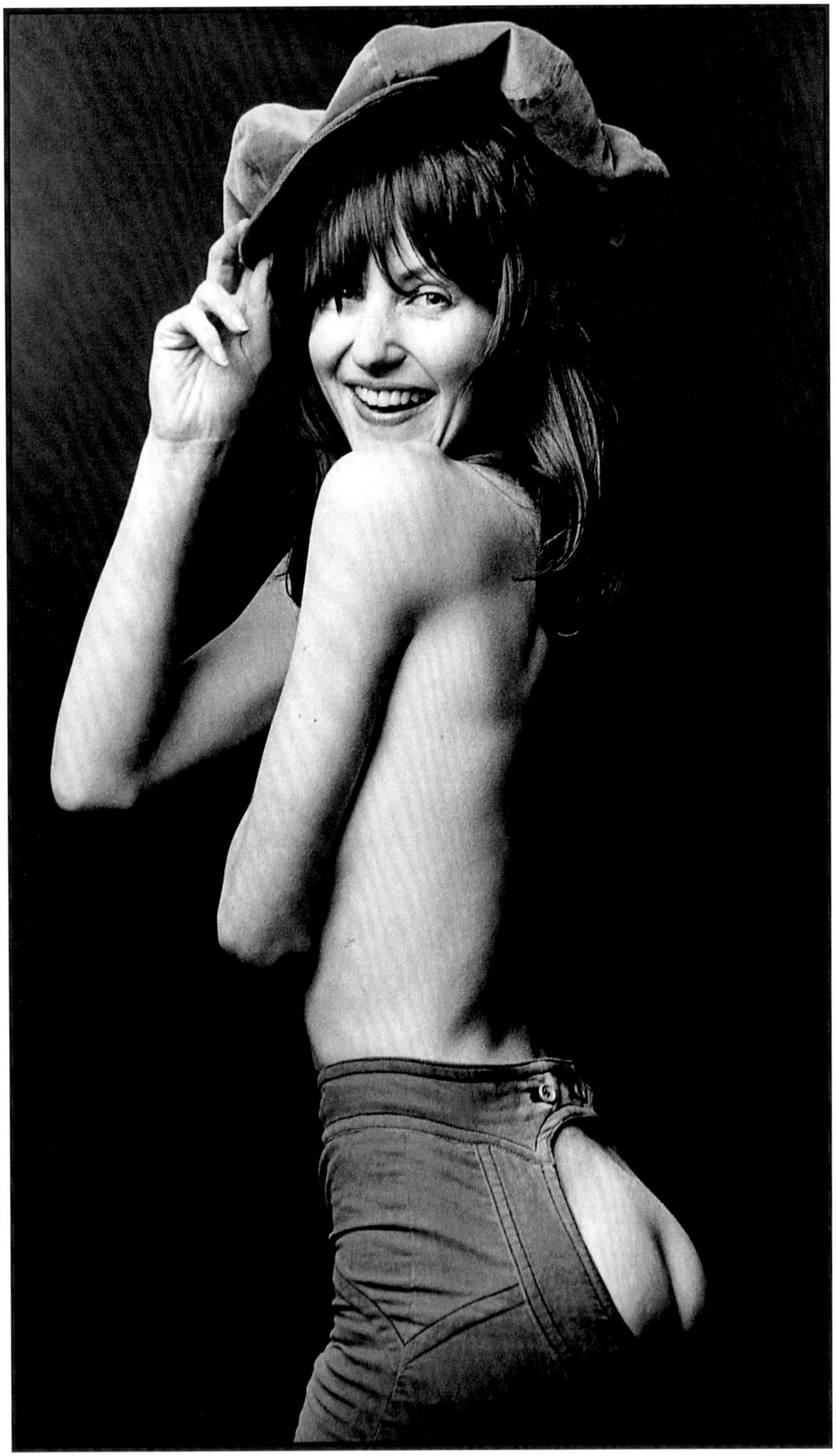

10.
Elton John
1976, Paris

I was sent to Paris to cover an Elton John concert. We had been invited by his Press Office, and they were picking up the tab for the whole weekend. Airline tickets had been sent from his office, and I set off on a great assignment. Arriving in Paris, I was picked up at the airport by a chauffeur driven limo and taken to my hotel. The Georges V, if you don't mind. It was going to be one of those extravagant gigs! Elton himself was staying there of course, and, along with a small group of reporters and photographers, I was invited to join him in his suite a couple of hours before the concert was due to start. As you can imagine, this was a lavish drinks reception. Perrier Jouët champagne in beautiful 'Belle Epoque' decorated bottles accompanied the best caviar and canapés imaginable.

We were ferried off to cover the concert. At the end of the performance it was back into the limos and on to a very exclusive club for dinner and to enjoy the rest of the night in the disco. I had my eye on Elton's very pretty PR girl who had been looking after us. I made sure I sat next to her over dinner and we got on really well. Then it was time for a spell on the dance floor. We were 'boogying' away when the most incredible thing happened. Elton had joined us all in the nightclub, and made a bee-line to the dance floor. He came over to the girl I was dancing with, tapped her on the shoulder and whispered something in her ear.

Blow me down, if it wasn't an old fashioned 'excuse me', he just took over and danced with me! I was a bit embarrassed but just carried on, helped no doubt by all that champagne... the image opposite was taken the following day, nursing a hangover!

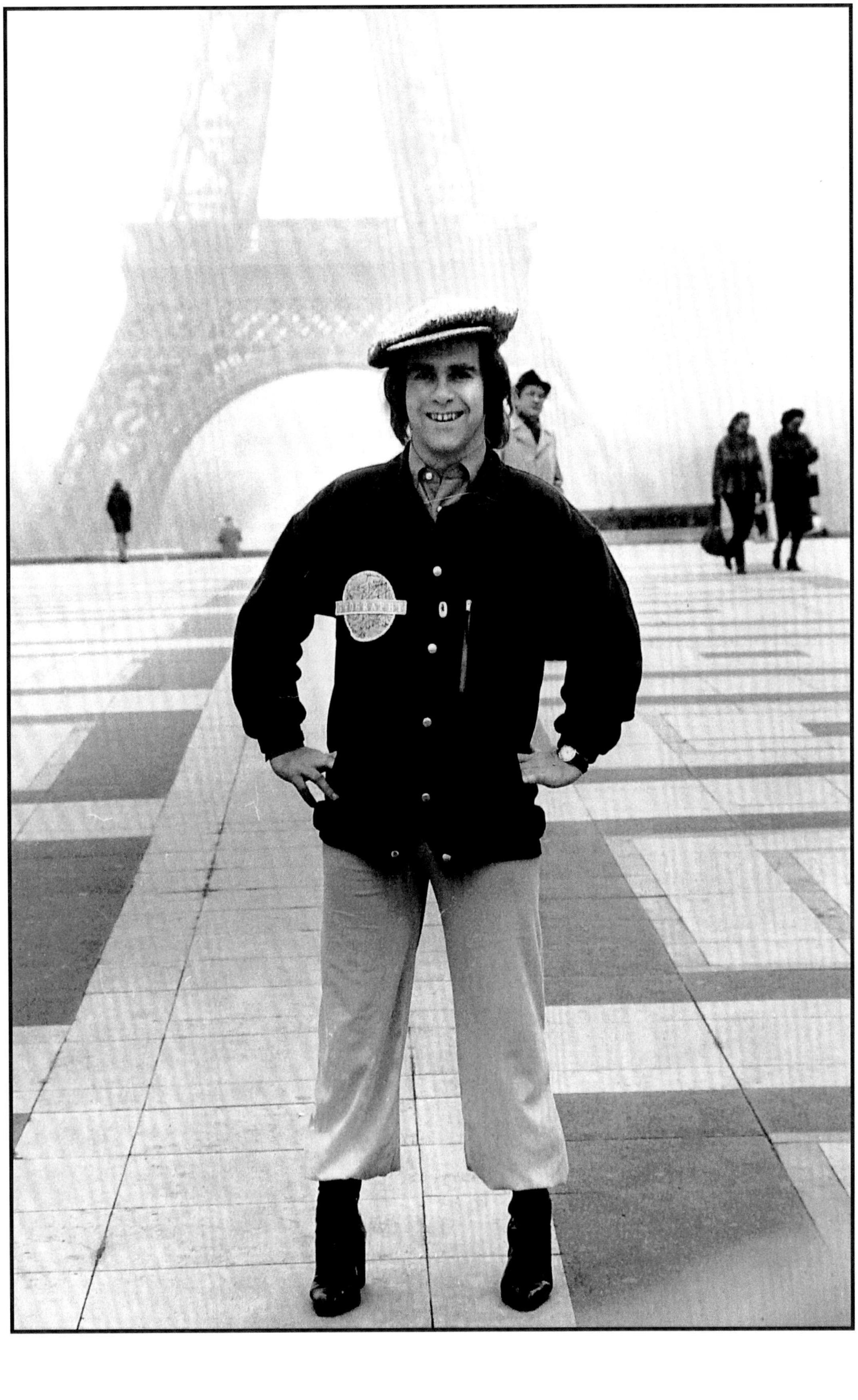

11.

Punks & Pensioners

1987, Kings Road

In 1987, a Cancer charity sponsored by the Duchess of York appealed to photographers across the country to capture a 'moment in time' on one nominated day. Winning pictures were published in a book entitled *'A Day for Life'*.

I decided to capture that moment by showing the contrasting cultures and generation gap between the Chelsea Pensioners and the Punks who habituated the Kings Road. I was pleased with my contribution, and *The Times* ran my picture as a poster captioned 'Sharp Pictures, Sharper Words'. It was later published in *The Times*' book '*A Century in Photographs*' to represent 1987.

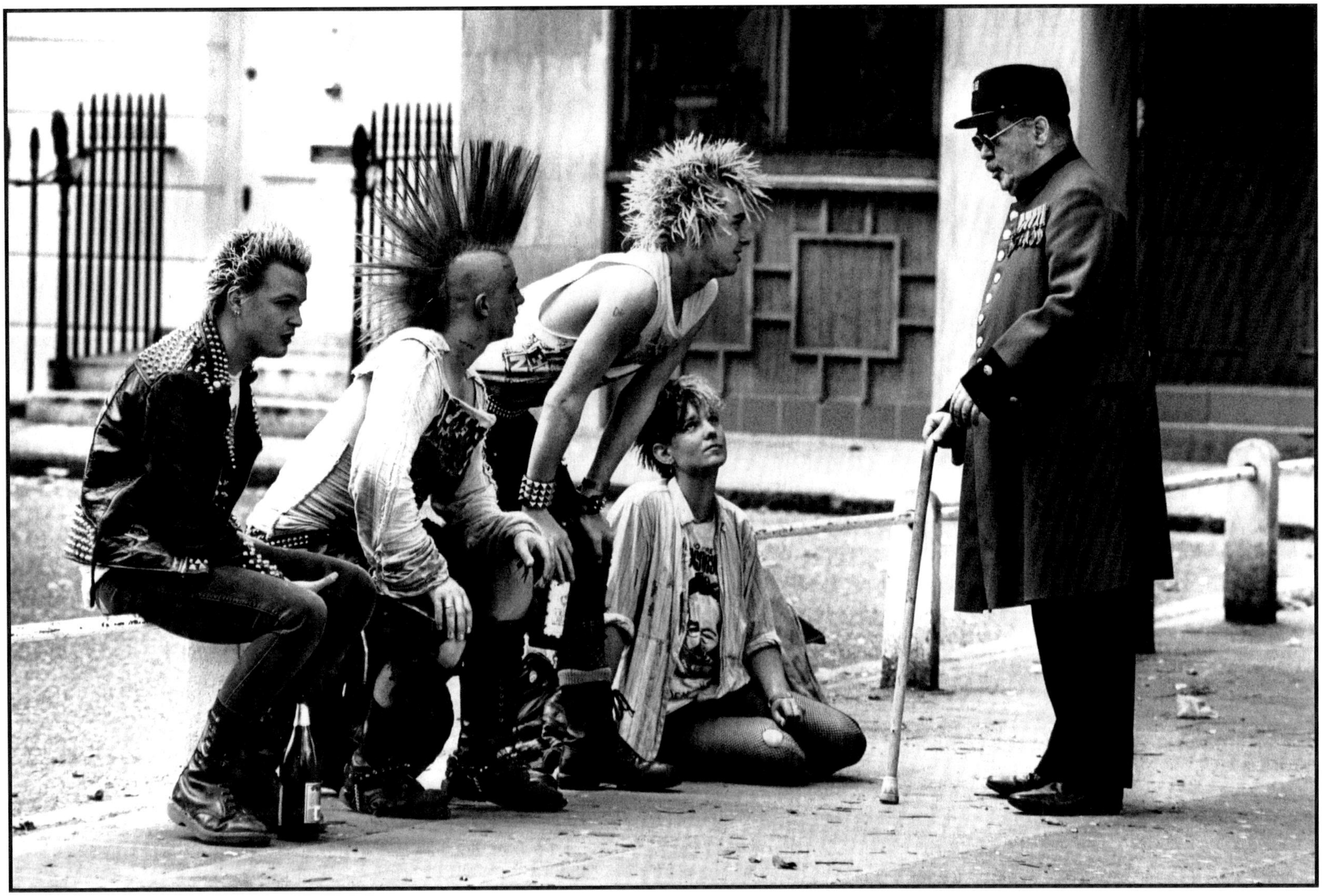

12.

Bowler Hats

1990, Hyde Park

The Combined Cavalry Old Comrades Parade and Memorial Service, held annually in London.
I took this picture as I thought it showed the idiosyncratic side of the British establishment.

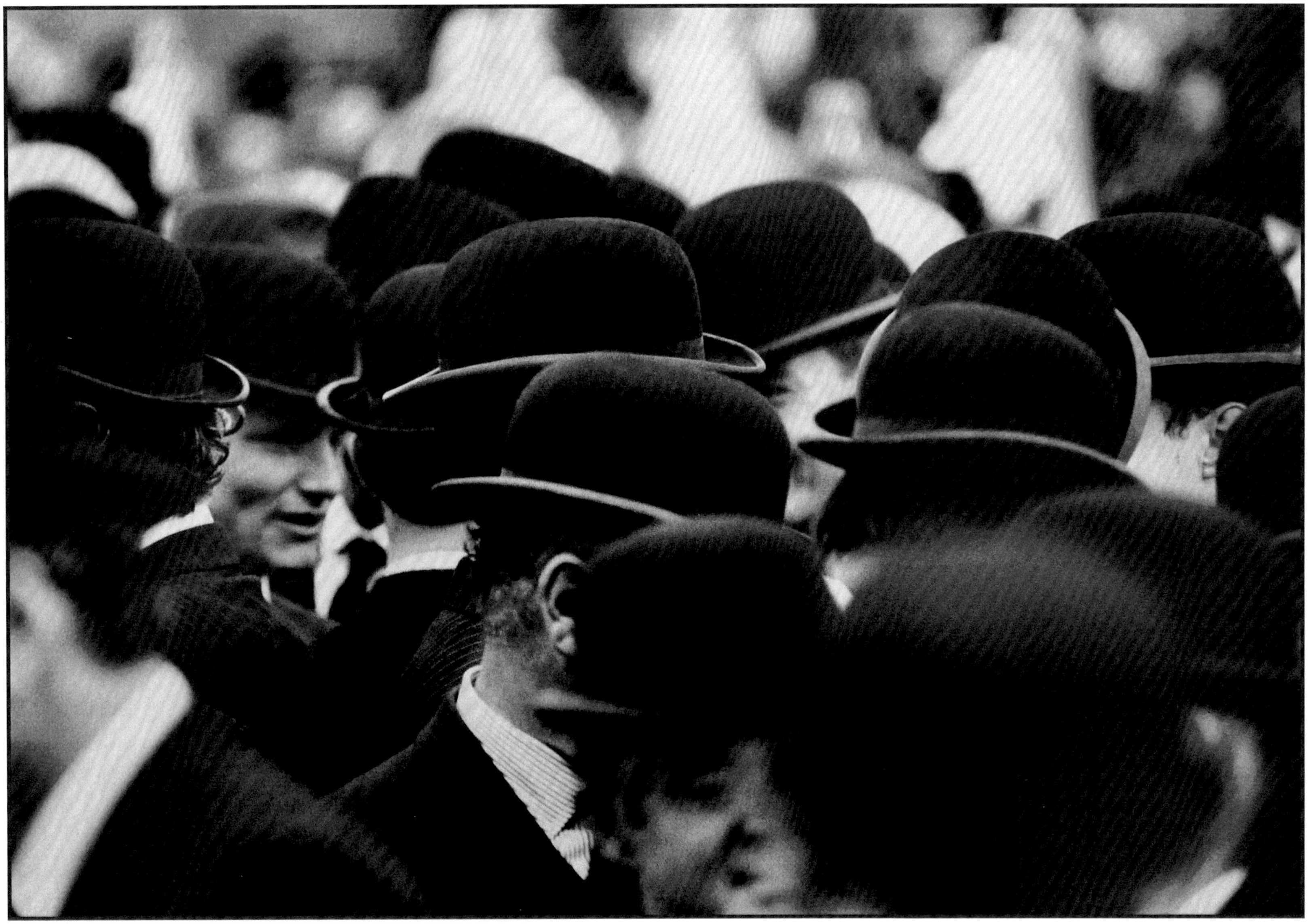

13.

Double Bass Player

1990, South Bank, London

I travelled with some Sinfonietta musicians on the Thames water bus to the Festival Pier at Queen Elizabeth Hall.
When we arrived I couldn't resist this image of one of them struggling with his double bass on the long walk from the Thames to dry land.

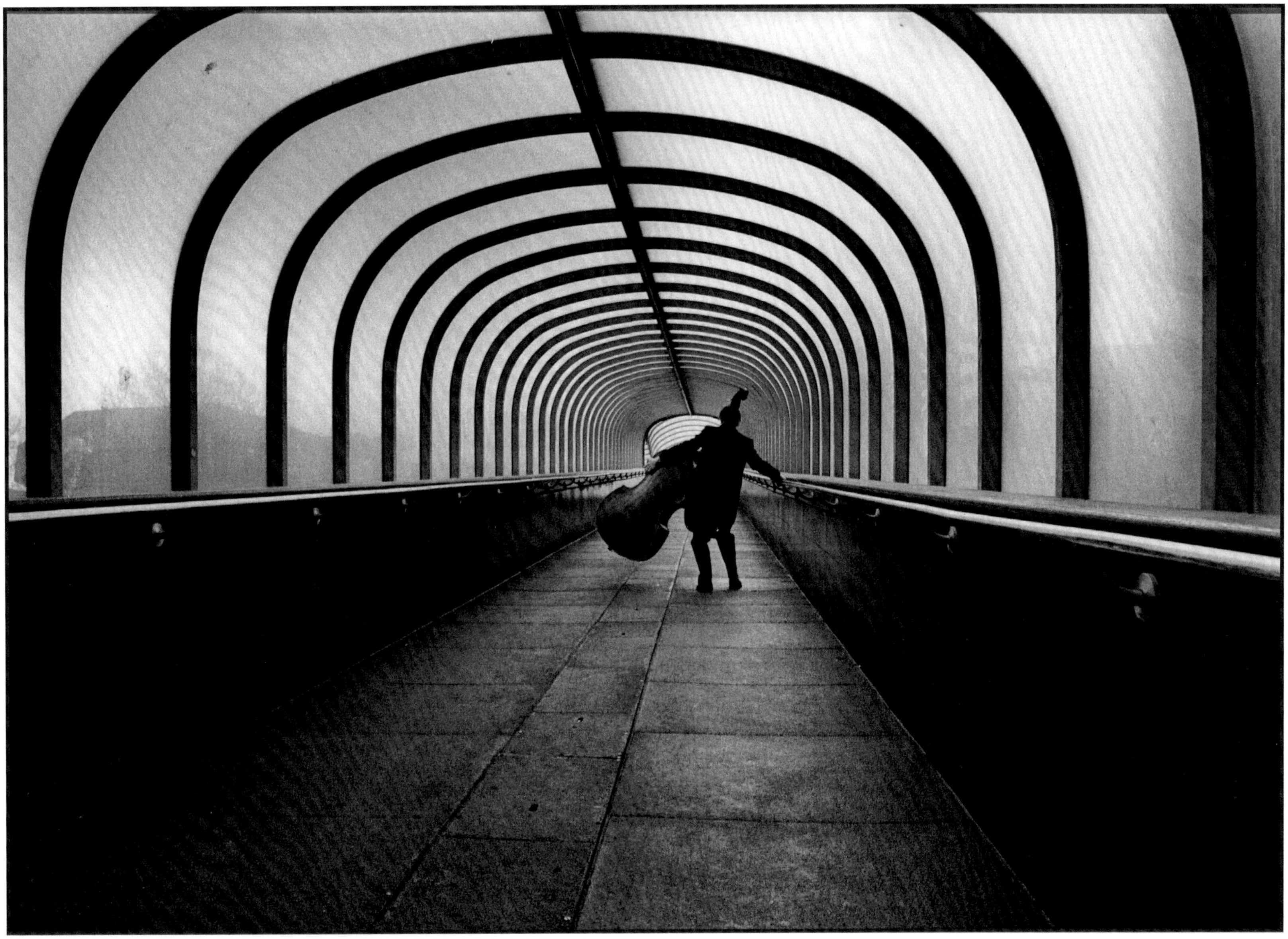

Part 2
Reportage

One aspect of working for a national daily newspaper was the certainty that somewhere in the world a major news story would be breaking. Not knowing in advance where I might be sent, or for how long, provided a regular adrenalin rush and the fact that I would often be witnessing and recording history in the making was perhaps the best part of the job.

14.

Great Train Robbers

1963, Linslade, Buckinghamshire

In 1963, when I had just started working for the *Daily Herald*, a Royal Mail train was audaciously robbed of £2.6 million (the equivalent of around £40 million today). The story made international headlines and the hunt for the perpetrators occupied the front pages for days. They were eventually caught and were being held at Linslade Police Station in Buckinghamshire.

This was my first major assignment for the paper. Ronnie Biggs and his accomplices, who had been dubbed 'The Great Train Robbers' are now infamous. I managed to get a shot of them, handcuffed together, as they were being transferred to prison.

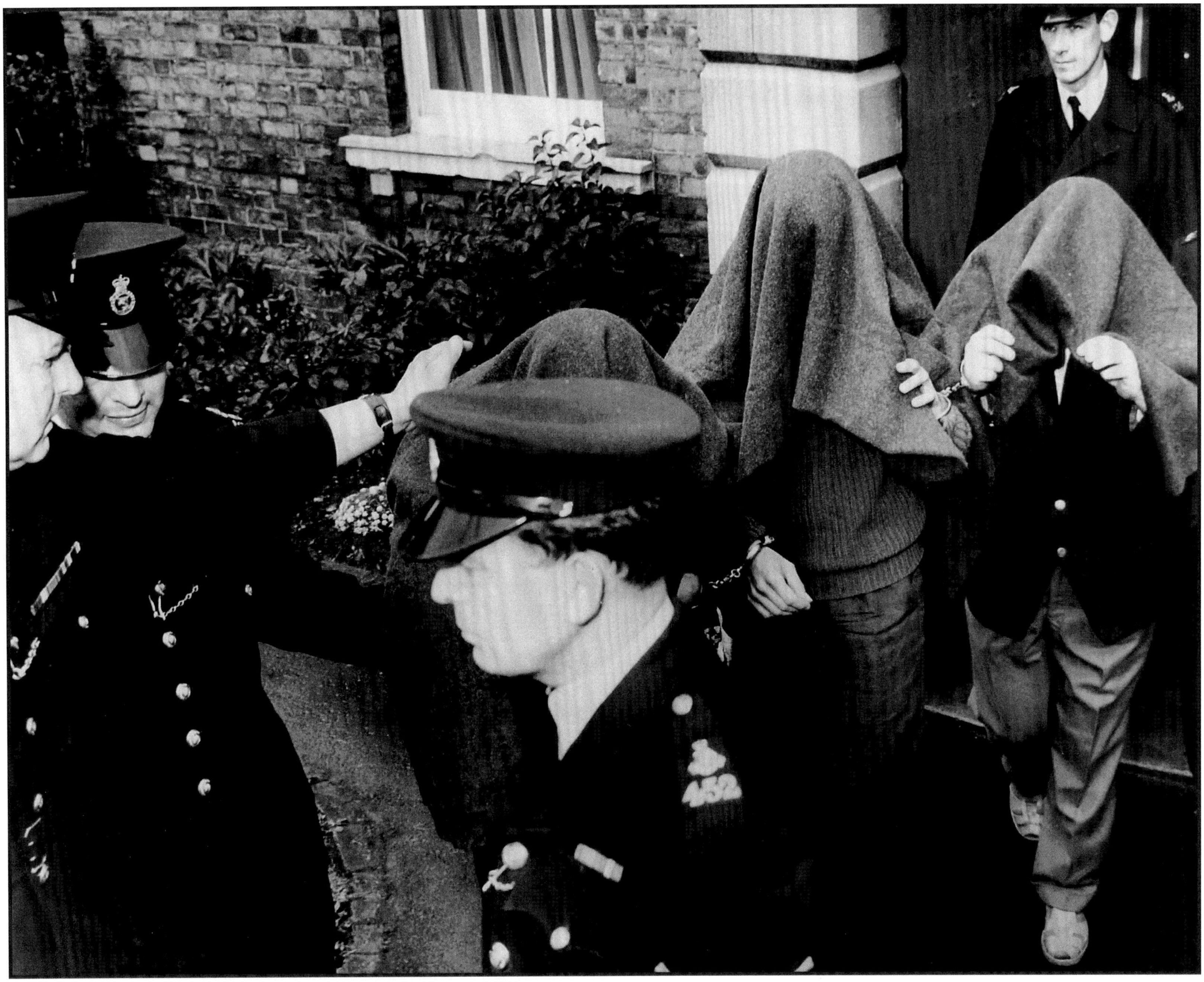
432

15.

Margot Fonteyn

1964, Heathrow

Margot Fonteyn is probably the most famous ballerina of all time and spent her entire career as a dancer with the Royal Ballet. She was appointed prima ballerina assoluta of the company by Queen Elizabeth. She married Panamanian diplomat and lawyer Roberto Arias in 1955 who became ambassador to Great Britain.

In 1959, they staged a coup d'état against President Ernesto de la Guardia of Panama, possibly with the support of Fidel Castro. According to Fonteyn, the plot was hatched when she and her husband were visiting Cuba in January 1959, with Castro promising to assist Arias with arms or men. The couple went fishing on their boat The Nola and during the voyage ordered fishermen to raise a buoy loaded with arms. The fishermen reported the couple, who decided that Arias should try to escape detection.

Fonteyn was arrested and deported. Arias took refuge in the Brazilian Embassy for two months and was then given safe conduct out of the country. Eventually the charges were dropped and, after a change of government, the couple were permitted to return to Panama.

In 1964 Arias was shot in an assassination attempt and returned to England shortly afterwards. I met up with Fonteyn in a cafe at London Heathrow airport whilst she was waiting for her husband's delayed flight. We spent about two hours together until the plane arrived. I photographed her greeting her husband in the back of an ambulance.

He was treated for 18 months in British hospitals, and spent the rest of his life in a wheelchair as a quadriplegic. One of the reasons Fonteyn continued to dance so late in her life was to pay Arias' enormous medical bills.

The couple moved back to Panama where she nursed him until his death in 1989. She died in poverty in 1991.

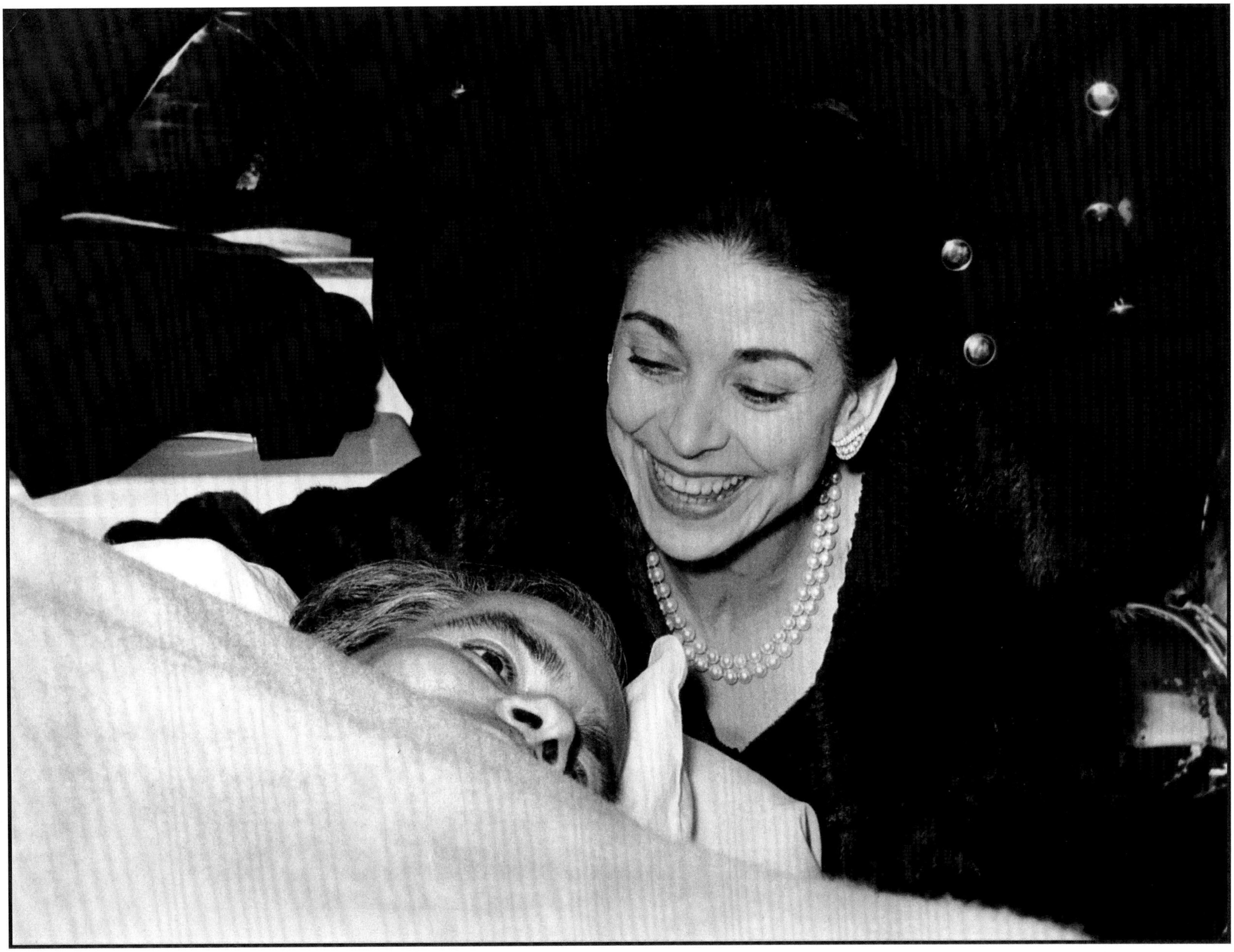

16.

Jackie Kennedy & Randolph Churchill

1965, London

Jackie Kennedy, widow of assassinated U.S. president John F. Kennedy, seen here with Winston Churchill's son, Randolph, one of several men she dated after JFK's death. This candid shot was the result of a tip-off that they were dining at Wilton's Oyster Bar in Jermyn Street, Piccadilly. I waited in a doorway for an hour and captured this picture of them. Their bodyguard wasn't too pleased.

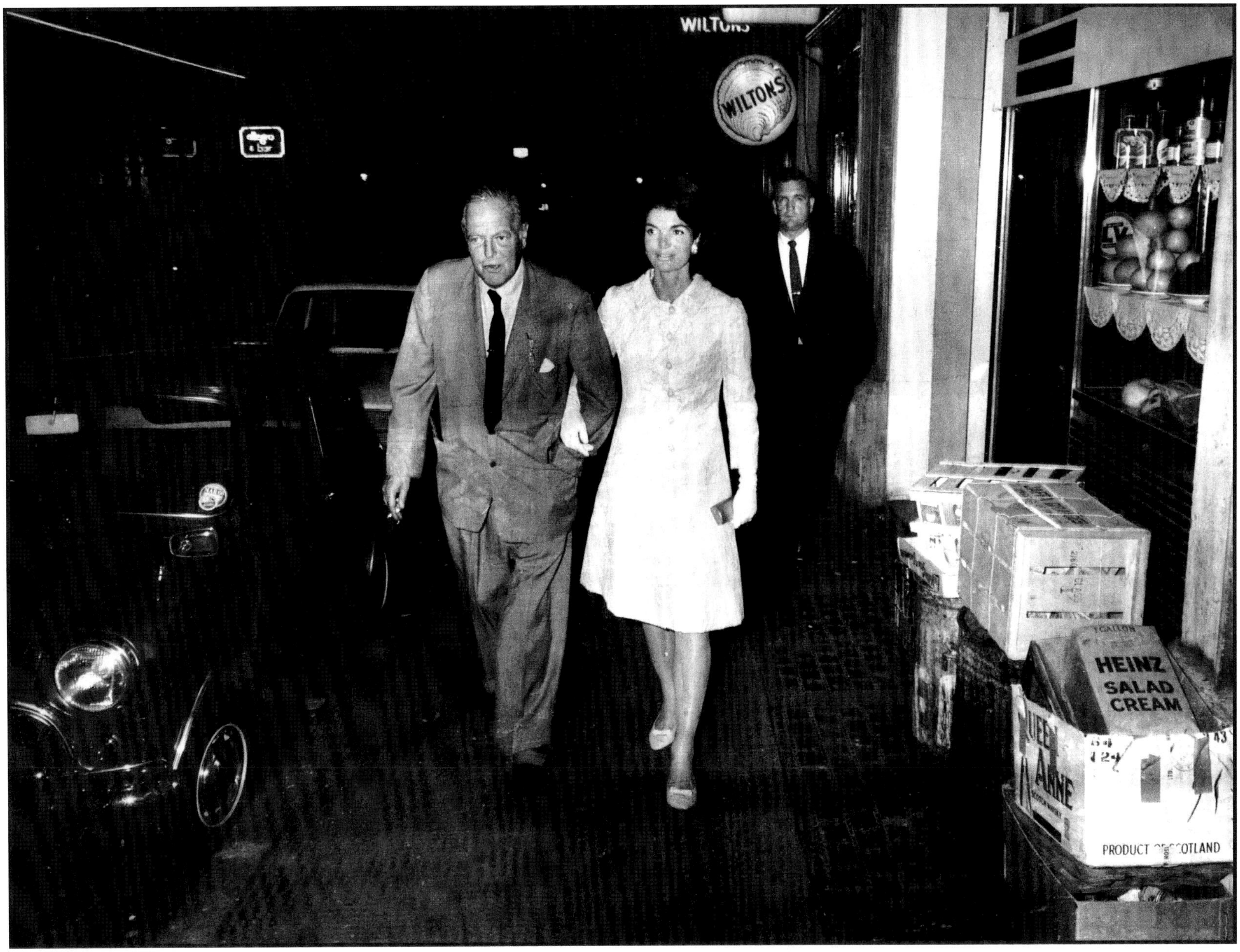
WILTONS
HEINZ
SALAD
CREAM

17.
Sorbonne Student Riots
1968, Paris

In May 1968 I was given one of my most exciting assignments. The student riots in Paris had crippled France. All airports were closed. There was very little, if any, phone communication, and it was developing into a major news story.

The Editor, Sydney Jacobson, called me to his office and told me to get to Paris in any way possible and as quickly as I could. As there were no commercial flights in or out of France, I made arrangements to fly to Germany to meet up with our Bonn correspondent, Dennis Newson.

As planned, he met me at the airport in his car. We knew that it would be impossible to get petrol in France, so Dennis had bought some jerry cans and filled them up. The boot was completely stashed with cans of petrol. I dread to think what might have happened if another car had shunted us in the rear.

Anyway, off we set to drive the long haul to Paris, which I think was about 800 miles. We did it non-stop, apart from one incident when we were driving through a sleepy village in Belgium. Suddenly, a horse with a large black plume attached to its head came from around the corner. It was pulling a hearse, followed by mourners. Screeching to a halt, Dennis swore abuse at the delay until the line of followers came quickly to an end and we were on our way again. I heard Dennis mutter 'Thank God he wasn't popular!'

We got to Paris in the early hours, completely exhausted, with no idea what to expect but we knew it wouldn't be pleasant. We based ourselves in a hotel on the Left Bank, around the corner from The Sorbonne, right in the thick of things. Students had barricaded the streets and a lot of the cobble stones had been dug up to hurl at the CRS - the French riot police. The popular chant was 'CRS...SS', and I have to say they were ruthless.

As each day went by, the rioting became more and more violent. Pitched battles, with the CRS smashing everybody they could with their batons. I learnt later that this riot force was drawn from the French Foreign Legion, known to be brutal. I took the precaution of buying a motor-cycle helmet to protect myself, but still took a few nasty blows to the head.

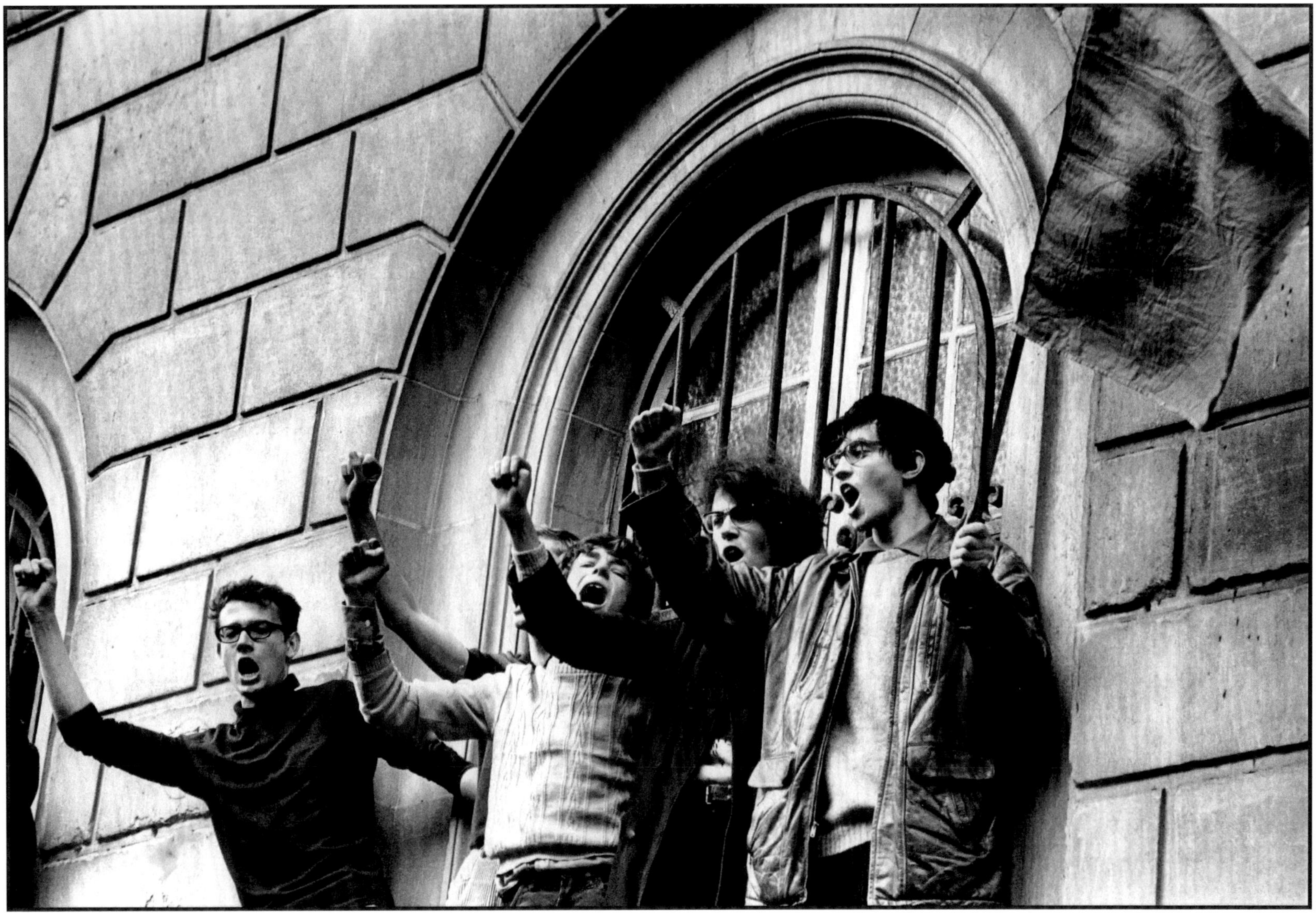

18.
The Sorbonne War Hospital
1968, Paris

By a very fortunate coincidence, Angela Burgess, a girlfriend from London, was studying at the Sorbonne at that time, and we saw quite a lot of each other. Indeed, she was instrumental in helping me get a major world exclusive. All eyes were on the Sorbonne, which the students had taken over and barricaded.

Press were barred by the students, who were manning every door to the university. Angela, was a volunteer worker for the Red Cross. Together we devised a scheme to get me into the Sorbonne. She lent me her Red Cross pass and I copied it, forging as best I could. Next, I needed a white coat, which Angela borrowed from a medical student friend. I was all set, except for the technical problem of taking pictures without being noticed. There was no way I could use a flash gun as I would have been rumbled straight away. However, Kodak made a specialist film called 'Recording Film 2475', which was the most sensitive film on the planet for working in subdued available light. I managed to find a roll and next day, armed with my 35mm Leica M2 (which was small and quiet) hidden under my white coat, I cooly presented myself at the side door of the university. I was nervous, but I flashed my 'Red cross' pass and, lo and behold, I was in!

I wasn't sure what to expect. It looked like a scene from a war film. Hundreds of students milling around with volunteer doctors and nurses tending the injured as they were brought in from the streets. The Rector's room was transformed into an operating theatre and the opportunity for pictures, albeit clandestine, was enormous.

Of course, having great pictures in my camera was one thing. Getting them back to England was quite another. Under normal circumstances, I would have a mobile team with me to transmit the pictures back to London which required telephone lines but as there were none working, that wasn't an option. An alternative would have been to put the film on a plane, but no commercial flights were operating, nor were there any ferries. I studied a map, looking for private airfields and found one outside Paris. I hoped to find a private plane to charter and was in luck. I paid a pilot to fly my film to Shorham airfield on the south coast of England.

I still had no way of communicating with my picture editor to tell him of my coup, nor tell him where the film was so I briefed the pilot to ask Air Traffic Control to relay a message to the paper and ask for a motor cycle despatch rider to collect the film. I was limited by the 36 frames available on that single roll of film so finding a means of getting the film out of France, and trusting the pilot to ensure its safe delivery was a challenge and a risk.

When I eventually got back to England, I was knocked out by the hero's welcome I received. I was shown the edition with my world exclusive images on the front page as well as a full inside spread.

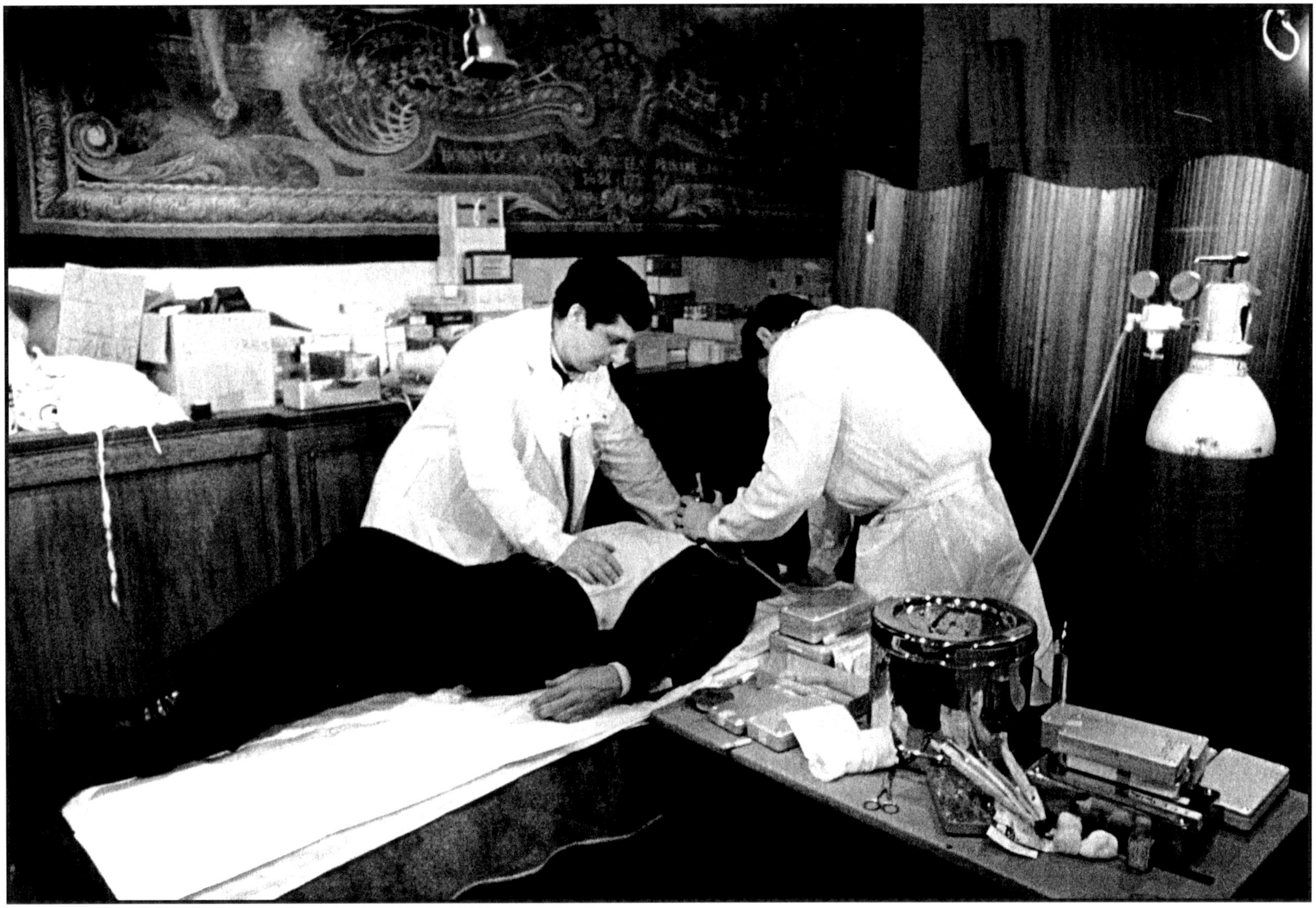

19.

Front Page Exclusive

Angela (opposite - right) helped me forge a Red Cross pass but made me promise not to identify any of the doctors.

INSIDE THE SORBONNE WAR HOSPITAL

SUN EXCLUSIVE

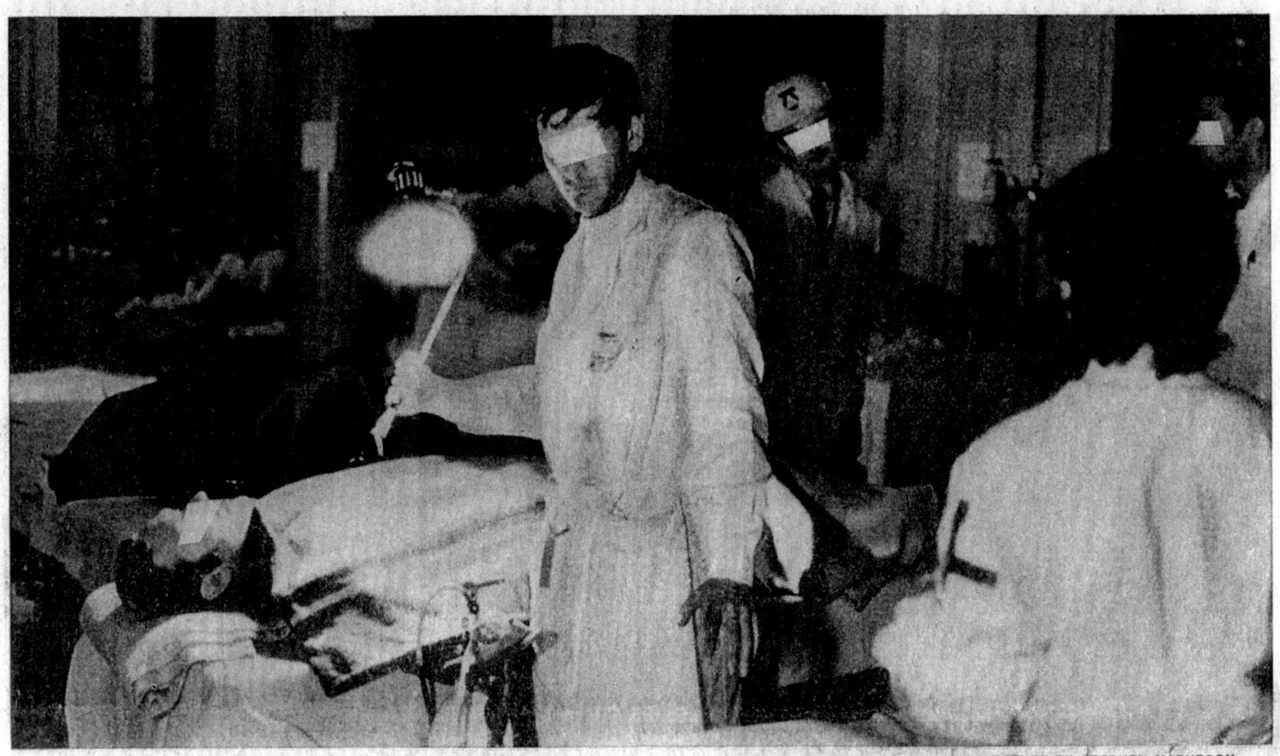

PICTURE BY STEPHEN MARKESON

The casualty station in the Sorbonne rector's room. Faces have been masked at the request of the students

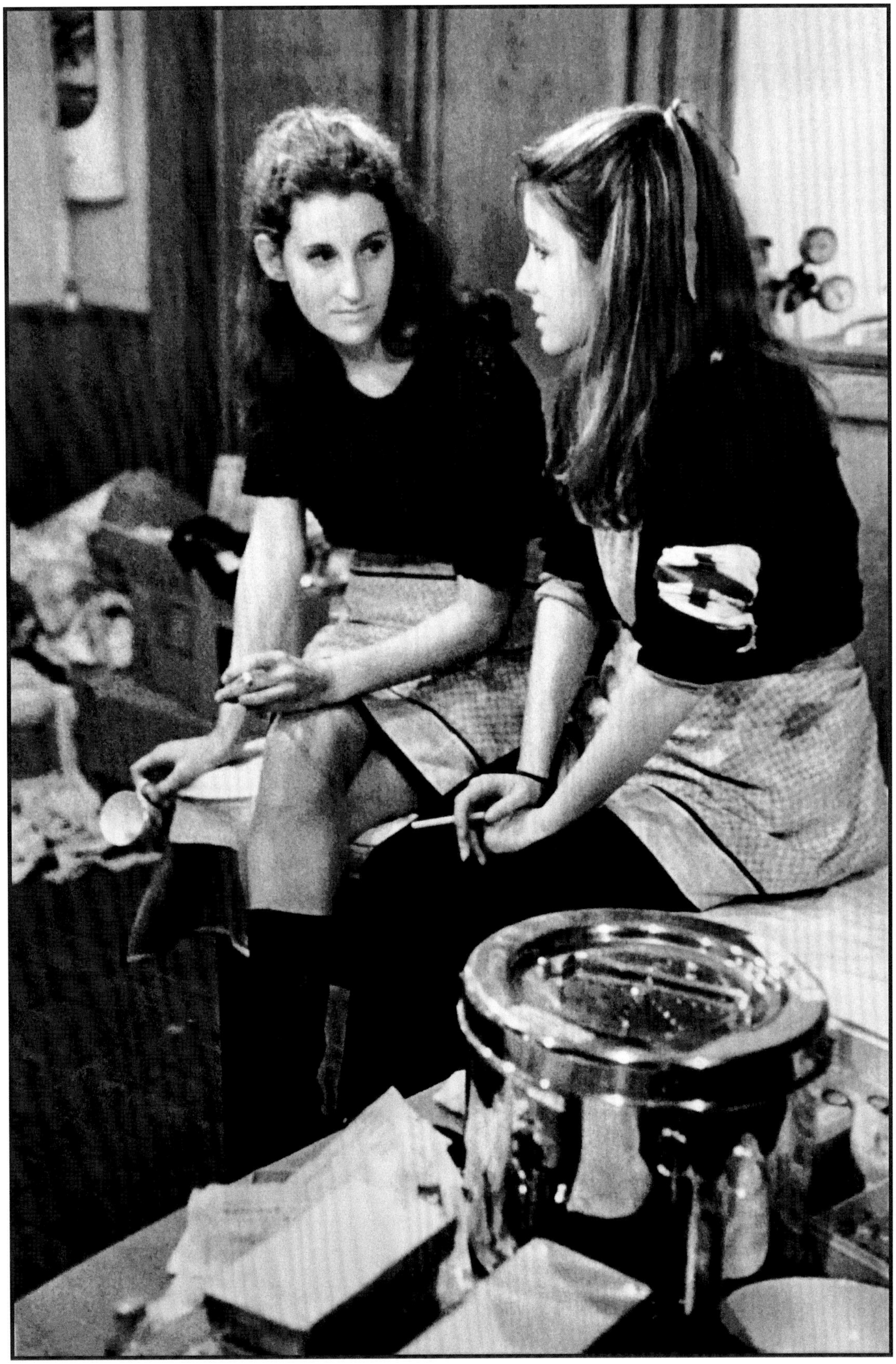

20.

Danny Cohn-Bendit

1968, London

Danny Cohn-Bendit was a student leader during the Paris unrest and wanted by Interpol.
He is now a Euro MP.
A fellow conspiritor was Tariq Ali (seen here by Bendit's left shoulder) - he is now a renowned writer and *Guardian* columnist.
They were in London after the rioting to give a press conference. In order to get this shot I persuaded a doorman to let me into a nearby first floor office. A five pound note changed hands.

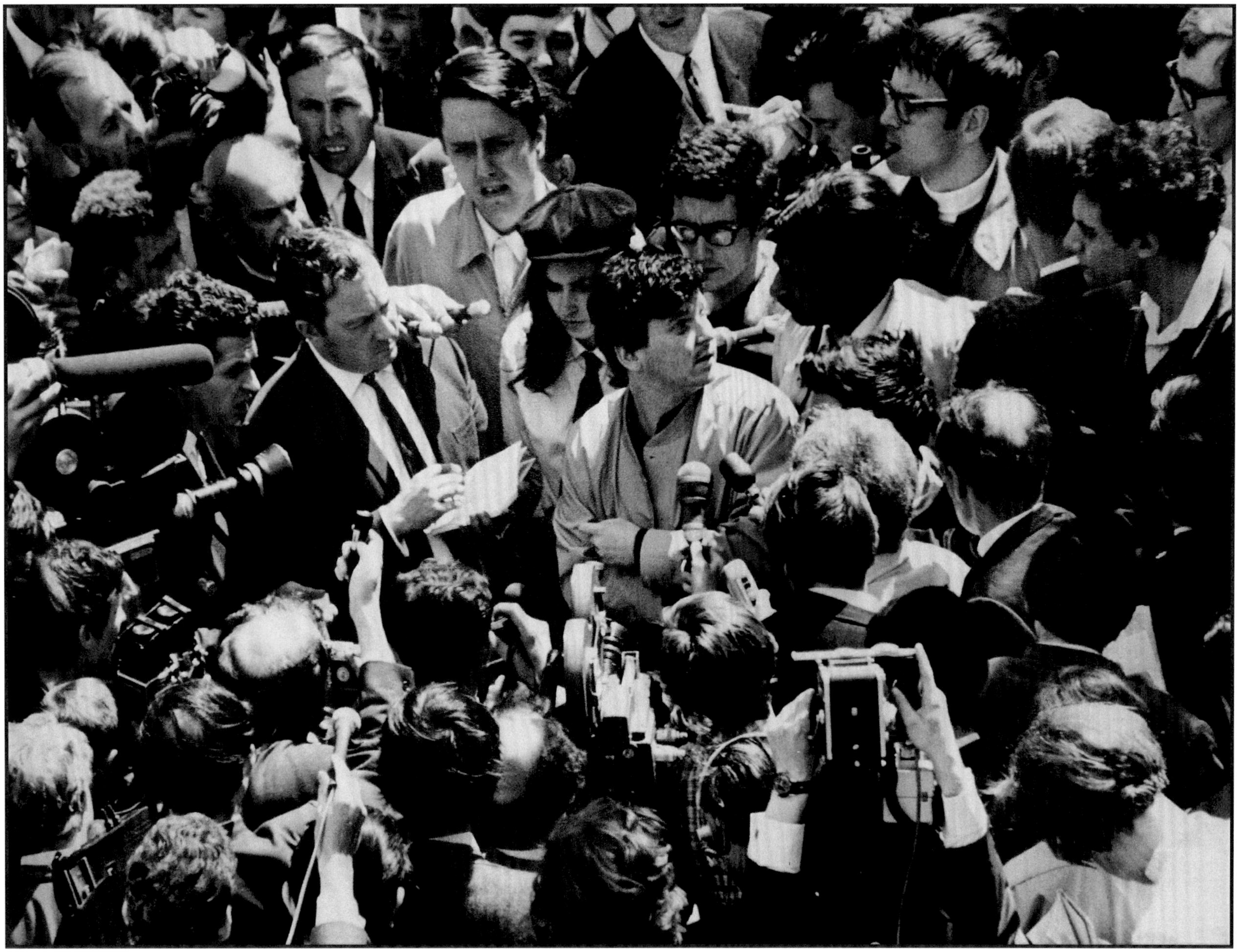

21.

Illegal Abortion Clinic

1969, Harley Street

It was the late sixties and the subject of abortion, which at that time was illegal, was of great public interest. There was a highly emotive campaign to have terminations legalised. In those days there was no freedom of choice and women were forced to use unregulated practitioners who charged extortionate fees and often endangered lives. I was working for *The Sun* and we had a tip-off from our crime reporter that a private clinic in London was performing many such operations. Women and girls, some under-age, from the UK, Southern Ireland and Italy were thought to be paying a lot of money to have their pregnancies ended.

I was briefed to get a job as a hospital porter in an attempt to get pictures to illustrate the story. I worked there for about ten days, pushing patients about the place on trollies, before taking clandestine pictures with my Leica M2, which I had hidden under my white coat.

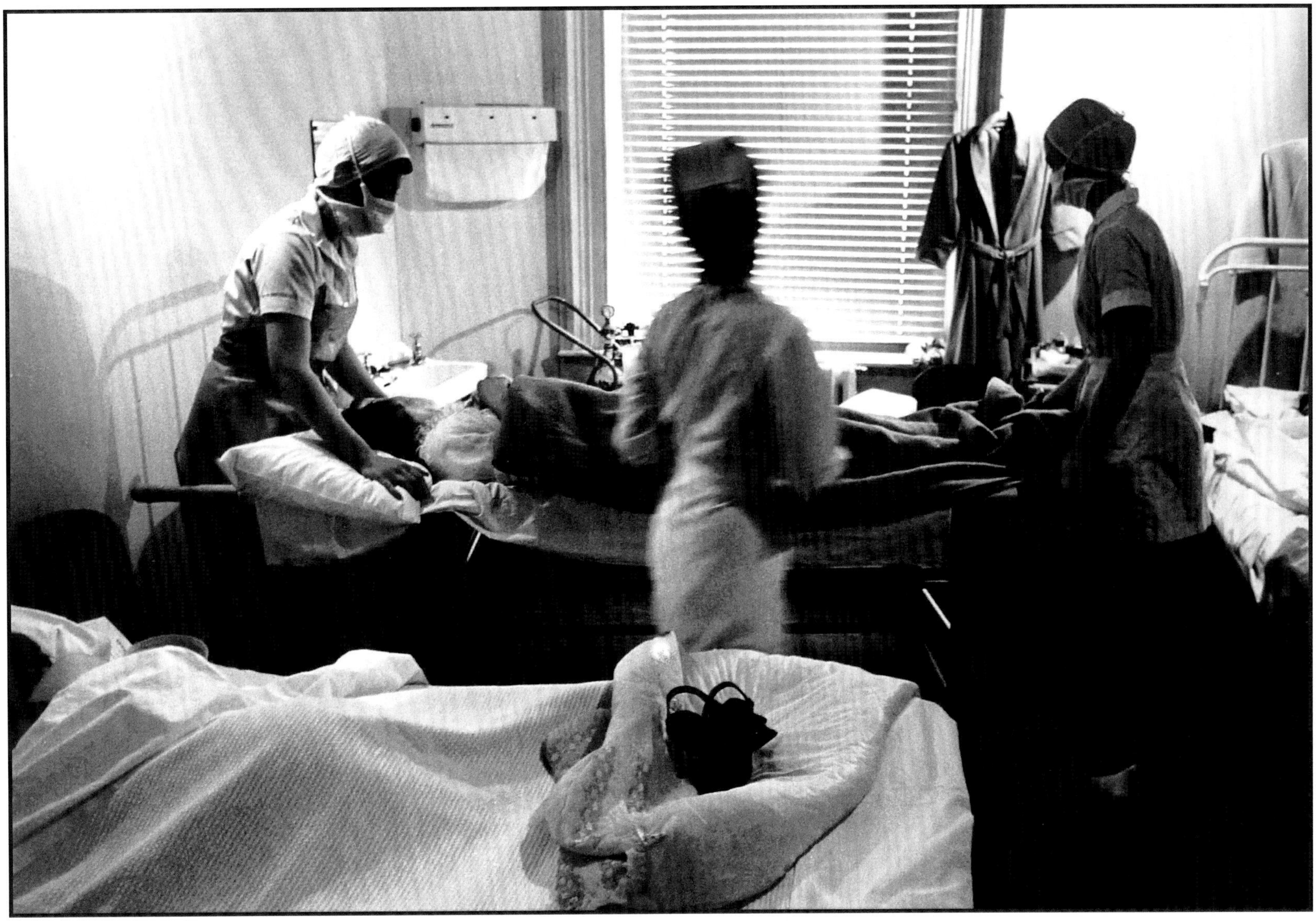

22.
Shot Policeman
1969, Northern Ireland

When British troops moved into Northern Ireland in 1969, I was part of a team sent to cover 'The Troubles'.
We were based at the Europa hotel in Belfast, where we set up an office, a darkroom and a wire machine.
I was in Northern Ireland for almost three years and during that time took many graphic images and had a couple of nasty injuries, including three broken ribs after being hit by a rubber bullet and a patch on my lung from tear gas poisoning.
It was 'Bloody Sunday', there was rioting everywhere and I was naturally quite scared. I saw a Royal Ulster Constabulary officer cautiously moving down a side turning towards some very active rioting and decided to follow him. He noticed me joining him and told me to be very careful, as there were barricades and missiles everywhere. At that moment, a hail of bullets rained down on us both from a rooftop sniper. I hurled myself into a chemist shop doorway, instinctively taking a photograph from my hip as I hit the ground. The officer had been shot in the back of the neck and, sadly, I don't think he survived. I was incredibly lucky not to have also been shot, but was pinned down in that doorway for an interminable and very frightening two hours before being rescued by the army in an armoured car.
I had inhaled so much tear gas that I was coughing up blood.

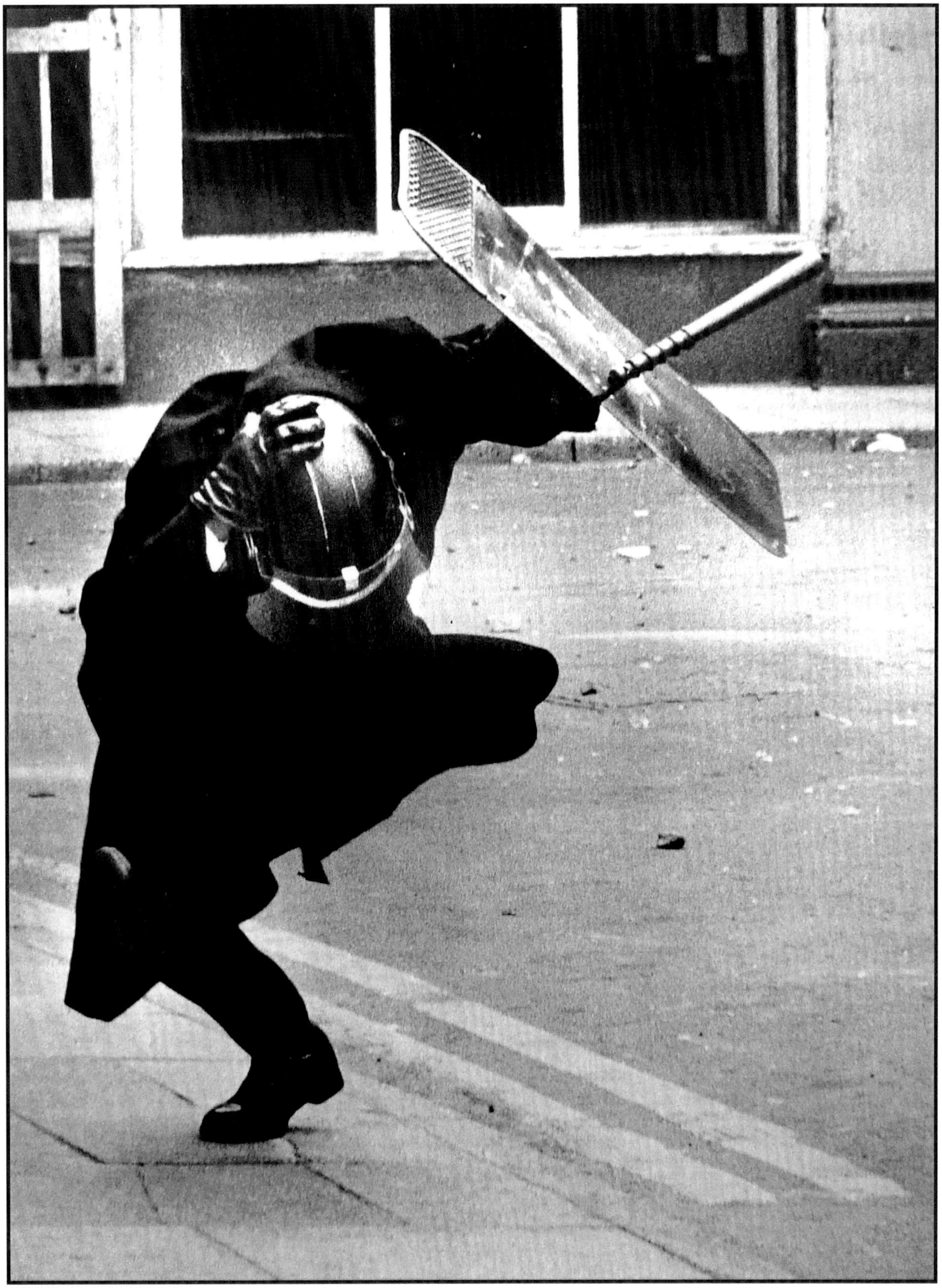

23.
Tear Gas
1969, Northern Ireland

Whilst at the Europa hotel I had some lucky escapes. The hotel was a prime target for the IRA, and it was bombed three times whilst I was inside. I can't say that I was unhappy to leave Belfast, and my eventual departure was a far from pleasant experience.

I'd received an anonymous note. It wasn't typed or handwritten, but letters cut from a newspaper and stuck on a sheet of paper. 'We don't like what your newspaper is printing. Leave now or else...' I was scared and felt physically sick.

I immediately rang the editor in London, who ordered me straight back on the next plane. I packed my bag and cameras as quickly as possible and set off in my hire car towards Belfast airport. Then a very fortunate twist of fate. To this day I'll never know why I changed my mind, but I had driven no more than half a mile when I decided that it would be quicker to return to the Europa and take a taxi. I drove into the forecourt, handed the keys and paperwork to the doorman and asked him to get the car picked up by the rental company.

I jumped into a taxi and we set off for the airport. We had been driving for about 15 minutes when there was a traffic jam ahead of us. As we crept slowly forward, I saw a handful of heavily armed masked men standing by the side of the road with a blackboard with a list of car registration numbers. It was one of the illegal road blocks set up by dissidents on the look out for various targets (many of whom were tortured, murdered, or simply disappeared). My eyes scanned the list and, to my horror, the registration number of my hire car was there. Call it luck or instinct, fate was definitely on my side that day.

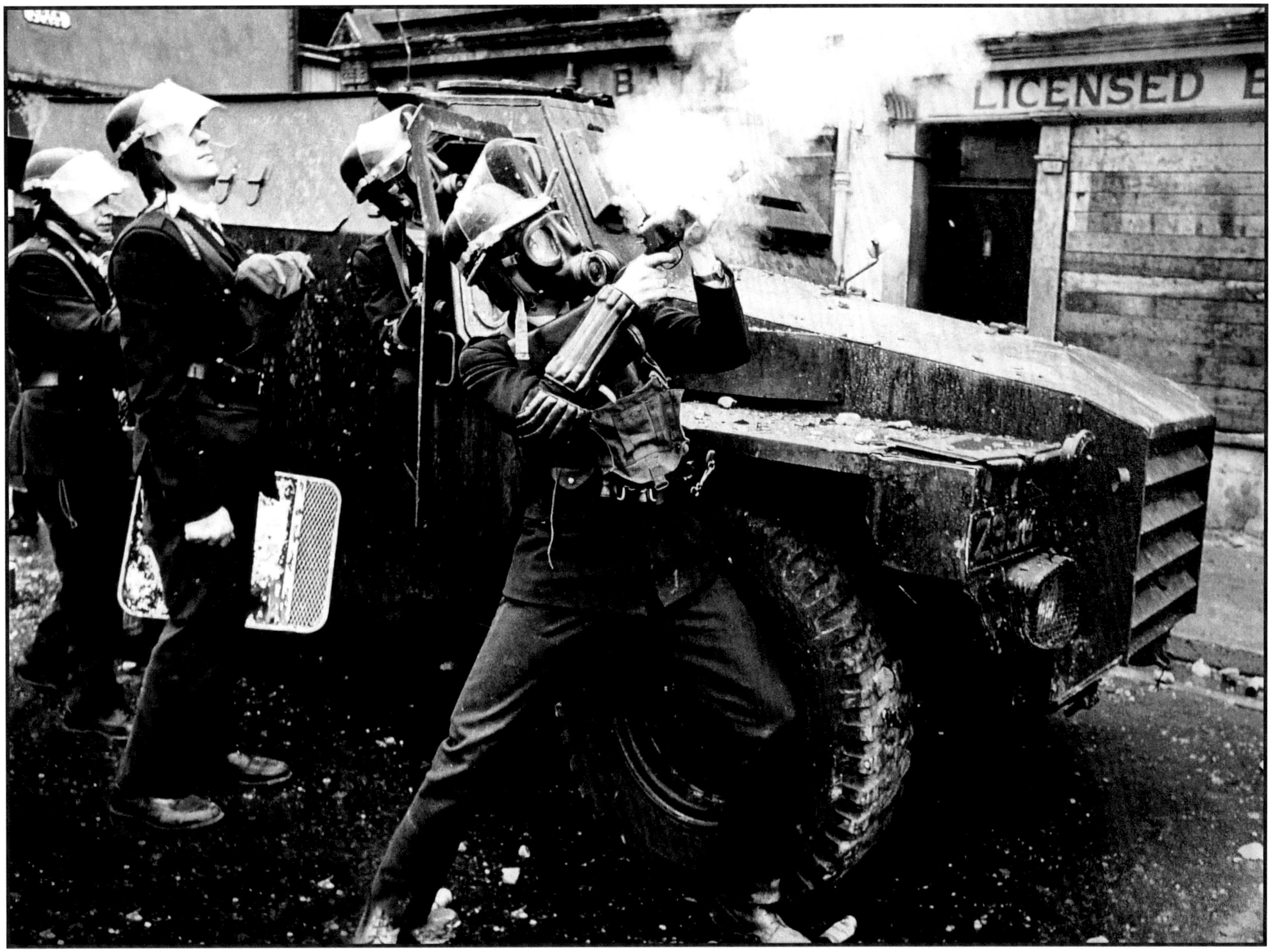
LICENSED

24.

Troops with captured 'Molotov Cocktail' petrol bombs.

1970, Northern Ireland

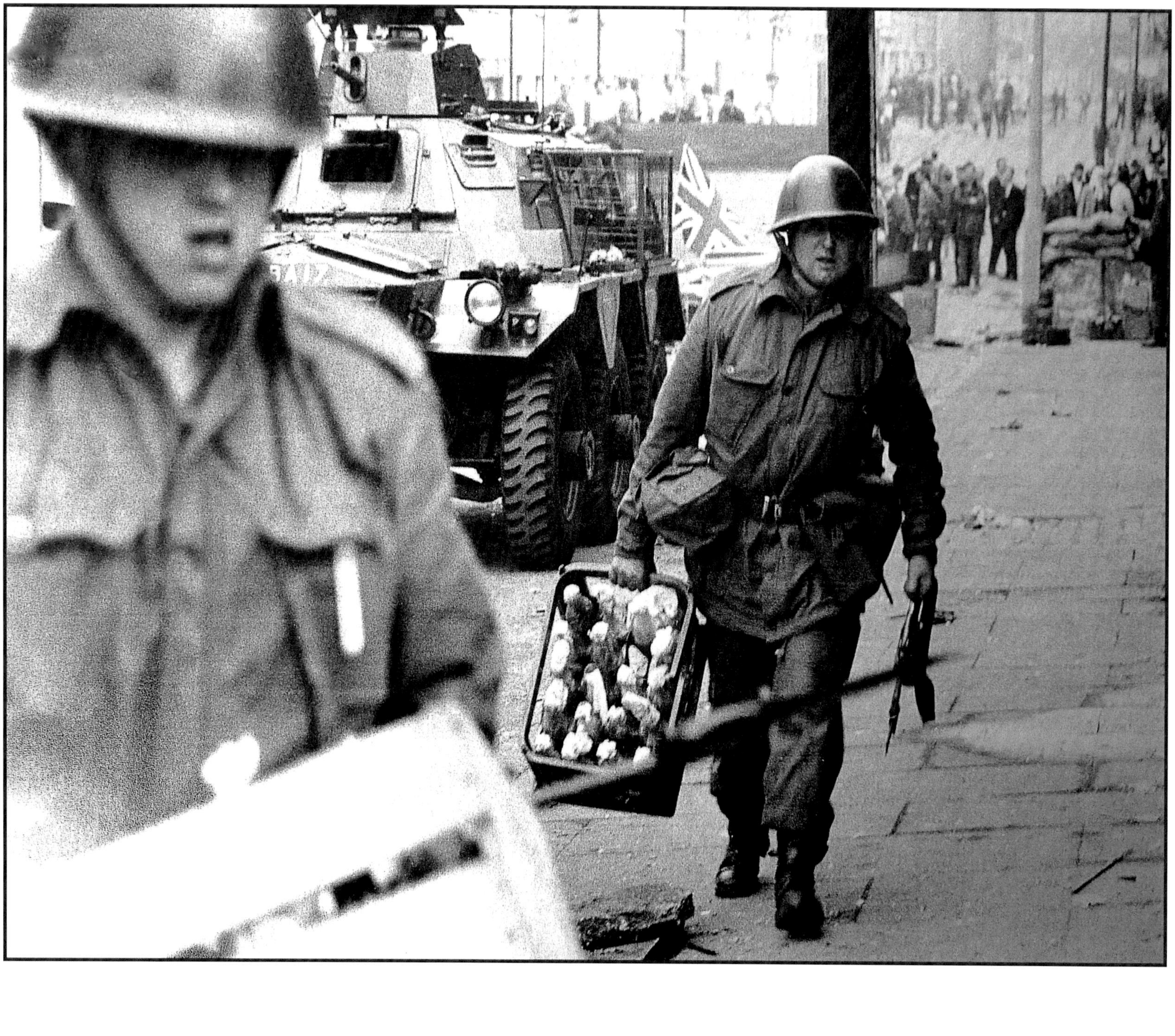

25.

Policeman Leaning on a 'Pig'

1970, Northern Ireland

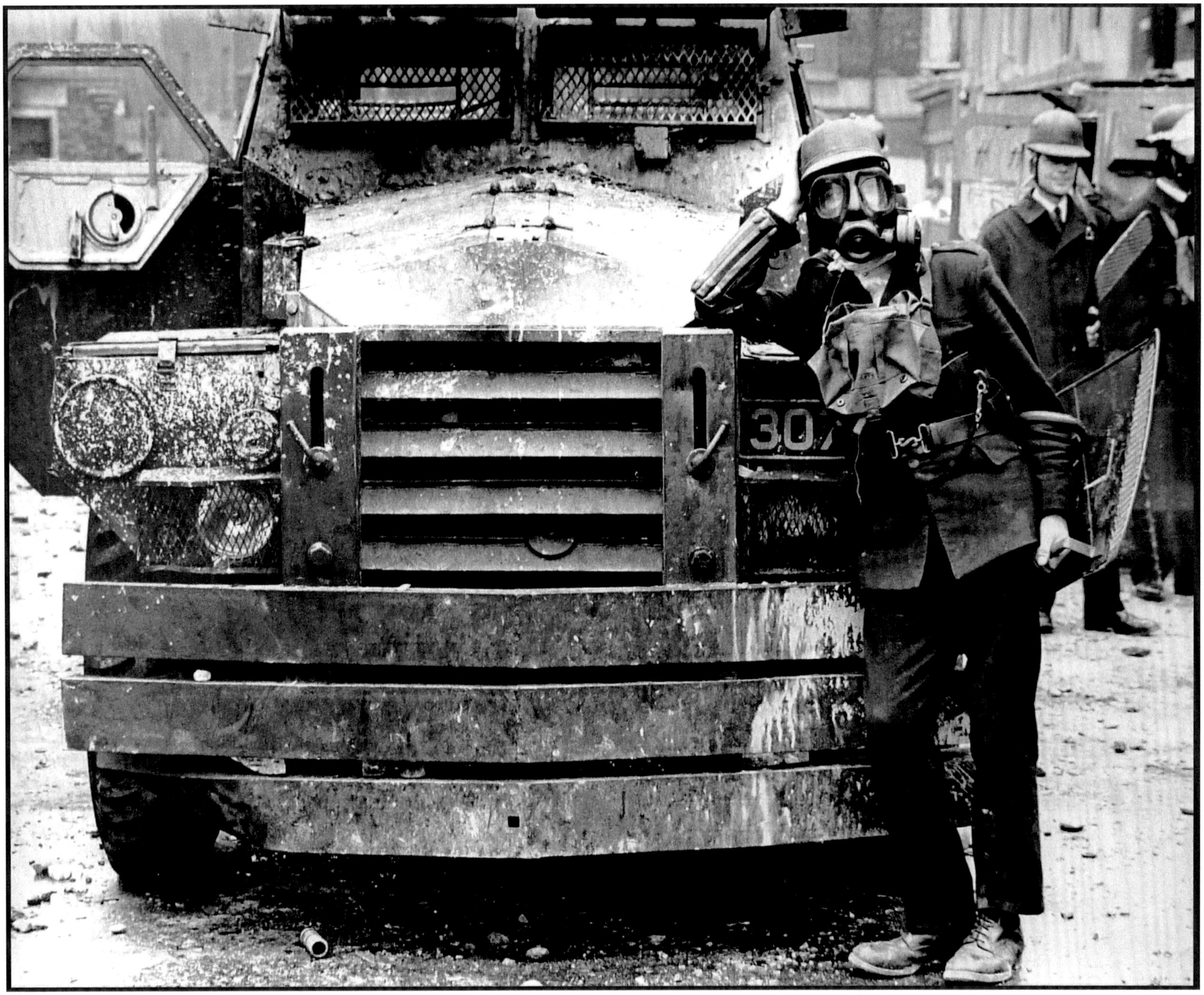

26.

Fire Rages

1970, Northern Ireland

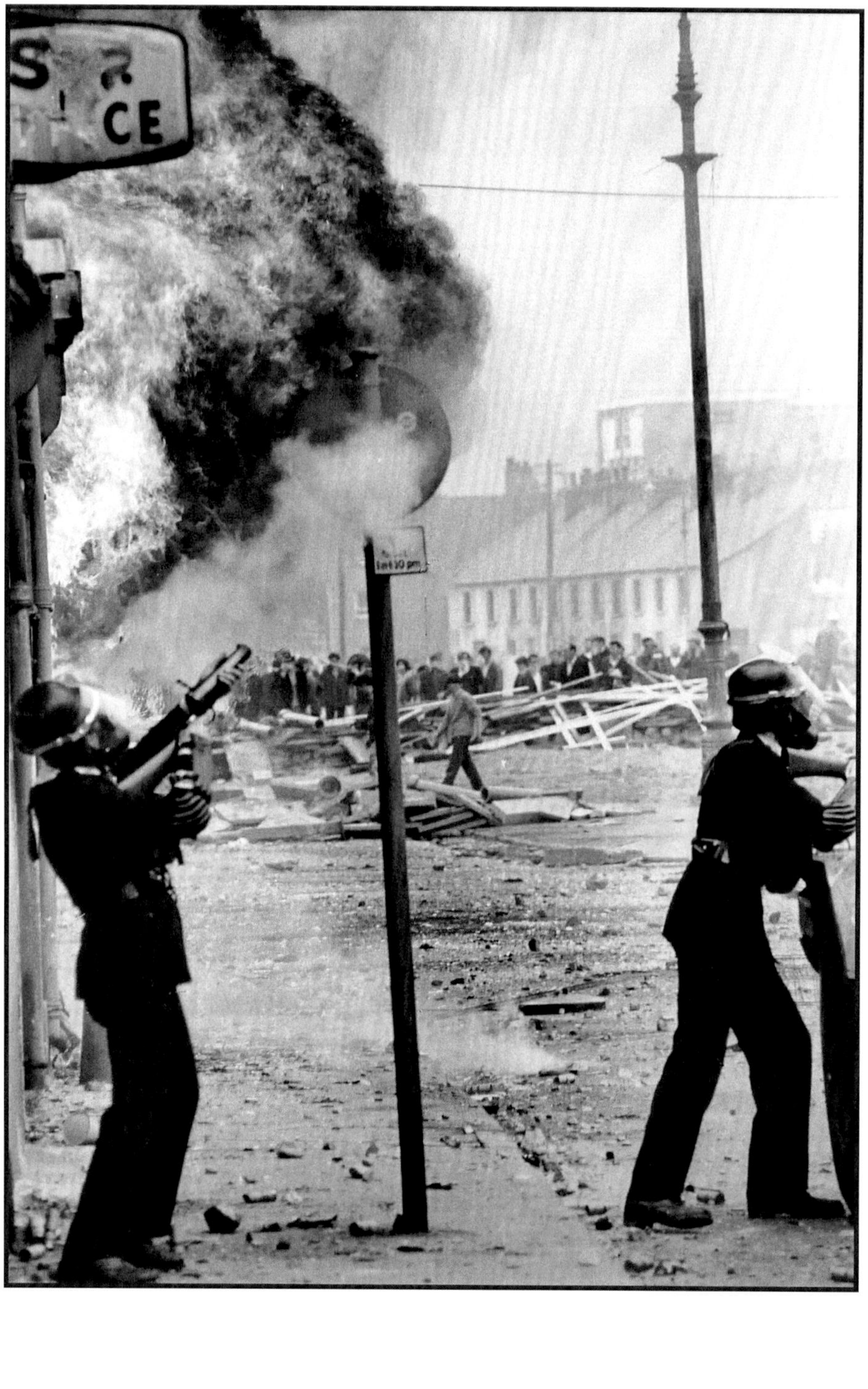

27.

Riots

1970, Northern Ireland

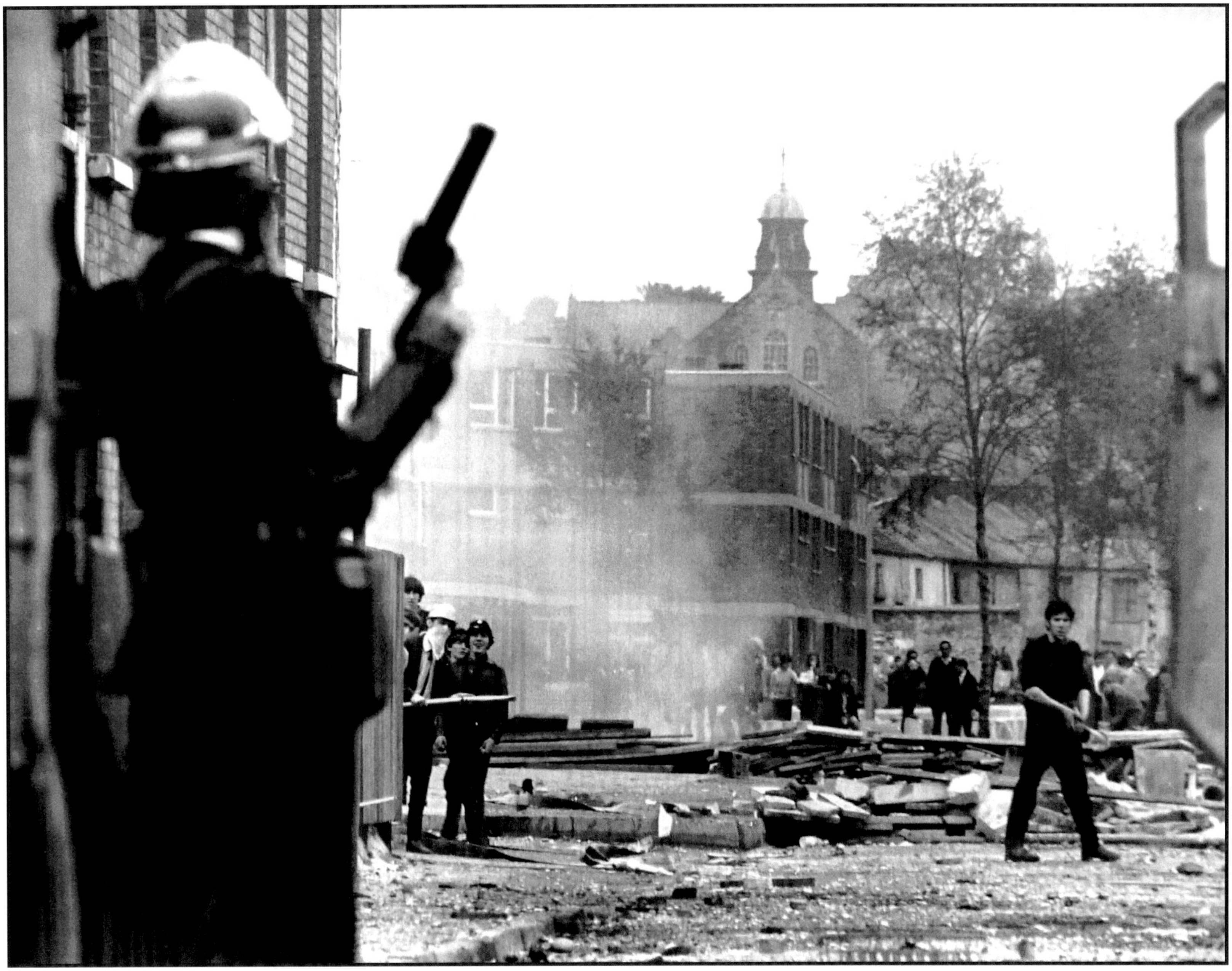

28.

Army Barracks in Belfast

1970, Northern Ireland

Taking no chances on the way to the washroom.

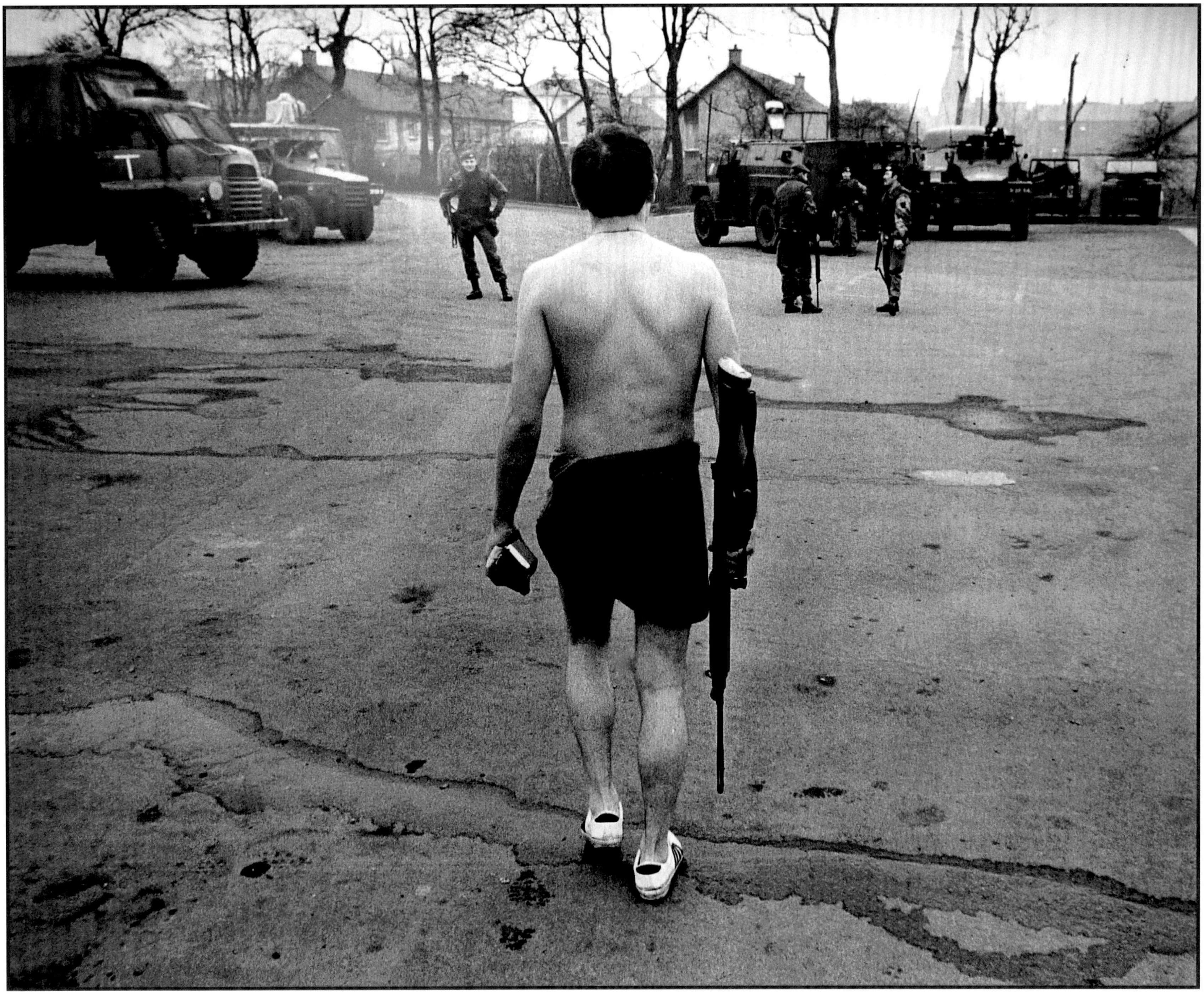

29.
Natalie Wood
1971, London

Natalie Wood, acclaimed actress who was the recipient of four Golden Globes, and three Academy Award nominations, with her second husband Richard Gregson and their assorted children.
Natalie's agent had arranged for me to meet up with them in Green Park, Piccadilly.
Later that year Wood filed for divorce from Gregson and went on to re-marry her first husband Robert Wagner. She drowned in suspicious circumstances in 1981 whilst sailing off Santa Catalina island aged 43. Wagner was named a person of interest in the investigation into her death.

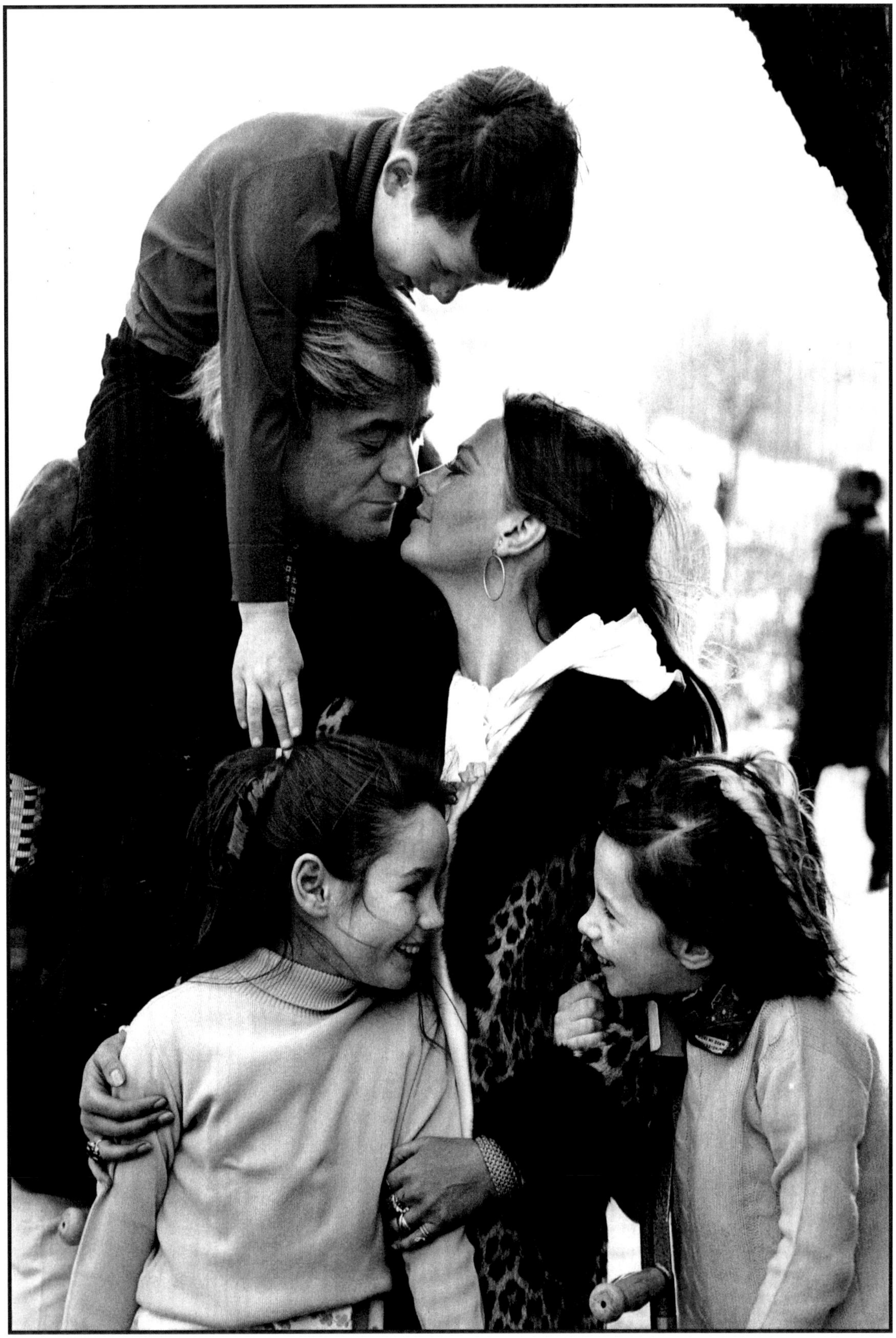

30.

Demo with Brolly

1972, Whitehall

The 70s was a time when there were a lot of protests and street riots in London.
The CND 'Ban the Bomb' movement was particularly active and there were all manner of political protests, some of which turned quite ugly. Having been on the receiving end in some violent clashes I knew how important it was to be cautious, nevertheless in order to get graphic images like this I needed to be in the thick of things. This demonstration in Whitehall produced my picture of a protestor pinned down by policemen, but still hanging onto his umbrella for dear life!

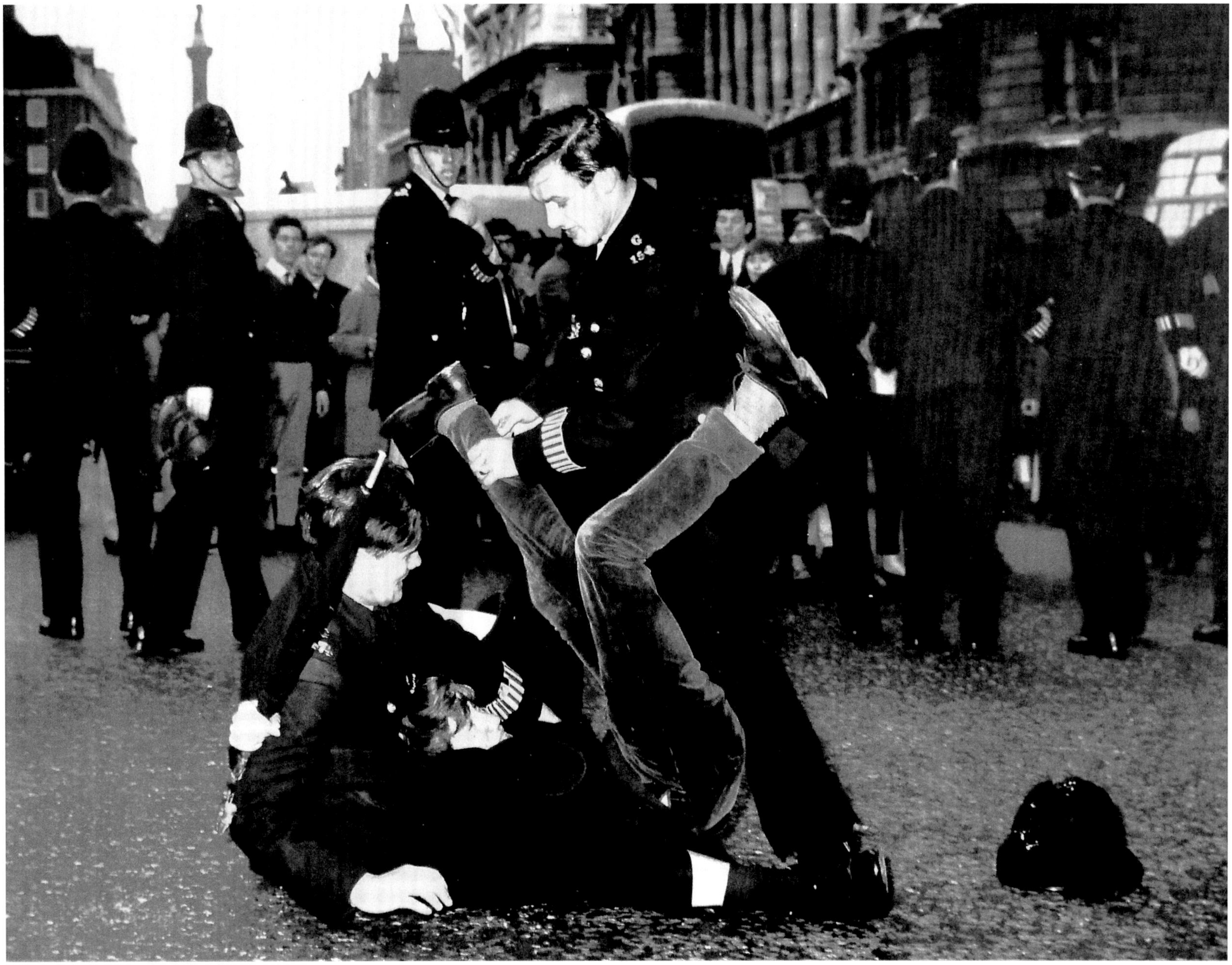

31.
Air Disaster
1974, Paris

In 1974, whilst I was working for *The Sun*, a Turkish airliner bound for London via Paris crashed on the outskirts of that city near Senlis, killing all 346 passengers and crew. This was a major disaster and, along with a reporter, I was briefed to get to Paris as soon as possible. We went straight to the airport, where many friends and relatives who had been waiting for the doomed plane were gathered. I seem to remember that there was an industrial dispute at Heathrow at the time, making it virtually impossible to get a normal flight out, but speed was imperative. It was decided that the quickest option was to charter a Trident to get us to Paris and we offered a ride to any of those waiting who wanted to come with us.

When we got to Paris, the reporter and I jumped in a taxi and headed for the scene. It was horrendous. The plane had ploughed through a forest, cutting a swathe through hundreds of trees. As I walked through the smouldering wreckage, the devastation and the stench of burnt wood and flesh was sickening. It was obvious that nobody could have survived.

Heading towards me was a Turkish man with his head in his hands. He had been on our chartered plane from Heathrow, and was looking for his wife. It was a harrowing experience and a sight which is indelible in my memory.

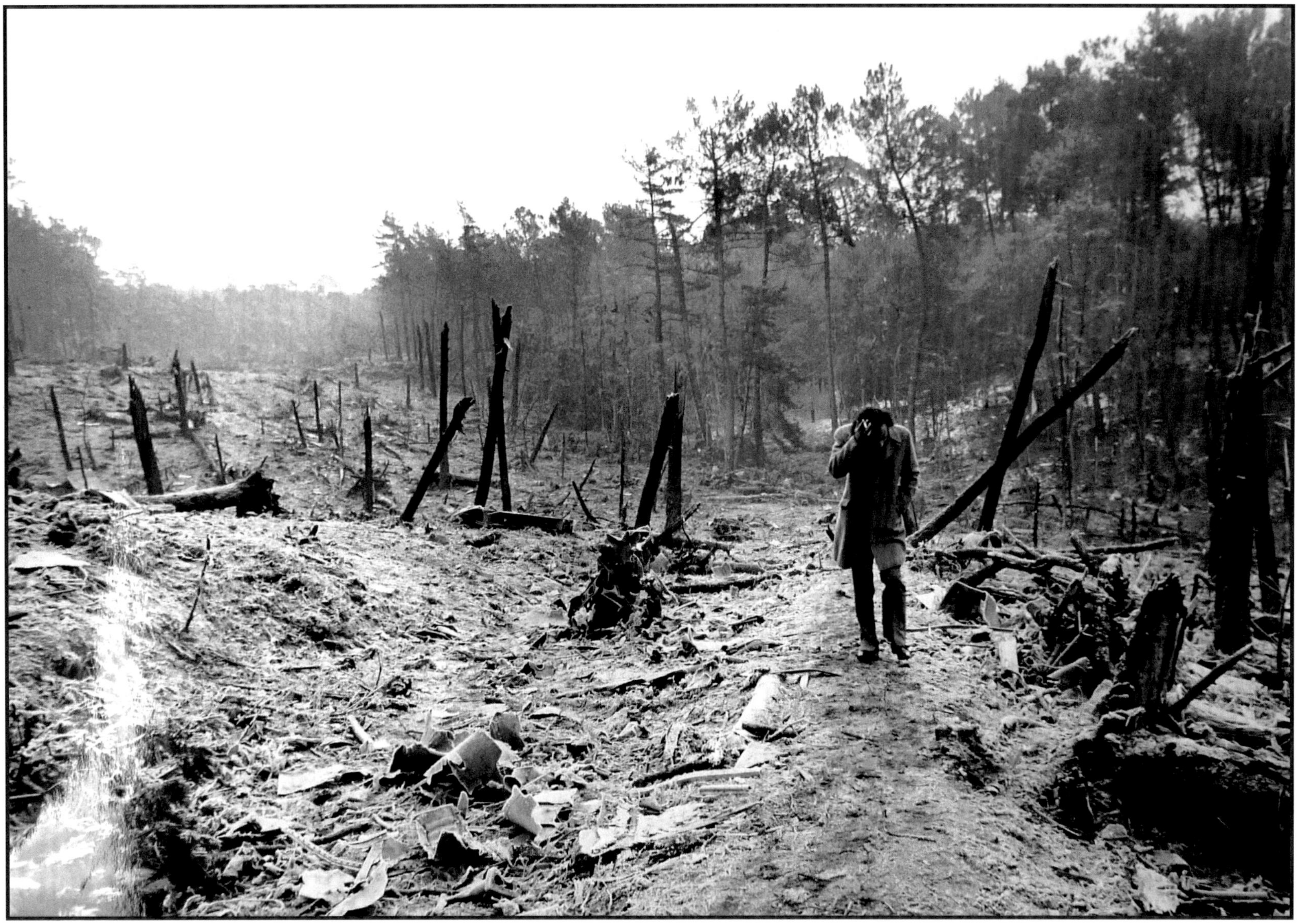

32.

Charles & Diana Wedding

1981, London

In 1981 Prince Charles married Lady Diana Spencer.
The Royal wedding was a huge logistical exercise for newspapers as so many locations and vantage points had to be researched to achieve maximum coverage. I was assigned a position on a statue at the entrance to Admiralty Arch. It was a tense moment as the royal carriage approached, I knew there would only be time for one shot before the carriage swung into the Mall. The picture was syndicated around the world.

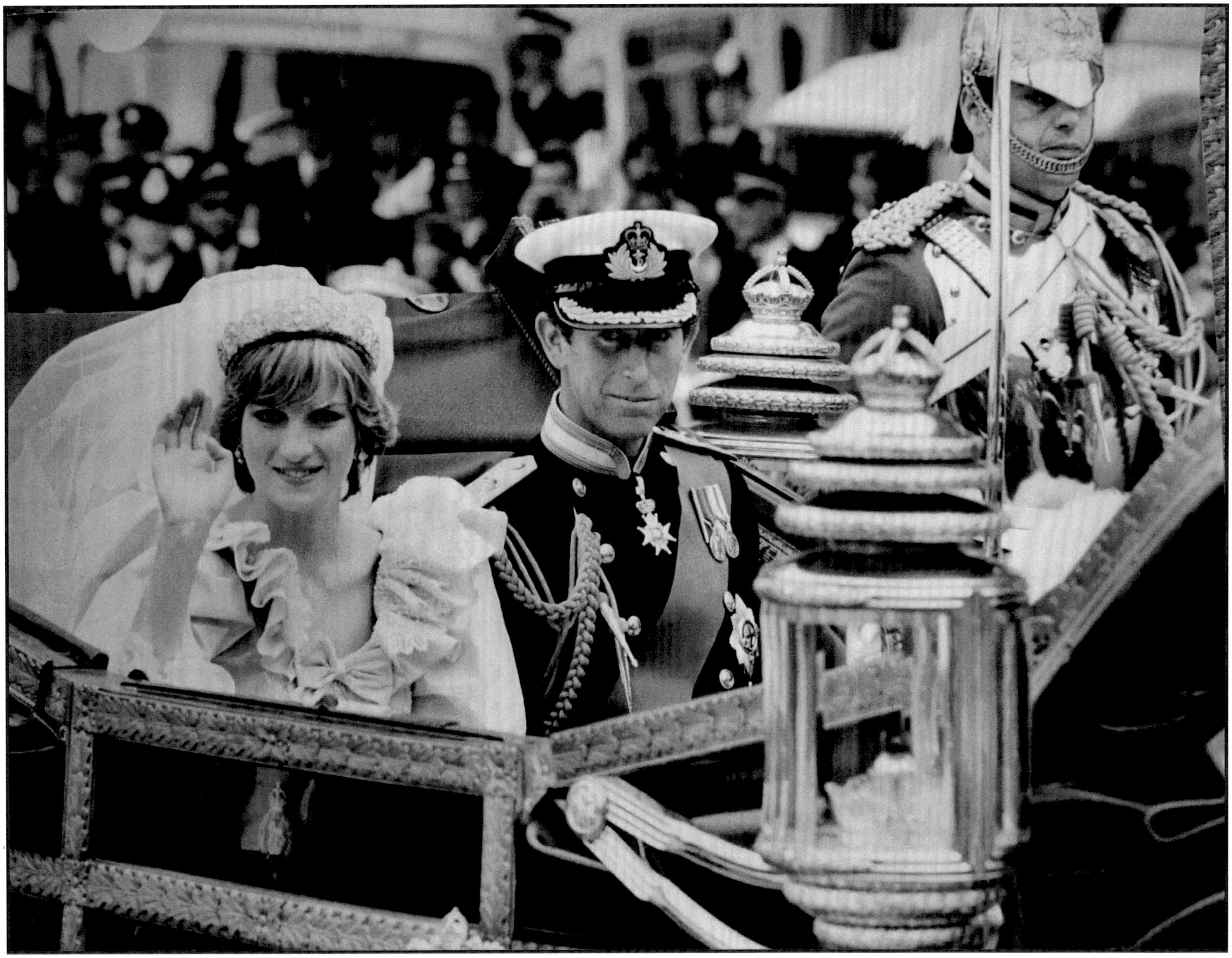

33.
The Pharaohs' Secrets
1988, London

Between 1985-1990, Charlie Wilson was editor of *The Times*. One day in 1988 he called me to his office. He said that he wanted me to be involved in a story that was of great importance, particularly for *The Times*.

Back in 1924, English Egyptologist Howard Carter made the sensational discovery of the treasures of Tutankhamun in the burial chamber hidden in the Valley of the Kings in Egypt. *The Times* had secured a world exclusive, and was the first newspaper to run the story. As a result, a *Times* correspondent was appointed for the dig and the paper was given sole rights to distribute dispatches on the excavation.

Howard Carter was sponsored by Lord Carnarvon, whose family home was Highclere Castle, in Berkshire. Charlie Wilson told me he had just taken a call from the present Lord Carnarvon. He had revealed that his butler at Highclere had made an amazing discovery and Lord Carnarvon wanted to continue the close ties with the paper and give us another world exclusive. The butler had noticed a cupboard that had been painted-in for years. Curious, he forced the door open to discover some boxes full of forgotten treasures from Tutankhamun's tomb. When Howard Carter returned in triumph with his haul to show his sponsor, the 5th Earl of Carnarvon, he had separated what he considered to be the important pieces and 'junked' the rest. They had remained in the cupboard, unseen since 1924.

Charlie was very excited about the story, particularly because of the historical ties with the paper.

I drove to Highclere Castle the next morning. Lord Carnarvon was charming. After showing me all the boxes of treasure, I needed to find a suitable location to set up my temporary studio. As luck would have it, Lord Carnarvon showed me to a part of the castle that had also been closed off for years. His ancestor, the 5th Earl of Carnarvon who had sponsored Howard Carter's expedition to Egypt, had been a keen photographer when the art was in its infancy, and had converted an attic room into a studio. Nobody had been in there since he died in 1923. It was a great location for me to set up my camera and lights and it was fitting that I should be using his studio to photograph some of the treasures that had belonged to him. I spent several days photographing all the objects and every day after processing the film, drove to Charlie's house in London to show him my work.

I returned to my Highclere studio one evening to pack everything up. As usual I was on my own in the attic studio, which was in a very remote part of the castle. Suddenly, I could smell burning. There was smoke pouring out of the lighting wires. A loud bang and I was plunged into darkness. The electrics in that wing had not been used for so long they just over- heated and the whole lot fused. I had no idea where the fuse board was and had no torch anyway. I managed to make sure the wiring that had been smoking was secure and not a fire risk, before trying to find my way out of the castle.

I couldn't help thinking about the alleged curse linked to those who had been involved with the excavation of Tutankhamun's tomb. I had done my research and remembered reading that rumours of such a curse had been rife in the world's press at the time of the excavation, fuelled by the sudden death of the 5th Earl in Cairo aged 56, at the same time as the light's suddenly went out in the city. Could the curse be true? I'd been working in that studio for days...Luckily, I lived to tell the tale, not without being almost scared to death trying to find my way out of the castle, in the middle of the night, without a torch!

Charlie was thrilled with the results of my labours. We ran a full colour spread and it looked fantastic. All the pieces I photographed, along with copies of my photographs are now part of a permanent exhibition at Highclere Castle.

He told me how much he valued the way that I had handled the project, and wanted to show his appreciation. He asked me if there was anywhere in the world I would like to go, and he would pick up the tab. When I said that I would love to go to India and the Himalayas, he suggested covering an assignment in Dubai for the racing desk and that I could go on from there, maybe taking a few pictures for the travel pages, which I loved doing.

What a fantastic 'Thank you'.

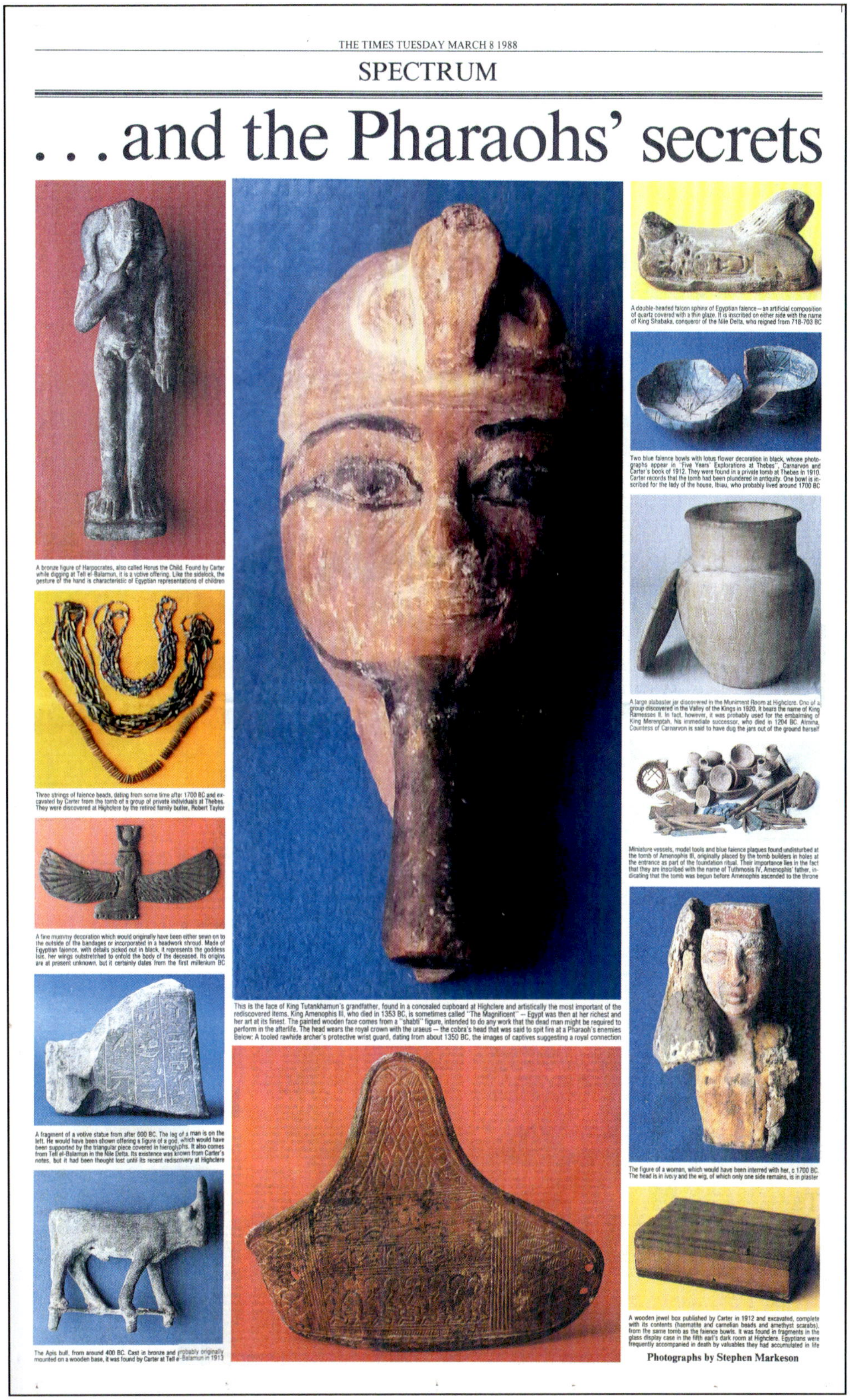

THE TIMES TUESDAY MARCH 8 1988

SPECTRUM

. . . and the Pharaohs' secrets

A bronze figure of Harpocrates, also called Horus the Child. Found by Carter while digging at Tell el-Balamun, it is a votive offering. Like the sidelock, the gesture of the hand is characteristic of Egyptian representations of children

Three strings of faience beads, dating from some time after 1700 BC and excavated by Carter from the tomb of a group of private individuals at Thebes. They were discovered at Highclere by the retired family butler, Robert Taylor

A fine mummy decoration which would originally have been either sewn on to the outside of the bandages or incorporated in a beadwork shroud. Made of Egyptian faience, with details picked out in black, it represents the goddess Isis, her wings outstretched to enfold the body of the deceased. Its origins are at present unknown, but it certainly dates from the first millenium BC

A fragment of a votive statue from after 600 BC. The leg of a man is on the left. He would have been shown offering a figure of a god, which would have been supported by the triangular piece covered in hieroglyphs. It also comes from Tell el-Balamun in the Nile Delta. Its existence was known from Carter's notes, but it had been thought lost until its recent rediscovery at Highclere

The Apis bull, from around 400 BC. Cast in bronze and probably originally mounted on a wooden base, it was found by Carter at Tell el-Balamun in 1913

This is the face of King Tutankhamun's grandfather, found in a concealed cupboard at Highclere and artistically the most important of the rediscovered items. King Amenophis III, who died in 1353 BC, is sometimes called "The Magnificent" — Egypt was then at her richest and her art at its finest. The painted wooden face comes from a "shabti" figure, intended to do any work that the dead man might be required to perform in the afterlife. The head wears the royal crown with the uraeus — the cobra's head that was said to spit fire at a Pharaoh's enemies

Below: A tooled rawhide archer's protective wrist guard, dating from about 1350 BC, the images of captives suggesting a royal connection

A double-headed falcon sphinx of Egyptian faience — an artificial composition of quartz covered with a thin glaze. It is inscribed on either side with the name of King Shabaka, conqueror of the Nile Delta, who reigned from 718-703 BC

Two blue faience bowls with lotus flower decoration in black, whose photographs appear in "Five Years' Explorations at Thebes", Carnarvon and Carter's book of 1912. They were found in a private tomb at Thebes in 1910. Carter records that the tomb had been plundered in antiquity. One bowl is inscribed for the lady of the house, Ibiau, who probably lived around 1700 BC

A large alabaster jar discovered in the Muniment Room at Highclere. One of a group discovered in the Valley of the Kings in 1920, it bears the name of King Ramesses II. In fact, however, it was probably used for the embalming of King Merenptah, his immediate successor, who died in 1204 BC. Almina, Countess of Carnarvon is said to have dug the jars out of the ground herself

Miniature vessels, model tools and blue faience plaques found undisturbed at the tomb of Amenophis III, originally placed by the tomb builders in holes at the entrance as part of the foundation ritual. Their importance lies in the fact that they are inscribed with the name of Tuthmosis IV, Amenophis' father, indicating that the tomb was begun before Amenophis ascended to the throne

The figure of a woman, which would have been interred with her, c 1700 BC. The head is in ivory and the wig, of which only one side remains, is in plaster

A wooden jewel box published by Carter in 1912 and excavated, complete with its contents (haematite and carnelian beads and amethyst scarabs), from the same tomb as the faience bowls. It was found in fragments in the glass display case in the fifth earl's dark room at Highclere. Egyptians were frequently accompanied in death by valuables they had accumulated in life

Photographs by Stephen Markeson

34.
Hidden Treasures
1989, Iraq

As a senior staff photojournalist on *The Times* I was given a free rein as I was expected to be self-generating, producing good pictures and stories on a global brief. The picture editor, Andrew Harvey, had supreme confidence in me. I would find stories anywhere in the world, and disappear for as long as it would take to get results.

Some years before the Iraq war I read an article in a specialist magazine about a major excavation underway in the desert in Northern Iraq. Archaeologists were unearthing treasures of the Assyrian Kings, including some fabulous jewellery, the most important find since the discovery of Tutankhamun's tomb in Egypt. I had never been to Iraq and it sounded like an assignment that would produce good colour material, maybe for a supplement, particularly bearing in mind *The Times*' well documented connections with archaeological discoveries.

I contacted the Iraqi embassy in London about getting a visa. They told me that it could take up to 12 months, which was far too long to wait. I decided to go through their press office, explaining my reason for wanting to go and the publicity benefits for the country. They decided to 'bend the rules' and get me a visa within a week. 'Much more like it', I thought!

I flew to Baghdad, arriving late at night. I was in the process of going through immigration and customs, when an officious officer in an army uniform told me to empty all my bags and camera case. The look on his face when he saw all of my cameras spelt big trouble. I was shunted into an office where two army officers cross-questioned me. I explained that I worked for *The Times* and was on my way to Mosul and Nimrud, in the north of the country, to photograph an archeological site.

They refused to believe me, insisting that a photographer only needs one camera. After an hour of interrogation I was getting very worried. They accused me of lying and wanted to know the real reason why I was there. My mind was racing. 'My god, they think I'm a spy. What the hell do I do now?' By good fortune, I had done my research before leaving London and had a note of the British Consulate in Baghdad. I managed, with extreme difficulty, to make contact and with their help was released. Not before a whole page in my passport had been scrawled over detailing my camera equipment.

(It was only on my return to the UK that it became clear why I had been detained and given such a hard time. Unbeknownst to me, the military and immigration were on high alert. A freelance journalist, working for *The Observer*, had been arrested in Iraq before I arrived there and was awaiting trial accused of spying for Israel. Farzal Bazoft was eventually executed, protesting his innocence to the end.)

Meanwhile, I had a job to do, and by this time it was very late at night. I found a taxi outside the airport to take me to my hotel. The name of the hotel escapes me now, but it was the best in Baghdad. We drove through some very unlikely streets and came to a stop outside a small, scruffy, hotel in the suburbs of Baghdad. The hotel indeed shared the same name as the one that I had booked, but this was clearly not the right one!

The driver couldn't speak English, so communication was minimal. I protested that this was certainly not my hotel, but he insisted, and emptied all my luggage onto the street. By this time it was about 3.00 in the morning. The streets were empty and I was exhausted. I took a view that the best option was to check into what was a real dump and review the situation when daylight came.

The hall was full of Iraqi men in their white cotton robes, sleeping on the floor. I managed to get a room and was so

- **COOKING:** NO-PODGE CHRISTMAS PUD
- **BOOKS:** HUTTON'S *KING CHARLES II*
- **SHOPPING:** CLASSY PARTY GLASSES
- **DRINKS:** PICK OF THE WINES BY POST

THE TIMES

REVIEW

SECTION 3

SATURDAY NOVEMBER 25 1989

HIDDEN TREASURE

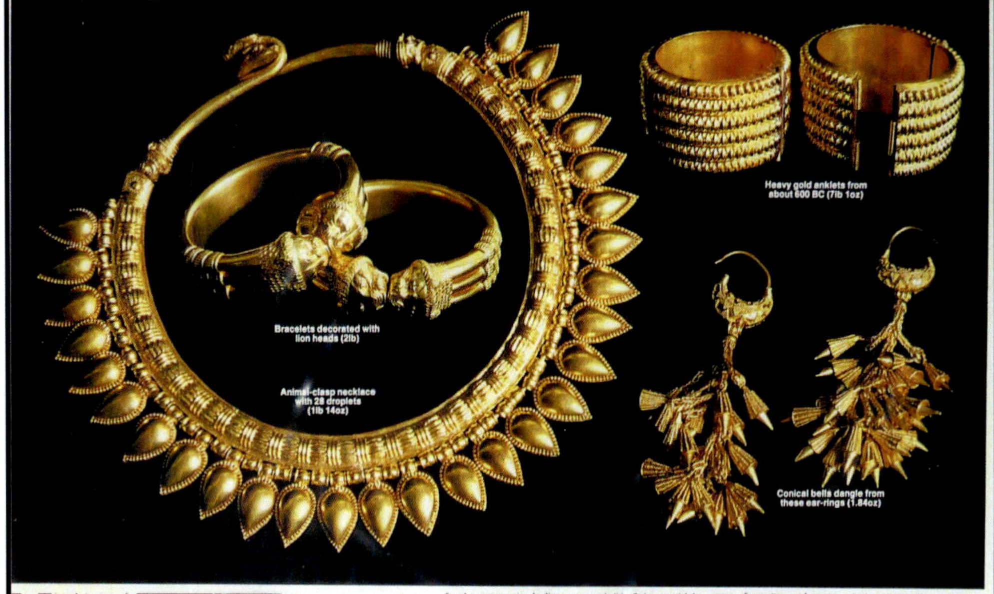

Heavy gold anklets from about 800 BC (7lb 1oz)

Bracelets decorated with lion heads (2lb)

Animal-clasp necklace with 28 droplets (1lb 14oz)

Conical bells dangle from these ear-rings (1.84oz)

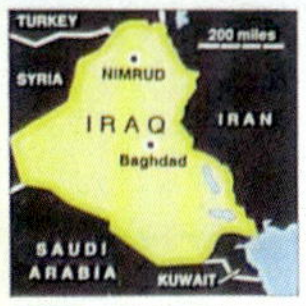

In the deserts of Iraq, archaeologists are unearthing the previously over-looked treasures of the Assyrian kings. **George Hill** reports on the most important finds since the discovery of Tutankhamun's tomb in Egypt. Photographs by **Stephen Markeson**

Nimrud is one of those pregnant mounds of rubble, scattered here and there in the deserts of the Near East, which archaeologists regard as the cradles of human civilization. In other words, they are the vast charnel heaps of unwept and detestable tyrannies over-thrown thousands of years ago – concentrations of litter, bones and, occasionally, gold, which bear witness to ancient squalor, cruelty and pride.

Tremulously referred to in the Bible as Calah, "the great city", Nimrud was for centuries a capital of Assyria, perhaps the most ferocious of all the bloodthirsty empires of Mesopotamia. Its presiding deity was Ninurta, god of war. Its ruins were among the first to be excavated by the high-handed archaeologists of Queen Victoria's day: any visitor to the British Museum must have seen the majestic, human-headed, winged lions and bulls which archaeologist Sir Austen Henry Layard took from a dead empire to embellish a living one.

Between 1949 and 1958, Nimrud was painstakingly re-excavated by Sir Max Mallowan, the husband of Agatha Christie, who used her first-hand experience of digs in torrid climates as the setting for one of her most intricate mysteries, *Murder in Mesopotamia*. But Layard and Mallowan never knew that they missed a treasure at Nimrud more glittering than anything they unearthed. For Mallowan in particular, the failure was a tantalizingly near thing. He actually cleared debris away from a small paved room in the labyrinthine ruins of the royal palace, little knowing that just below his feet lay a treasure which has been compared to the legendary finds made a generation earlier in the tomb of Tutankhamun in Egypt.

The upshot is that these superb crowns, necklaces, fragile glass-work and massive golden bracelets, which lay within a few yards of the spot, have gone to the Iraq Museum. Appropriately, they will thus be preserved and displayed on what was once Assyrian soil, in Baghdad, instead of thousands of miles away in Bloomsbury. The parts of the collection which have already been put on display fill two rooms of the Iraq Museum, and the richest finds are not yet ready to go on show.

"I don't think you can blame Mallowan for missing them," says Dr John Curtis, keeper of Western Asiatic Antiquities at the British Museum, who is now in Nimrud as head of a British team excavating another part of the site. "You can't dig under the floor of every single room on the off-chance that there might be a grave there. Mallowan excavated only one of the three rooms where the tombs were found, and there was nothing remarkable about the room in itself."

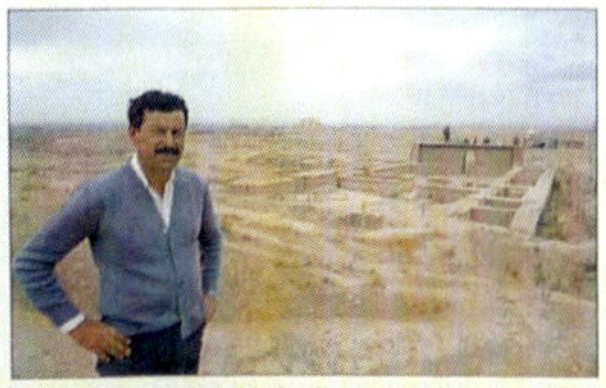

City of gold: Muzahim Mahmud, of the Iraqui archaeological team, at Nimrud

Curtis believes that the new discoveries show that the part of the palace where they were found must have been the harem wing, where the queens of Assyria lived. A carved inscription identifies one of the tombs as that of Yaba, "palace woman", or queen, of King Tiglath-Pileser III, a soldier who seized power in a military coup in 744 BC and extended the empire in a series of slaughterous campaigns to what may have been its greatest expanse, from Azerbaijan to Syria and the Persian Gulf.

"It was common practice in the Near East to make burials under the floors of buildings," Curtis says. "Knowing what we know now, I think there is more gold under the floor of the palace. It would be very tempting for an archaeologist to go rushing round from room to room after a discovery like this, looking under the pavements and forgetting to do careful research. But the archaeologists from the Iraq Department of Antiquities have been extremely responsible in keeping to their programme of excavation and restoration since making the finds."

The first of the three separate treasure-burials was discovered last year by Muzahim Mahmud, head of the Iraqi team at Nimrud, below the room which had been cleared by Mallowan. The tomb contained golden jewellery, including a large pomegranate-shaped pendant, an ornate brooch with a chain, and ear-rings decorated with delicate flowers. Muzahim was granted permission to resume the search this season.

Recently, he told our photographer, Stephen Markeson, who visited the site and took pictures of some of the finds, how he came across the second and much richer tomb, within 50 yards of the first, in April this year. "Fifteen days after we had started to dig, we found a pottery pipe leading down to the top of a stone barrel-vault. Further digging showed that we had found the roofs of two chambers built in a T-shape. We looked for the entrance, and found one, blocked by two big stones."

This doorway led into an ante-chamber, empty save for a stone tablet with a long inscription in cuneiform script. At one end was an opening which had been bricked up. Breaking through the bricks, Muzahim's team entered a vaulted tomb-chamber containing a sarcophagus nearly eight feet long, covered by two large slabs of stone. He levered a slab off and shone a torch into the coffin.

"I saw the gold, very bright in my eyes, mixed with bones and clothes and dust," he said. "There was gold from head to toe – many, many pieces – a crown, ear-rings and necklaces, and bangles and rosettes fixed on the dress."

The sarcophagus contained a vast array of grave goods, including nearly 90 necklaces, more than 80 gold ear-rings – many of them with elaborate clusters of pendants – and an exquisite golden diadem made from fine wires plaited together in a herring-bone mesh, with a tasselled fringe at the front and tiger-eye rosettes at the sides and at the rear, where the golden ribbon would have flowed down the wearer's back.

There were four heavy gold bracelets inlaid with brightly coloured stones, showing winged figures kneeling beside sacred trees. A gold bowl, embossed with a pharaoh hunting crocodile in a papyrus thicket, appeared from its style to have come from Phoenicia, 500 miles away on the western borders of the Assyrian empire – a unique example of Phoenician gold.

Other vessels, in gold, alabaster and rock crystal, are inscribed with the names of Yaba and the queens of the next two kings of Assyria (remains of at least two skeletons were found in the tomb, and there were burnt ashes which may have been a cremation burial).

Four months after making these finds, Muzahim found a third burial a few yards to the south. This was a more complicated and puzzling collection: three bronze coffins were found higgledy-piggledy in an ante-chamber, filled with an astonishing variety of goods in gold and ivory, with bones and also perishable materials such as wood and light linen fabric. The items even include an ornate glass jar, inlaid with blue plaques and rows of tiny human figures, showing that Assyrian craftsmen had an entirely unsuspected mastery of the art of glassmaking.

Stone double doors turning on carved stone hinges led into a vaulted tomb-chamber like that of the second tomb. It contained a huge stone sarcophagus with an engraved lid, fitting so tightly inside the chamber that the latter must have been built round it. The lid had to be broken before it could be removed. But the searchers found that the coffin was, mysteriously, quite empty.

However, the treasures in the ante-room were even more remarkable than what had been found in the second tomb. As yet they have not been publicly shown, so relatively little is known about them. But they include 440 gold objects, weighing 23 kilos in all – almost twice the weight of the gold in the second tomb.

Among them is a crown, perhaps the masterpiece of the entire collection, which is in the form of a domed openwork hat in gold, decorated around the base with rows of rosettes and pomegranates. Above this, winged genies support an interlaced framework of vine leaves and grapes.

According to unofficial reports, some of the goods carry the name of the queen of one of the greatest and most implacable of all the Assyrian kings, Ashurnasirpal II. This would make them more than a century older than the remains found earlier. Ashurnasirpal reigned from 883 to 859 BC, and was the original builder of the palace. He boasted that he entertained 69,574 guests at its opening ceremonies. Surviving remains show that he had it decorated with superb limestone bas-reliefs showing battle scenes and symbolic fertility rites, in which he was depicted actively participating in both activities. His exploits are unusually well-recorded, for he took care to ensure that posterity would be well-informed about the details of his conquests, and about how he enforced Assyrian dominance over his enemies by beheading, flaying and impaling them – as well as by shuffling the survivors around the empire so that they should lose all sense of territorial identity.

Because Ashurnasirpal and his successors had such sanguinary tastes in interior decoration, few indications have come down to us of the softer side of Assyrian life, such as it was. That is one reason why the new discoveries at Nimrud are so revealing. "The astonishing fineness of the work on the

Continued overleaf

'THE GOLD WAS VERY BRIGHT IN MY EYES. MIXED WITH BONES. GOLD FROM HEAD TO TOE. CROWN, EAR-RINGS, NECKLACES AND BANGLES . . . .'

scared of being mugged, or worse, that I barricaded the door with any furniture that was in the room, and sat on the edge of the bed, trembling. I was too scared to sleep and just waited for daybreak. I couldn't wait to get away, and took my suitcase, camera case and lights down the stairs and onto the street. I couldn't find a taxi anywhere. Desperate situations require desperate solutions. I walked into the middle of the road and stopped the first car that I saw. Luckily the driver spoke some English. Explaining my predicament, I offered him some money and he very kindly took me to the correct hotel. What a relief!

I was so exhausted that I went to bed and slept for hours. The following day I had to get to Mosul, some 250 miles to the north. I tried to hire a car and failed, so there was no alternative but to get a taxi to take me. In a way it was fortunate as it was a tortuous journey on some very rough roads. All the road signs were in Iraqi script, which of course I couldn't understand, so a taxi turned out to be a good idea. Arriving in Mosul, I checked into my hotel, this time without a hitch.

When researching the story in London I had made contact with the curator of the Mosul Museum, who had said that he would welcome me and take me to the site at Nimrud. I couldn't believe that things could carry on going wrong, but go wrong they did. I got to the museum to find that the curator had gone away and wouldn't be returning to Mosul for three weeks! His deputy, who had no instructions about my arrival, just said that I would have to come back when the curator returned. I explained that it would be impossible, as I had to get back to England. He did at least arrange for me to visit the dig, but a large quantity of the beautiful excavated jewellery and artefacts , which I particularly wanted to photograph, were already in glass cases in the museum. The deputy curator was implacable. I would have to wait. Then a masterly stroke. 'As I am here,' I said, 'why don't you let me take the photographs, and I will leave you all of the film for security.

When the curator returns, he will confirm that it is all OK and you can then post the film to me in England?' Luckily he agreed, as it appeared to be a good solution to the problem.

I was shown to the part of the museum where I was to work. I set up my camera and lights, and all the pieces were presented to me and the jewellery looked stunning. I shot a lot of film. Actually, I shot double the amount that I needed. Yes, one for me, and one to leave behind! I managed to hide the 'duplicate' film under the foam lining of my camera case, before presenting the deputy curator with 'all' the film for safekeeping!

If any trip was to provide challenges which stretched me, that was it. Surely nothing more could go wrong? Believe it or not, yes. There is a final chapter to the Iraq saga. Returning to Baghdad, I made my way to the airport in good time to catch the weekly British Airways flight back home. Standing in the queue to go through passport control and customs, I overheard a conversation between three English businessmen.

One said 'OK guys, are we all set with our paperwork - passports, Aids certificates...?' What was that, I thought, what Aids certificate? Curious and more than a little anxious, I asked them what they meant about an 'Aids certificate'. ' You must have one', they said, 'You wouldn't have got a visa in the first place without one'. It transpired, that I should have been tested for Aids before being issued with a visa in London, but of course, because I had short-circuited the system and gone through the press office for my visa, I was never told about it. The guys in the queue said that I wouldn't be allowed out of the country without that certificate, and that I would have to go back to a Baghdad hospital and be tested.

The line started to move forward and it was my turn next at passport control. Time to call upon sneaky resourcefulness again. The passport controllers, like the customs officers, were all in military uniform. I presented myself at the desk. 'Passport and papers', shouted the officer. 'Hmm... Now where are they?' I said. As I gave him my passport, I could see that he was getting very agitated and kept looking over his shoulder. 'Certificate?' he shouted, all the time getting more and more anxious. Then I could see why. A high ranking army officer, a General I think, was doing a tour of inspection, and all the passport controllers and customs officers were jumping to attention in a line. This was my opportunity. I said that I thought my certificate was in another case, and would he hold on for a few minutes? I was just using delaying tactics, which, thank goodness, worked. Eventually he lost his temper as the General was getting closer and he would have to jump to attention, too. 'Just go, go on, go through quickly!' I duly obliged. What a relief

Needless to say, that trip was pretty memorable for all the wrong reasons. Back in London, everyone was very happy with the results, and a full colour front page on the Review section was my prize. Oh, and that film I left in Mosul ? - it never did arrive!

35.
Maggie Thatcher
1990, Downing Street

In November 1990, I was called to Simon Jenkins office. He was Editor at that time, and wanted to see me for a 'very important' assignment. *The Times* had been told that Margaret Thatcher had been ousted as Prime Minister, and would be leaving No 10.
Simon told me he had been granted an exclusive interview with her the next day in Downing Street at mid-day. Arrangements had been made for me to go in advance, again exclusively, to photograph the 'Iron Lady'. I was told that I would be given at least an hour alone with her, and that it was going to be a 'World-beater' of a story.
I arrived at 10 Downing Street at 10.00 am, and was greeted at the door by Mrs.Thatcher. We had met on a number of occasions in the past. Well that was a good start. 'Stephen', she said walking up the large staircase, 'Follow me, we'll go up to one of the drawing rooms'. We arrived in a very spacious, formal, room at the back of the house. 'I'll leave you to set up your lights', she said, adding 'And I thought we would do the pictures there', pointing to a sofa beside the open fireplace. Well, in 'Maggie Thatcher speak', that meant 'You will take the pictures there!'
I had been agonising for hours over how on earth I would illustrate this story. A picture of her just sitting on a sofa simply did not tell the story of her imminent departure. Anyway, I did as I was told and set up my lights by the sofa. I went through the motions, all the time wondering how on earth I would get a good picture that told the story. I could hardly ask her to stand on the doorstep with a suitcase.
I carried on taking a few portraits, all the time wracking my brains. Then a 'Eureka' moment hit me! The room was sited at the back of the house, overlooking the gardens. The windows were large and had seats built into them. Now if only I could get her to sit in a window seat, I had a cunning plan...
'Have you finished Stephen?' she asked. 'Actually, I have an idea', I said. 'Why don't we do some pictures sitting in the garden?' (*I had no intention of taking such pictures...*) 'But it's drizzling with rain and windy, and I've had my hair done especially', she declared. She was quite right of course, it was an awful day, however, I was ready for that one. 'I know', I said, 'But why don't you sit over here in the window, I will go down to the garden and find a nice sheltered spot. Give me a few minutes, and I will give you a wave when I've found somewhere'.
'What a good idea', she said sitting in the window seat'. 'Gotcha!', I thought, and made my way down to the garden. I took my time as I wanted her to peer through the curtains looking for me. I waited out of sight with a long focus lens on my camera. I took a peek out, and sure enough she was looking for me. I took a couple of very quick pictures without her knowing, and then innocently gave her the sign to come down to the garden.
I continued the pretence and took some pictures of her sitting on a bench. She had no idea of the subterfuge. We returned to the warm and dry of the house, I said my farewells, and returned to Wapping.
Simon Jenkins, was about to leave for Downing Street to conduct his interview and I went to his office to tell him of my mischievous but successful session.

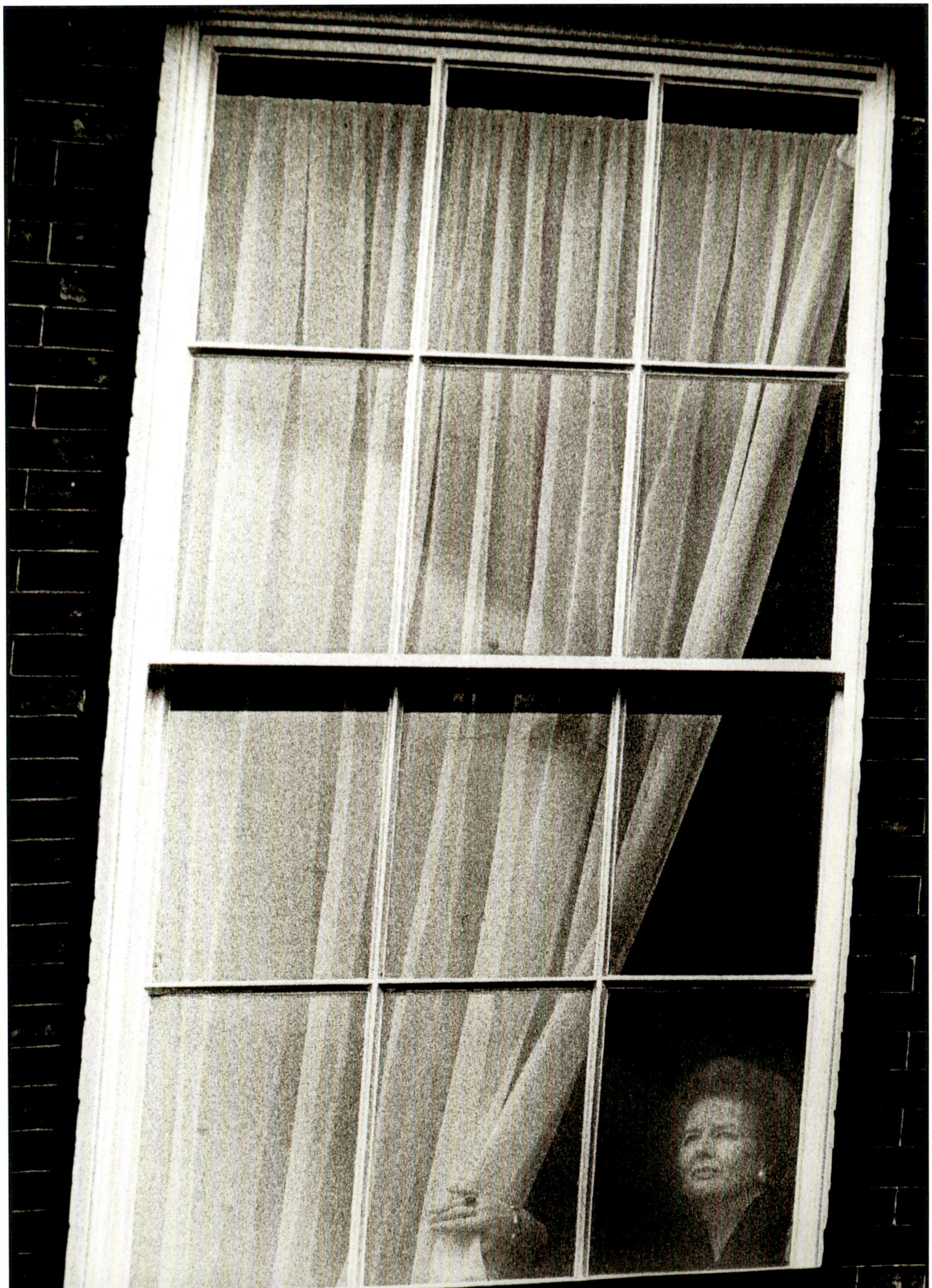

I explained that she had no idea of what I had done. As far as she was concerned, we had taken pictures in the drawing room, and in the garden. I explained to Simon that those pictures didn't tell the story, and how I wanted a picture of 'Maggie's last look out of Number Ten'. He thought it was great, but I wondered what the reaction might be from my 'victim' the next day.
The picture was published very large on the front page, and was also syndicated world-wide. The back of the house looked very similar to the front so everyone assumed she was gazing out over Downing Street! That morning Simon summoned me to his office. Oh my god, I thought, the proverbial has hit the fan. With more than a degree of trepidation I went into his office, where he was wreathed in smiles. 'Ive just taken a personal call from Maggie Thatcher, who wants you to know what a wonderful picture you had taken.' I cannot describe how relieved I was at hearing that. He went on to say 'She likes it so much, she wants you to arrange for a few large copies to be printed, and asked if you would take them personally to her'. 'Blimey', I thought, 'that's a result'. I duly had the darkroom make some 15 x 12 inch prints, and set off to deliver my ill-gotten gains.
I was greeted with compliments and thanks, and thought to myself that if I had been honest and declared my intentions at the outset, there was no way on this earth she would have agreed! All's well that ends well, and I don't suppose there are many people who can say that they got one over 'The Iron Lady'!

More recently, *The Spectator* magazine cartoonist copied my picture for the front page, substituting Theresa May at the window. I was subsequently asked to write 1000 words about how I took the original photograph.

THE SPECTATOR

The story behind my famous picture of Margaret Thatcher

Stephen Markeson

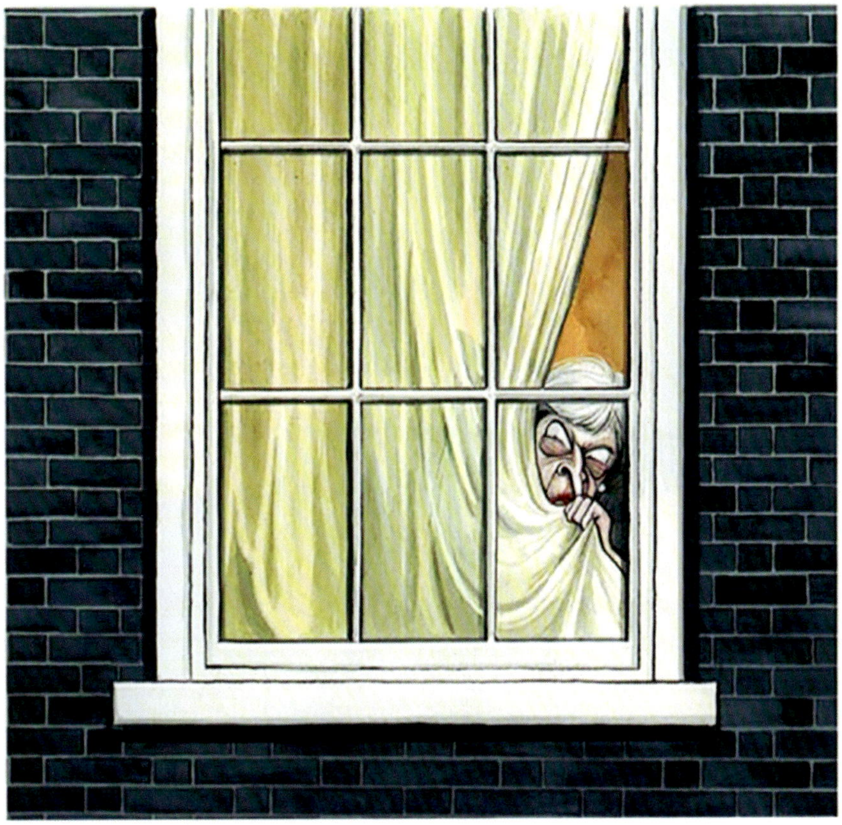

I was surprised and delighted to find Morten Morland's wonderful imitation of a photograph of Margaret Thatcher peering through the curtains of Number Ten on *The Spectator's* cover. It reminded me of one of my memorable experiences as a photographer with the 'Iron Lady'.

Stephen Markeson
29 September 2018
8:30 AM

PART 3
PORTRAITURE

Working for *The Times* was a great privilege. 'When *The Times* speaks the world listens'. Respected world-wide, it was considered the newspaper of record.

As a senior staff photographer I was not only briefed to cover the news but also to be 'self-generating', researching, arranging and covering stories anywhere in the world. I found that celebrities, politicians and other people of interest were usually only too pleased to let me photograph them for features in *The Times*.

However, newspapers were heavily controlled by trade unions. I had to be a member of the NUJ (National Union of Journalists) and union rules allowed me to take photographs but not to write stories.

In 1986 Rupert Murdoch revolutionised the industry by breaking the backs of the unions and opening up the News International plant at Wapping. No longer constrained by the old rules, I was now able to write as well as take pictures.

For a long period I wrote a weekly feature called *Off Duty* and some of my subjects are in this section.

36.

Barbra Streisand

1966, London

I waited in the rain for two hours near the stage door of the Prince of Wales Theatre in the hope of getting this shot of Barbra Streisand arriving to appear in the opening night of the hit Broadway show *Funny Girl*, in 1966.

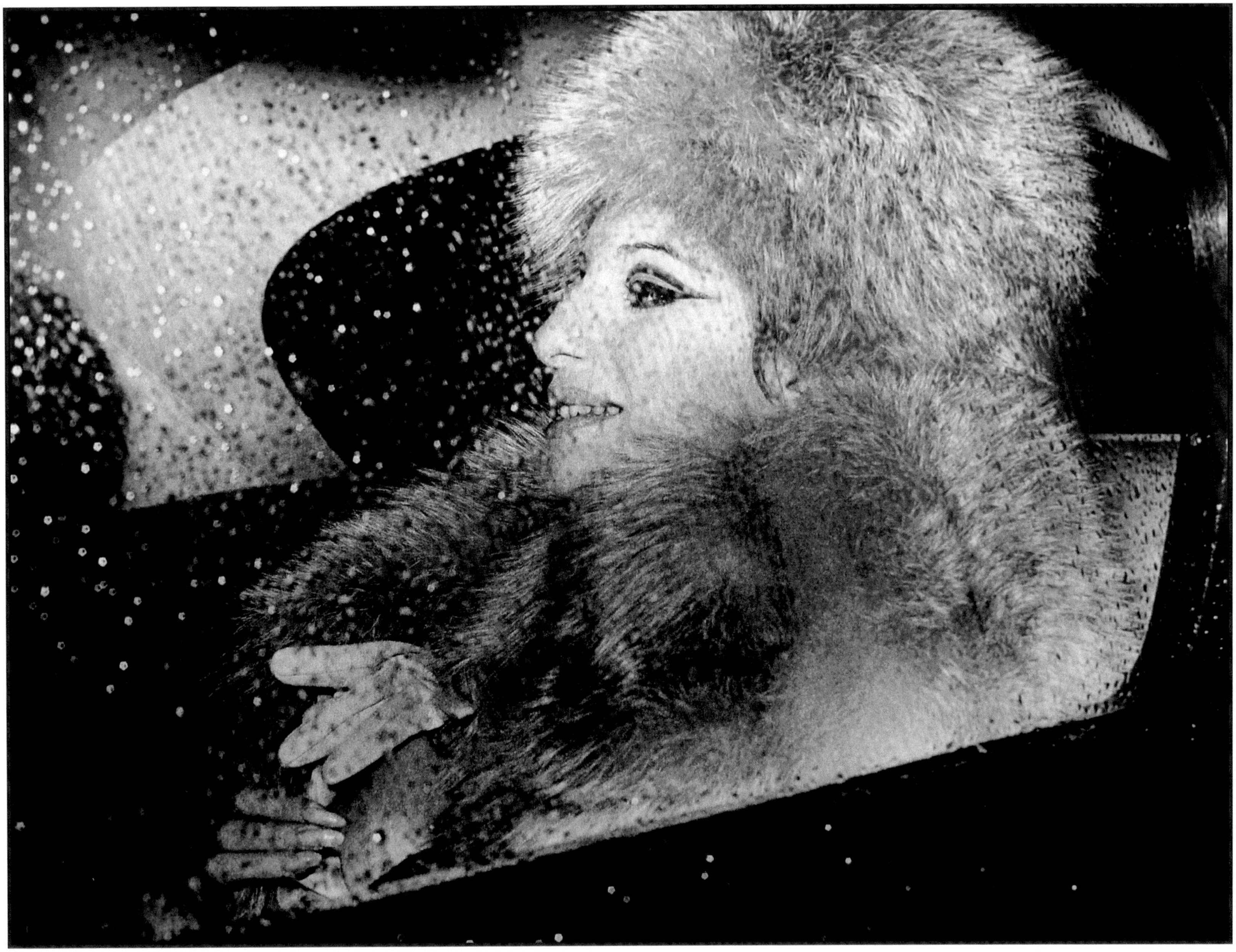

37.

Charlie Chaplin & Marlon Brando

1967, London

Celebrities have always been popular with readers and film premieres were considered major stories by newspapers, particularly as celebrity magazines were not as high profile as they are today.
I was sent to cover the world premiere of this British film *A Countess from Hong Kong*, written and directed by Charlie Chaplin. As you can see, it was a bit of a press-scrum.
I managed to get this shot of Chaplin with his wife, Oona, greeting Marlon Brando who played one of the leading roles.

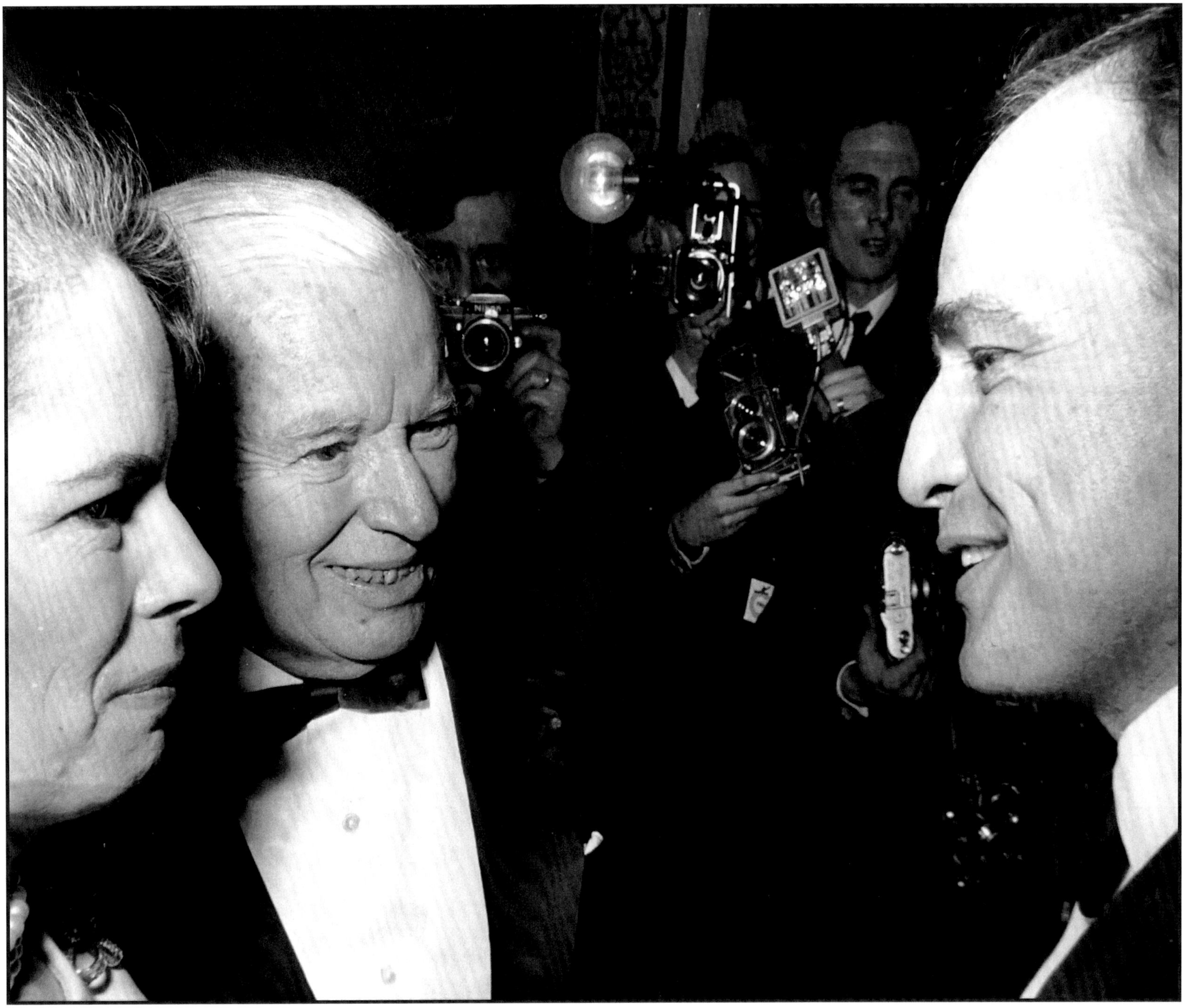

38.

Mia Farrow

1968, London

During a break in filming the Cold War thriller *Dandy in Aspic* in which she starred with Lawrence Harvey.
An American actress, activist, and former fashion model, Farrow has appeared in more than 50 films and won numerous awards, including a Golden Globe Award and three BAFTA Award nominations.
The producer had allowed me onto the closed set for ten minutes.

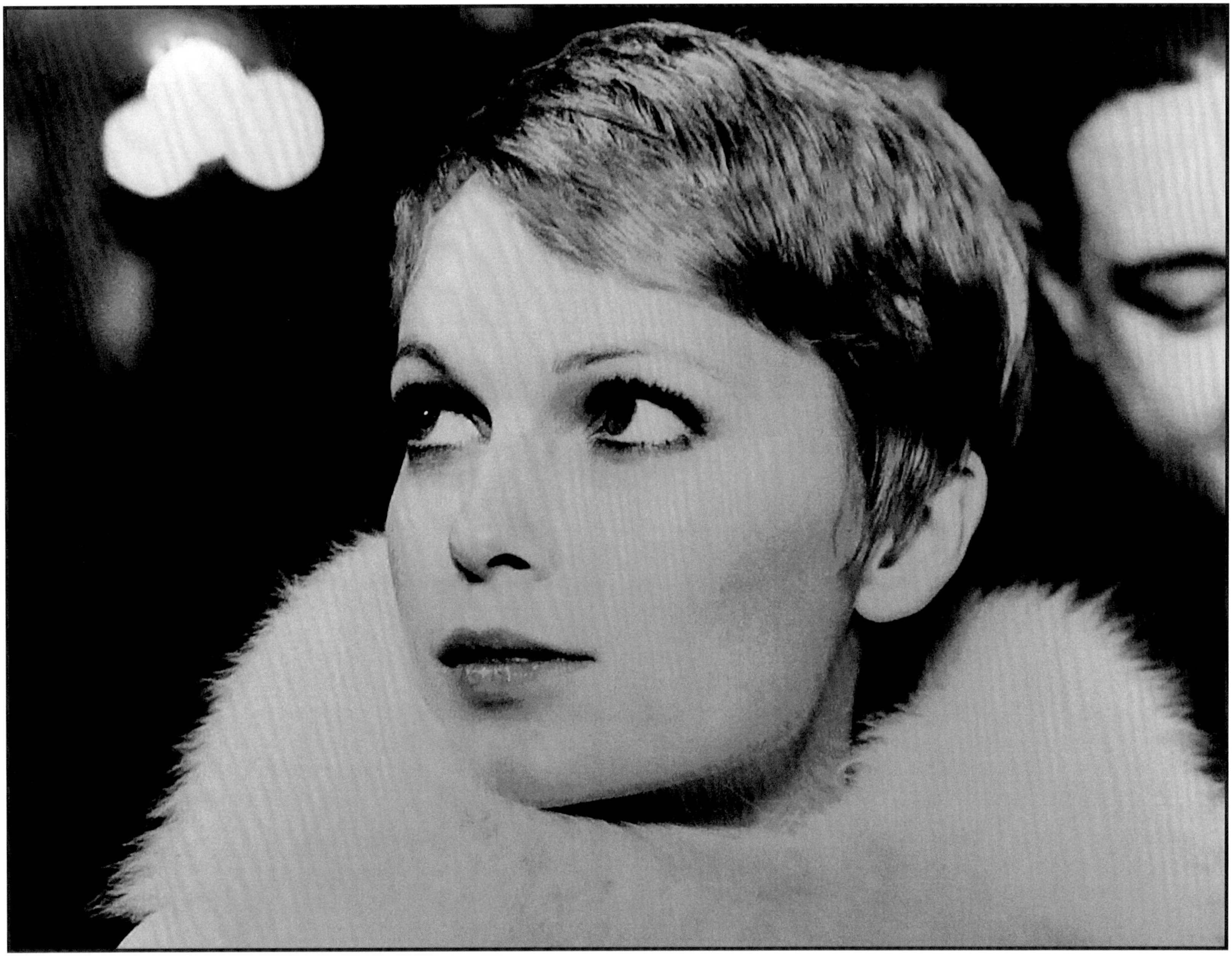

39.
Marsha Hunt
1969, London

Sixties icon Actress Marsha Hunt, star of rock musical *Hair* 1969.
(Partner of Mick Jagger and mother of their son, Karis).
The controversial musical *Hair*, which featured much nudity, had just opened in London and its 'leading lady' met me at the studios in Fleet Street.
An important ingredient in taking relaxed portraits is making friends with your subject quickly. I had seen *Hair*, which was a good start, and I mentioned that I had frequently photographed Mick in the early days of The Rolling Stones when I worked for Dezo Hoffman and the *Record Mirror*.
We got on like a house on fire.

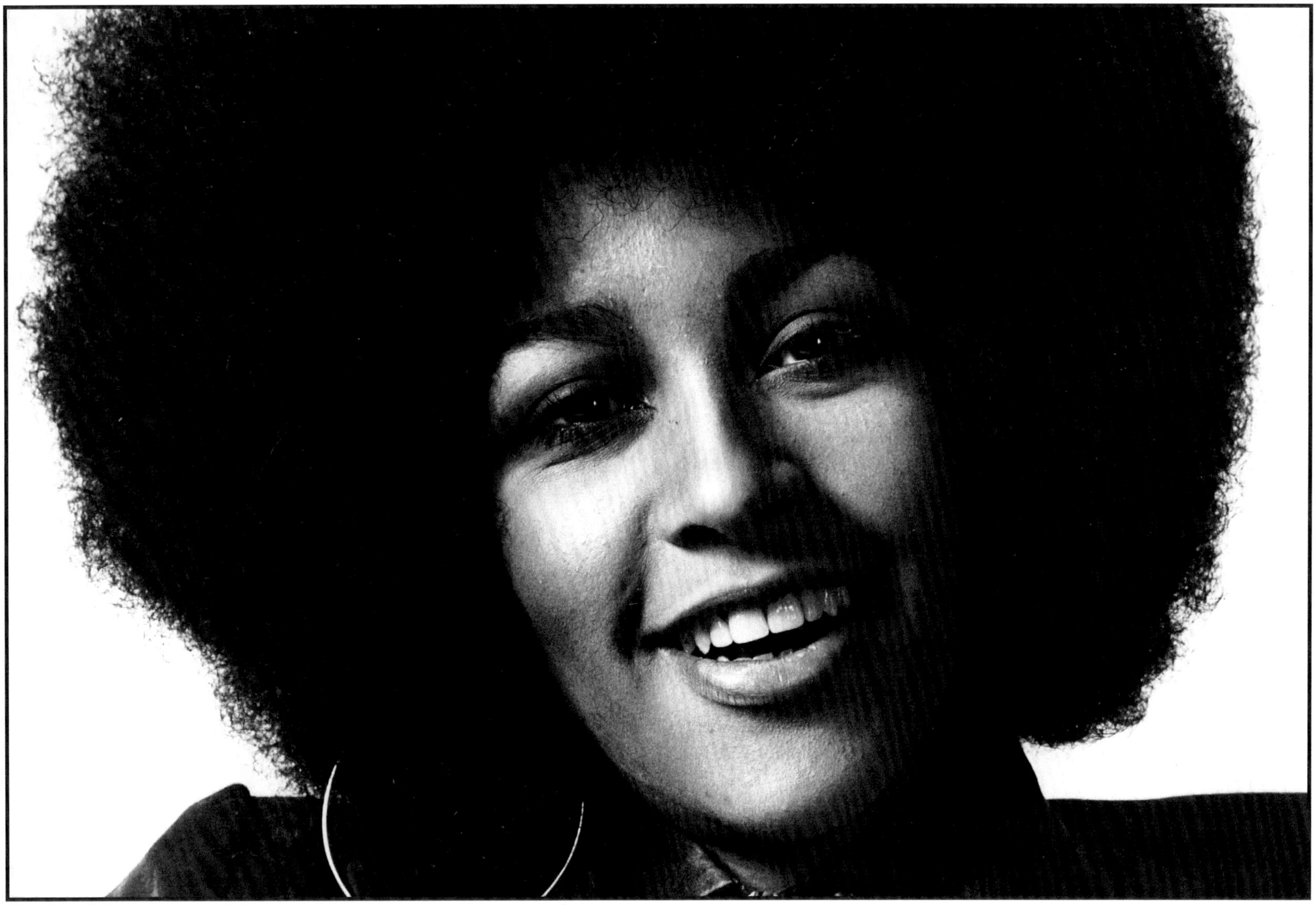

40.

John Lennon & Yoko Ono

1969, Heathrow

No prizes for guessing! Yoko greets John at London Heathrow airport on his return from a tour.
Famously, the duo staged a series of unforgettable 'bed-ins,' which were akin to the sit-in form of protest popular at the time.
Lucky to be in the right place at the right time I was fortunate to get this iconic shot of one of the world's great celebrities with his partner.
John Lennon, was shot and fatally wounded in New York City on 8th December 1980

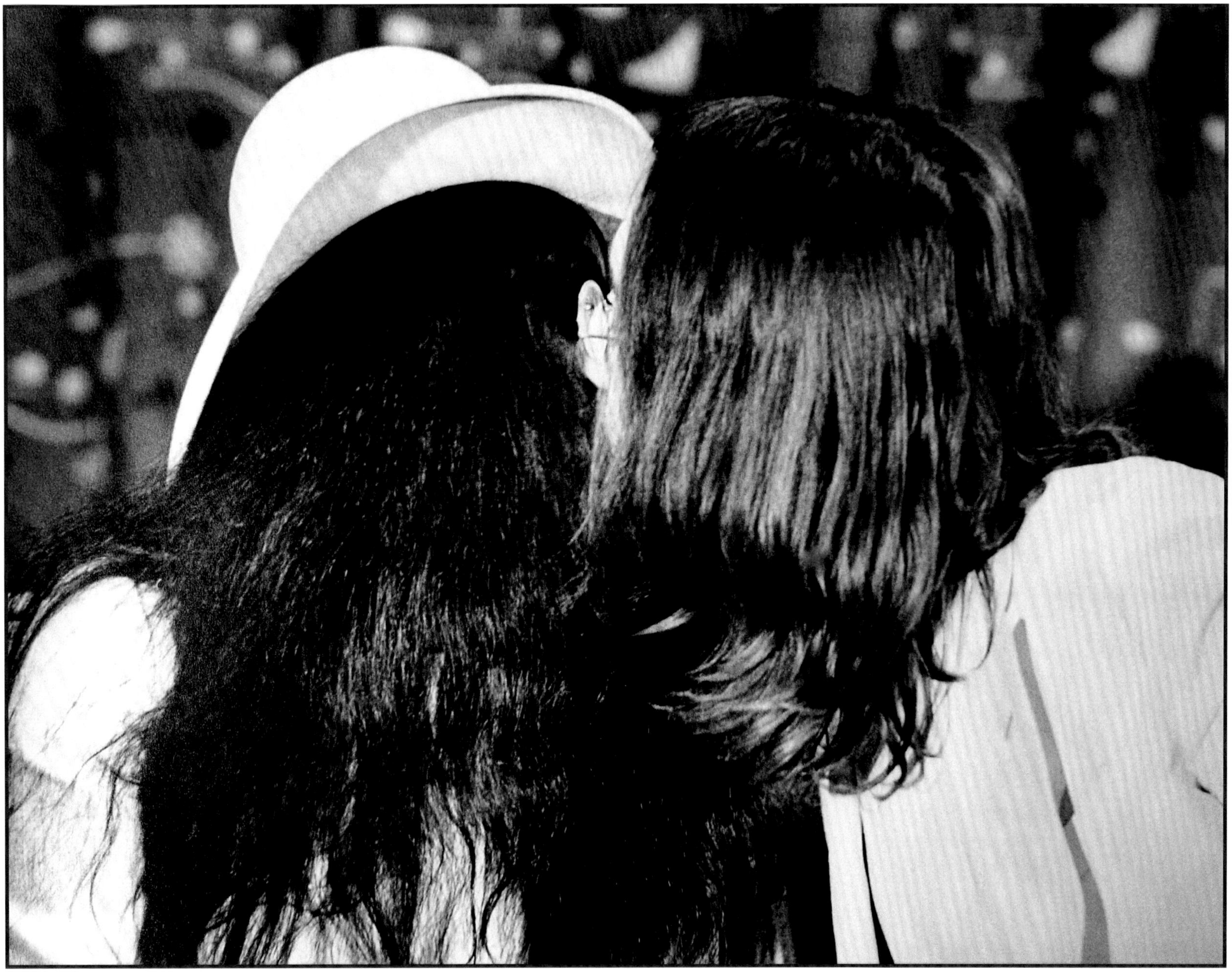

41.
Jochan & Nina Rindt
1970, Switzerland

In September 1970, I flew to Switzerland to photograph one of the worlds' leading Formula One racing drivers. Jochan Rindt was just 28 yeas old, and on the brink of winning the World Championship. He was about to compete in the Italian Grand Prix at Monza, and it was quite a coup to have him agree to be photographed with his beautiful Finnish wife, Nina.

It was a lovely sunny day, and I was given a lot of opportunities for family pictures before his historical drive. He had told Nina that he would retire from racing when he had won the World Championship.

We got on very well, and both he and Nina made me very welcome. When it was time for me to leave, I asked if they could arrange a taxi. Imagine my surprise when they telephoned their close friend and neighbour and asked him if he would drive me to the airport. It was none other than legendary racing driver Jackie Stewart. What a thrill!

On my return to London, I was driving from Heathrow when there was a news flash on the radio. Jochan had been killed in practice. I have to confess to being terribly upset, having just returned from seeing him in Switzerland. He became the first racing driver ever to win the Formula One World Drivers Championship posthumously, as he had amassed an unassailable lead in the points table.

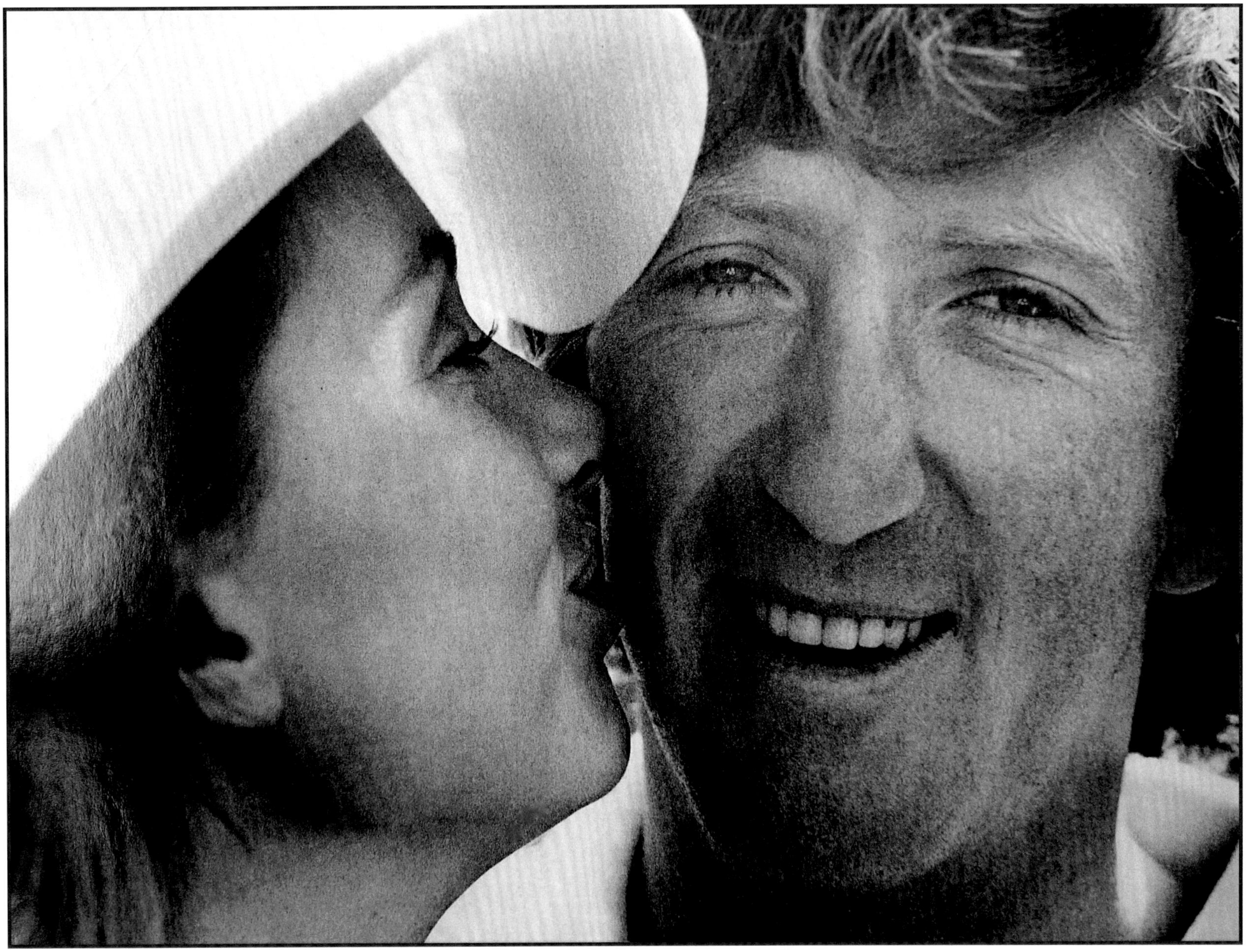

42.

Etta James

1975, Montreaux

As a huge jazz fan, I was thrilled to be given an assignment to cover the Montreaux Jazz Festival in Switzerland. The highlight was a performance by the legendary Etta James, doyenne of several genres including blues, R&B, soul, rock and roll, jazz and gospel.

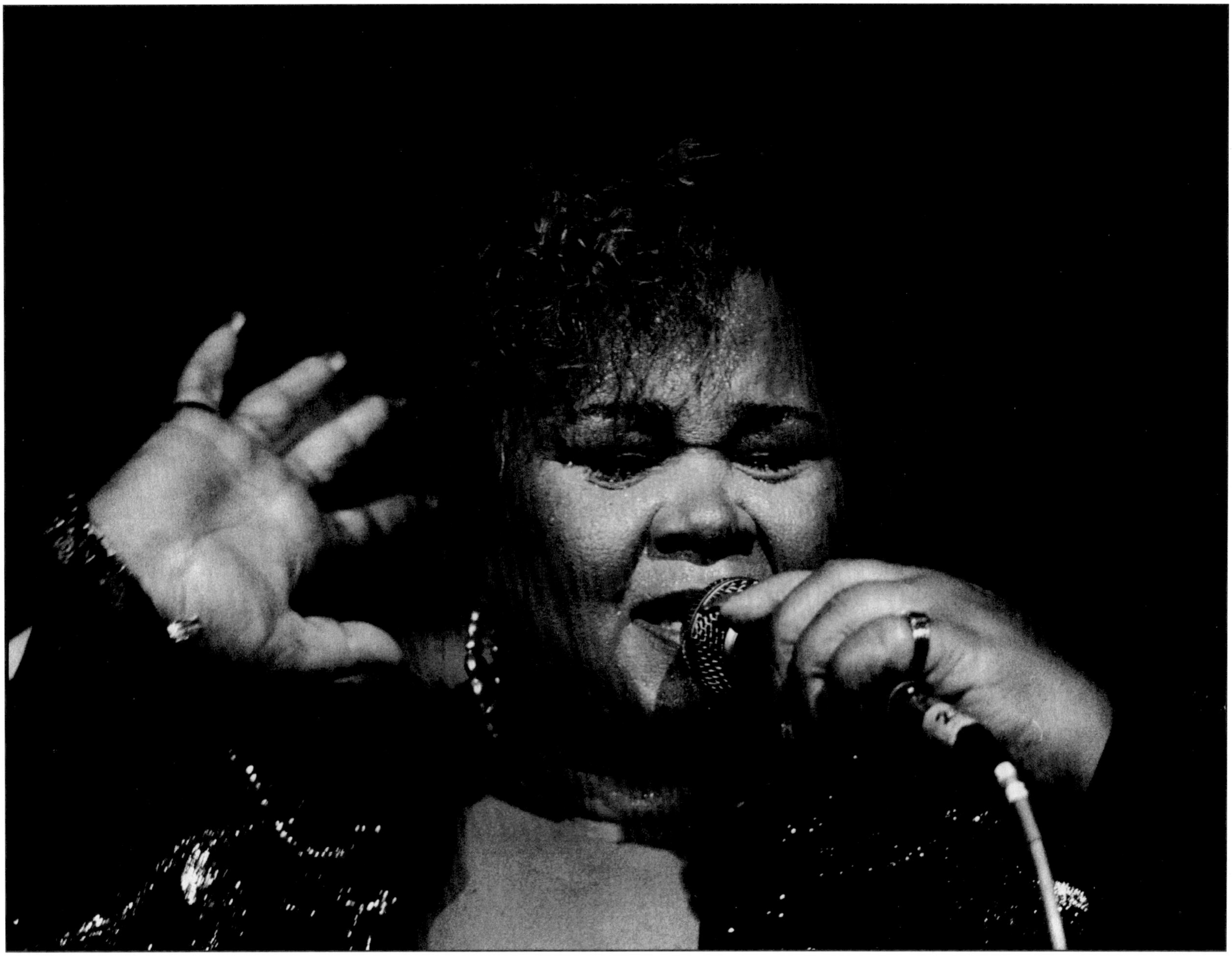

43.

The Queen Mother

1982, London

The Queen Mother waves to the crowd from her car during a tour in London. She was hugely popular with the public and press alike.
Newspaper photographers loved her.
On important photo-opportunities when surrounded by photographers she knew exactly how many were there and would make sure everyone got their shot.
On one occasion I was at Kempton Park races where the Queen Mother had a runner. I was standing alone in an enclosure below the Royal box and had just photographed her chatting to her trainer when I noticed her waving. I looked over my shoulder to see who she was waving at and to my embarrassment, realised that she had been waving at me. She graciously waved again in order for me to get a picture.

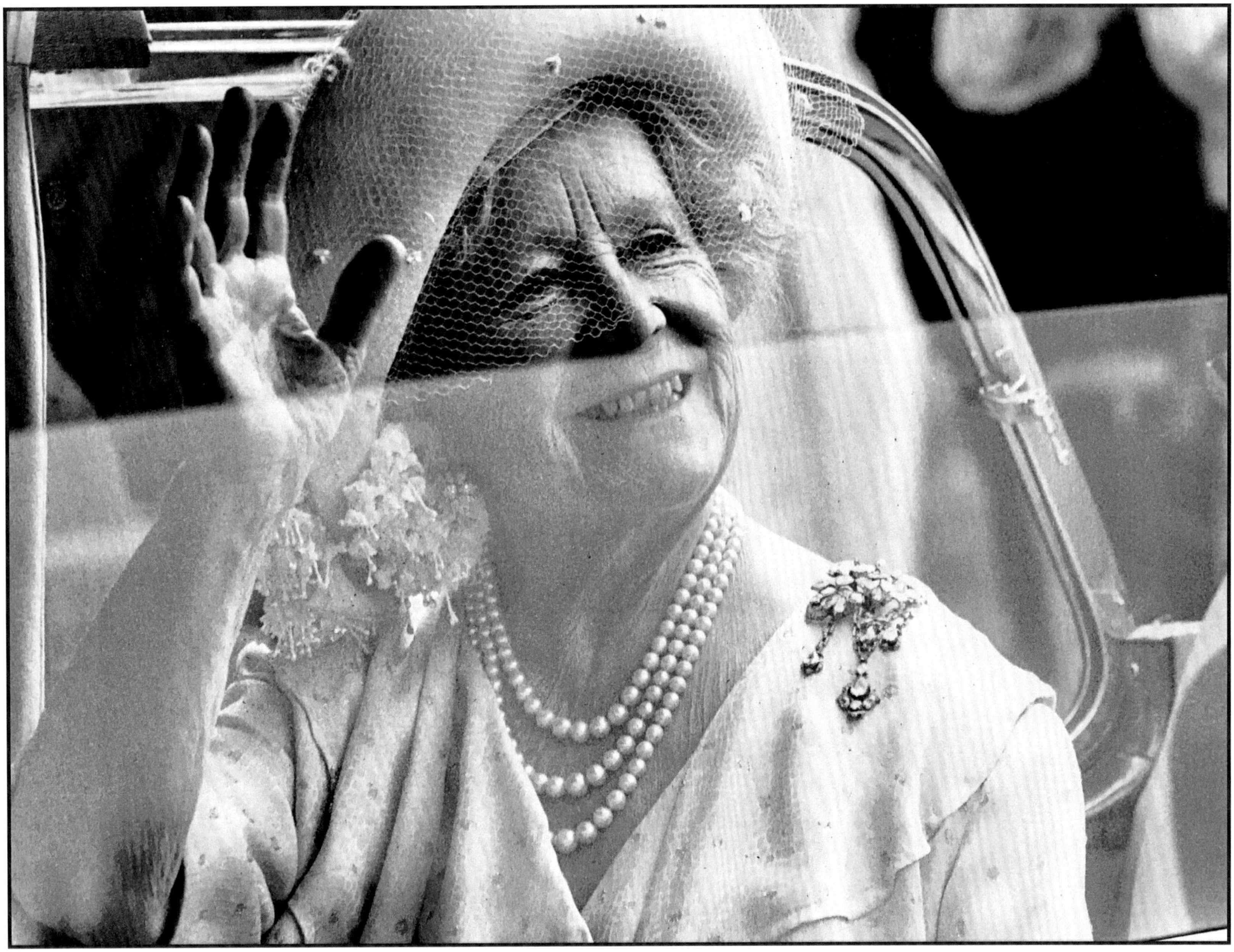

44.

Imran Khan

1987, London

One of my many *Off Duty* subjects, I met Imran Khan in his London flat to get a relaxed shot before interviewing him.
Imran was an international cricketer and captain of the Pakistan national cricket team which he led to victory in the 1992 Cricket World Cup, he is now Prime Minister of Pakistan.

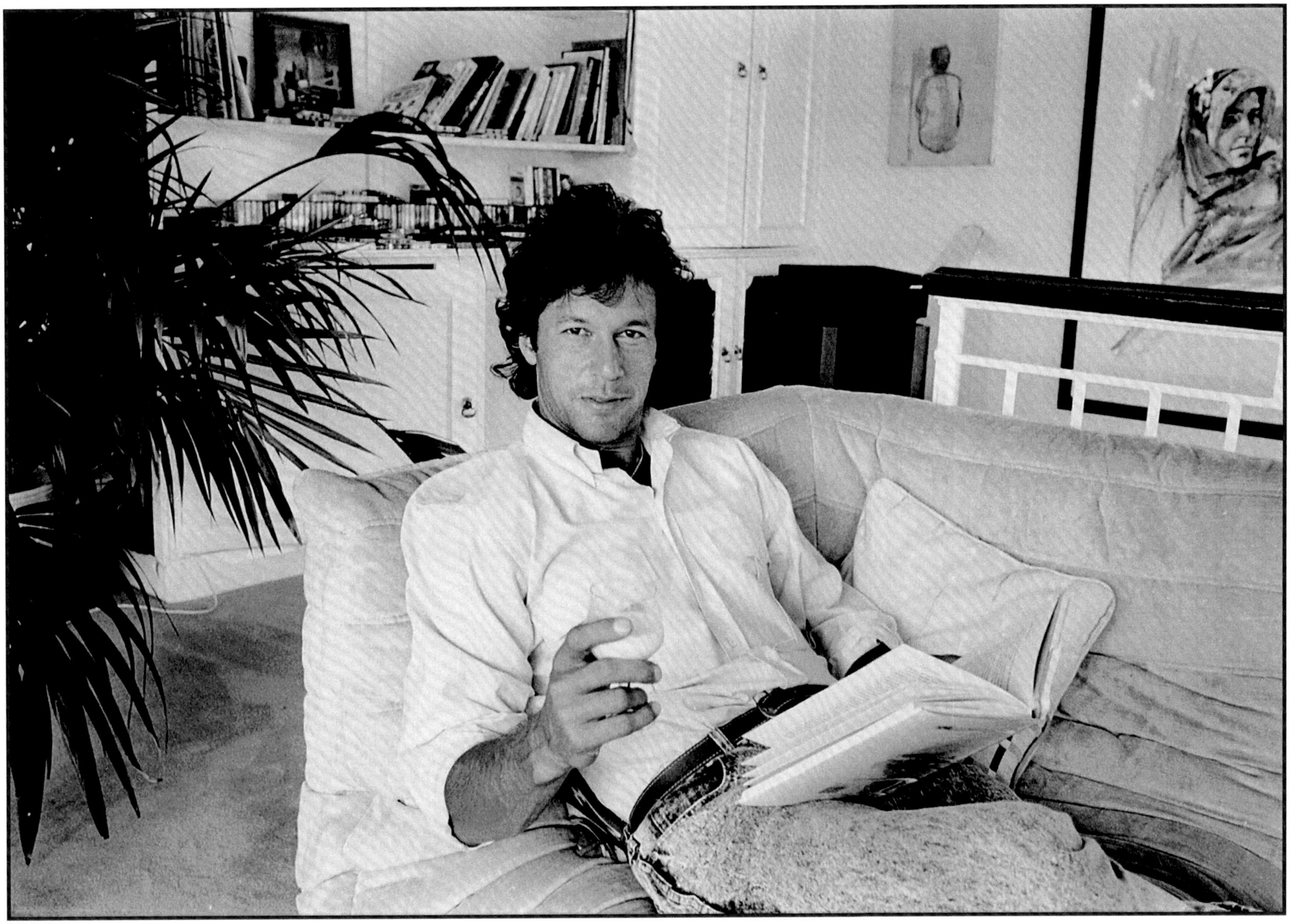

45.
Lord Snowdon
1987, Chelsea

One day in 1987 I was asked to make arrangements to photograph somebody who, in my opinion, was one of the worlds' greatest photographers - Lord Snowdon. I had met him socially many years earlier. I phoned his secretary and a date was made for me to see him in his Chelsea studio, where he was living at the time. I must confess to being more than a little nervous. Who wouldn't be?

I turned up at around 6.00 o'clock in the evening. He greeted me and took me into his studio. I wasn't at all confident, but I suspect he sensed that. After a few minutes, I reached down to my camera bag to start setting up. 'Hold on a minute', he said, 'There's no rush is there? Let's catch up, I haven't seen you for years'. We started to reminisce and he left the studio for a moment, returning with a bottle of wine and some glasses. By this time I had been there for over an hour, my cameras were still in my bag, and I was keen to get on with things. But another bottle was produced, and whilst the alcohol calmed my nerves to a point, I was certainly not sober! I kept repeating 'Do you think we should start?', but I seemed to be getting nowhere. He kept changing the subject, and then said, 'What do you think about this wine - nice isn't it? Let me get another bottle'. I began thinking that if we didn't get started soon, I would be incapable! It reached a point where I had to be really insistent, and whilst he agreed to sit in the studio, he seemed reluctant.

The session lasted about an hour, and when I was happy with what I had taken, he offered me another glass of wine. 'You've been trying to get me drunk all evening!' I told him that the alcohol had helped me overcome my nervousness about taking pictures of him, to which he exclaimed: 'What?, you think you were nervous? It was just delaying tactics, I was really nervous about having my picture taken, I needed to get some 'Dutch Courage' - I was terrified!'. I couldn't quite believe what I had heard, but I left a lot more confident than I had arrived, albeit a bit wobbly on my pins!

The Times published a very nice portrait and I followed that up by sending him a selection of prints.

A couple of days later a personal hand written letter arrived. He thanked me for 'taking such nice photographs, they really are splendid.' He apologised again for 'Being such a bad sitter - it just made me very nervous'. He continued that he thought 'they are the best that have ever been taken', and asked if they could be syndicated as his official portrait. What a huge compliment, I treasure the letter to this day.

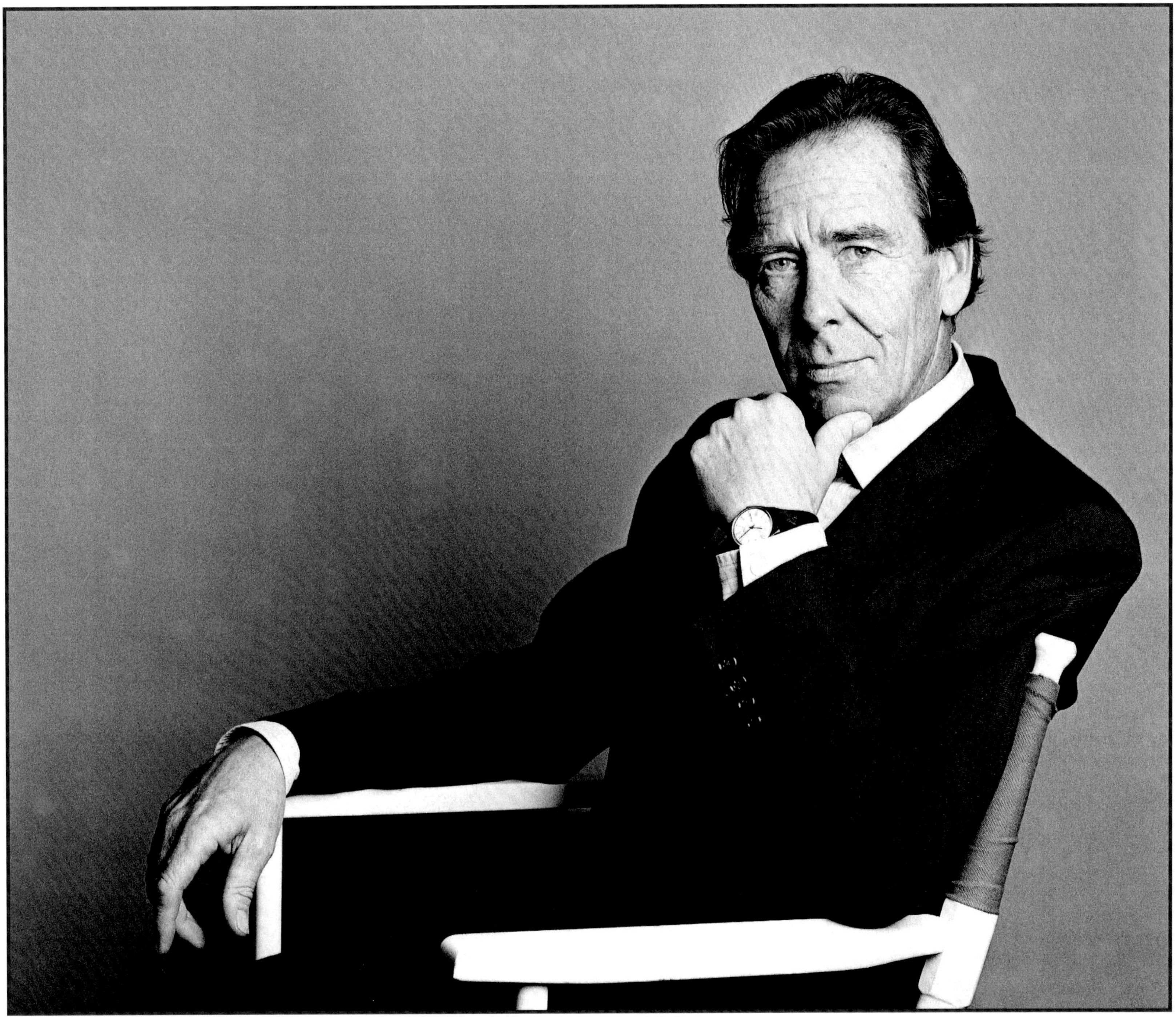

46.

Judi Dench & Daughter Finty

1988, London

Judi Dench was a great subject to have in my *Off Duty* feature.
Judi has won countless awards including an Oscar, many BAFTA awards, seven Olivier awards, two Golden Globes and a Tony.
I really like this affectionate picture with her daughter Finty Williams who is also an actress.

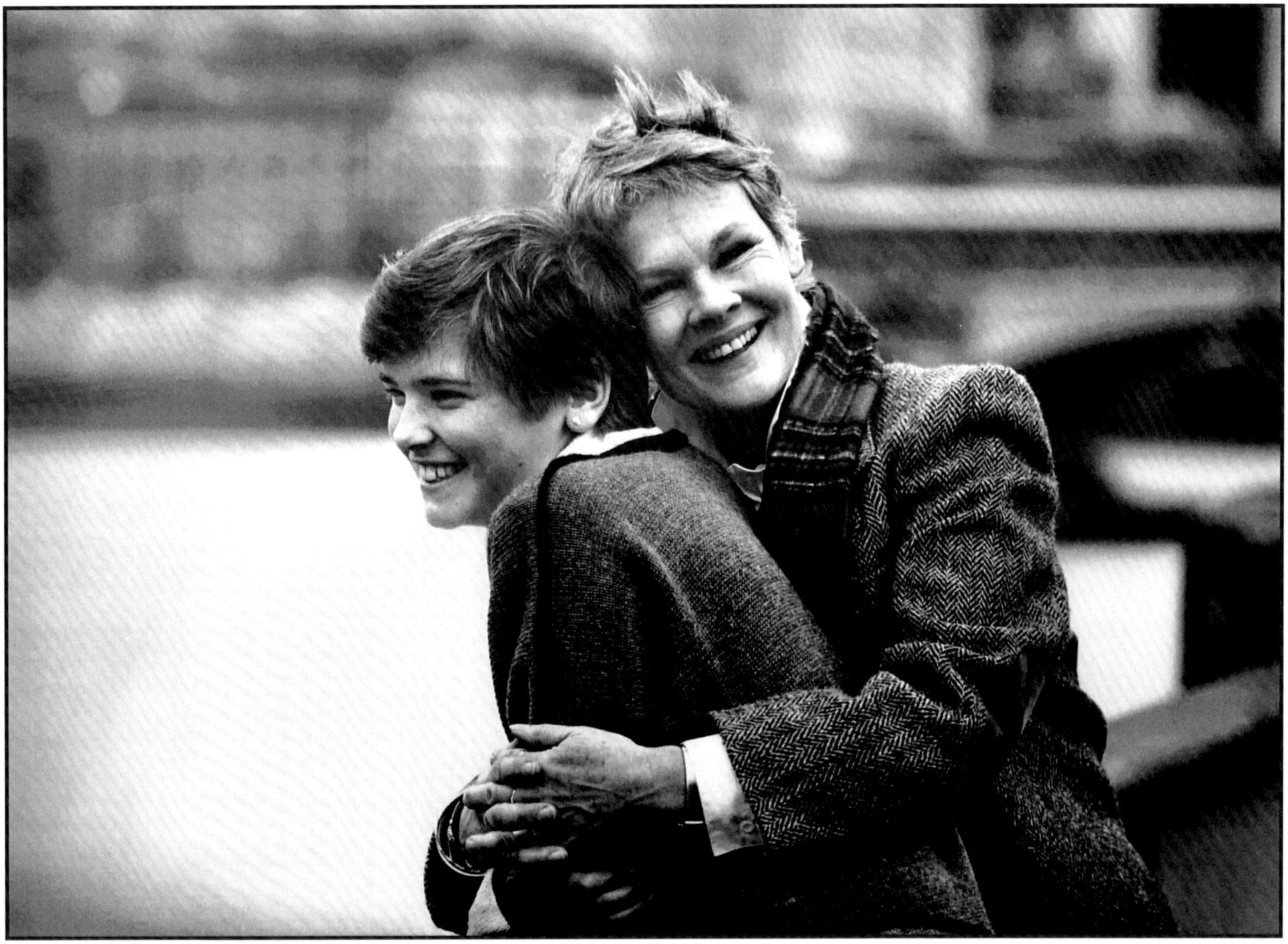

47.

Peter O'Toole

1988, London

O'Toole was an Irish-British stage and film actor. As a relatively unknown actor, he achieved international recognition playing T.E.Lawrence in *Lawrence of Arabia* (1962) for which he received his first nomination for the Academy Award for Best Actor.

He holds the record for the most Academy Award nominations for acting without a win.

I was briefed to meet up with him at an apartment in Soho. We chatted for ages over a drink or three and voila - an easy going portrait!

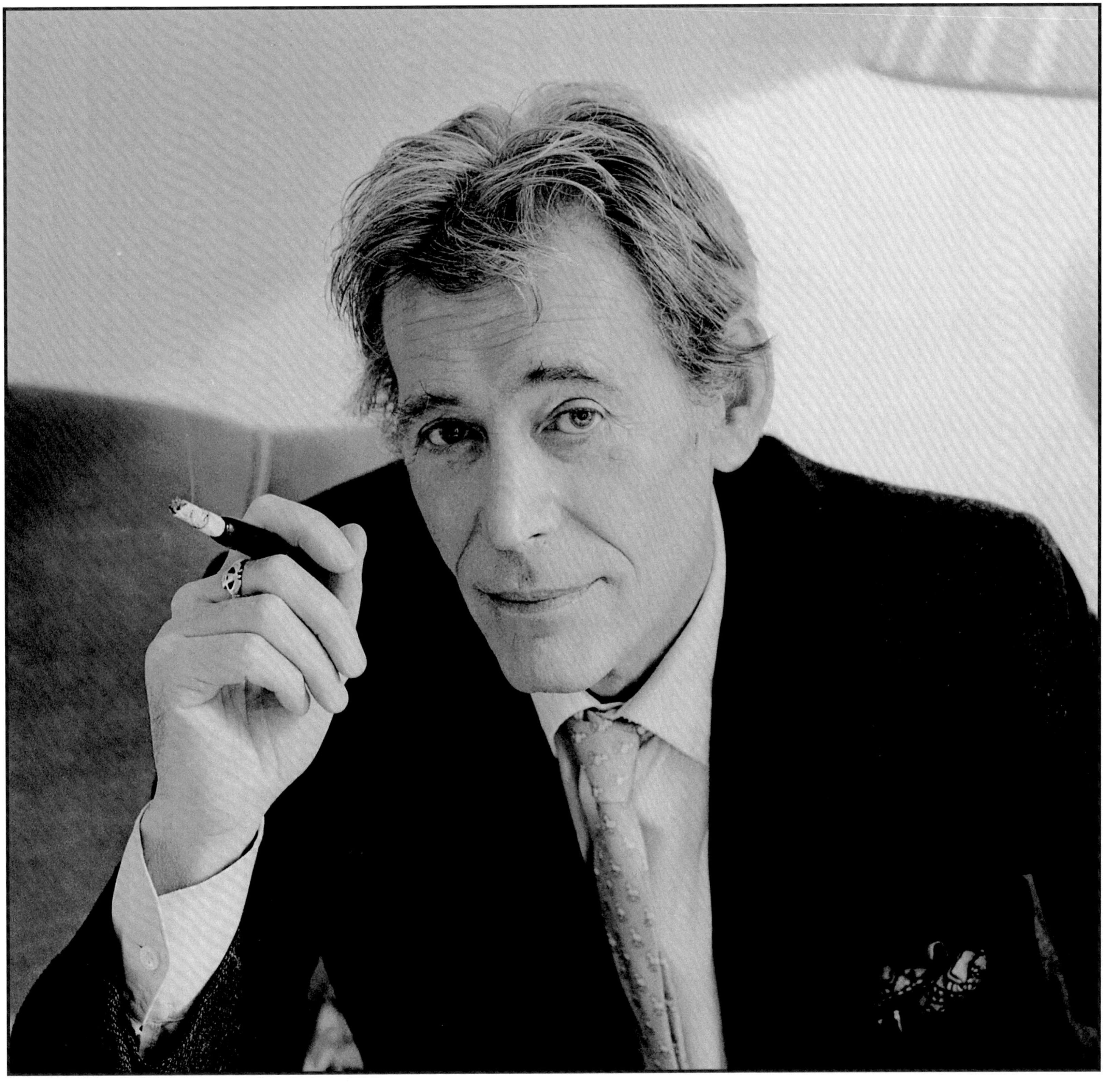

48.

Mickey Rooney

1988, London

This *Off Duty* shot of the legendary star of stage and screen, seen here during a break in rehearsals for the London run of the Broadway hit musical *Sugar Babes*. The ultimate laid-back relaxed portrait, and such fun to take.

Mickey was also a comedian, radio entertainer, and producer. In a career spanning nine decades and continuing until his death, he appeared in more than 300 films, and was among the last surviving stars of the silent era. Mickey was married eight times including to Ava Gardner.

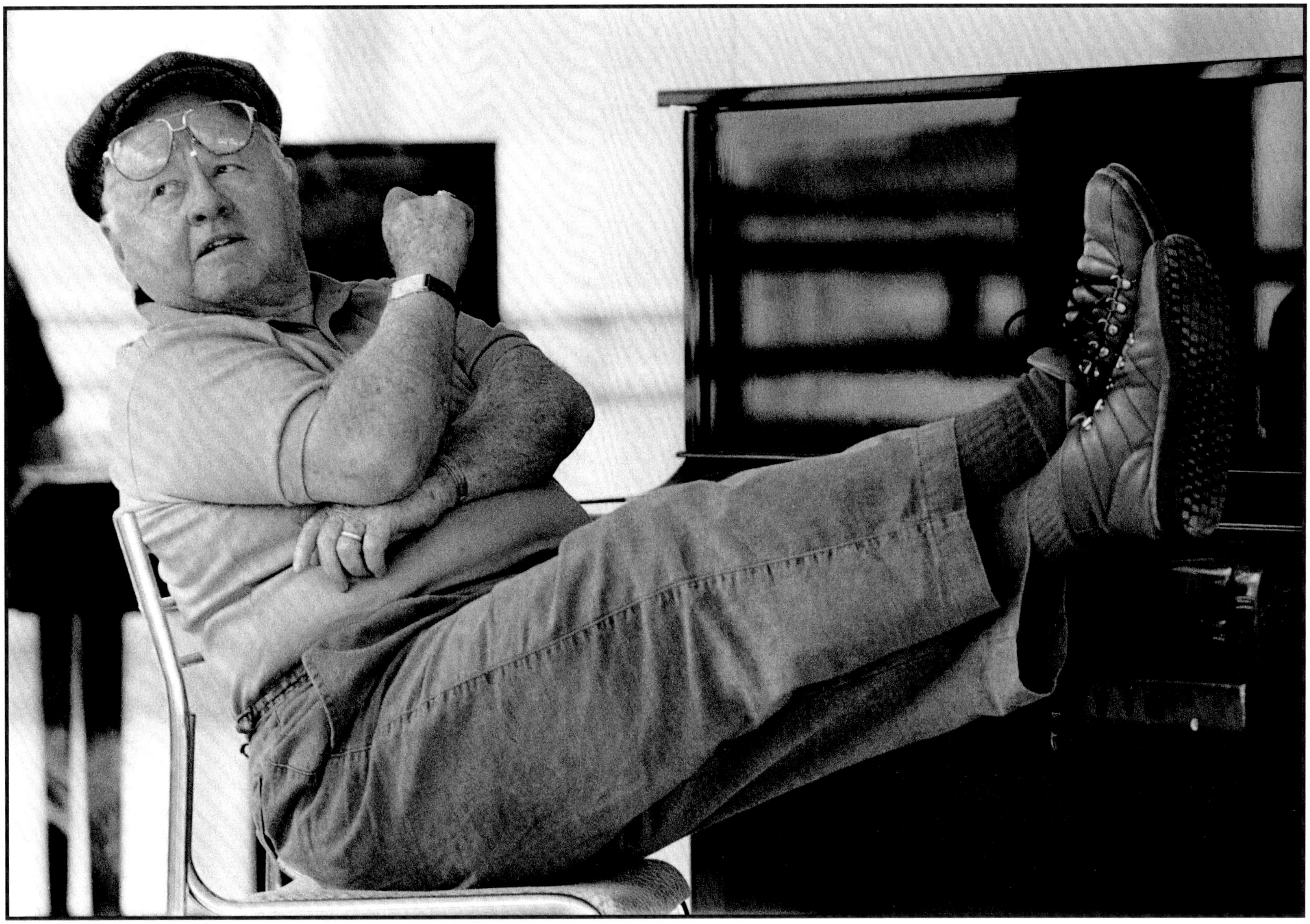

49.

Bob Hoskins

1989, London

I always enjoy meeting actors. I seem to have have an affinity with them and was pleased that Bob Hoskins agreed to my *Off Duty* request. Star of *Who Framed Roger Rabbit*, Bob Hoskins was preparing to go on a charity fund-raising expedition to the Sahara to raise money for Algerian refugees, who had been living in camps for thirteen years after their homeland was annexed by Morocco.

I photographed him with his pet dog, Dixie, at a local pub on Hampstead Heath before conducting the interview.

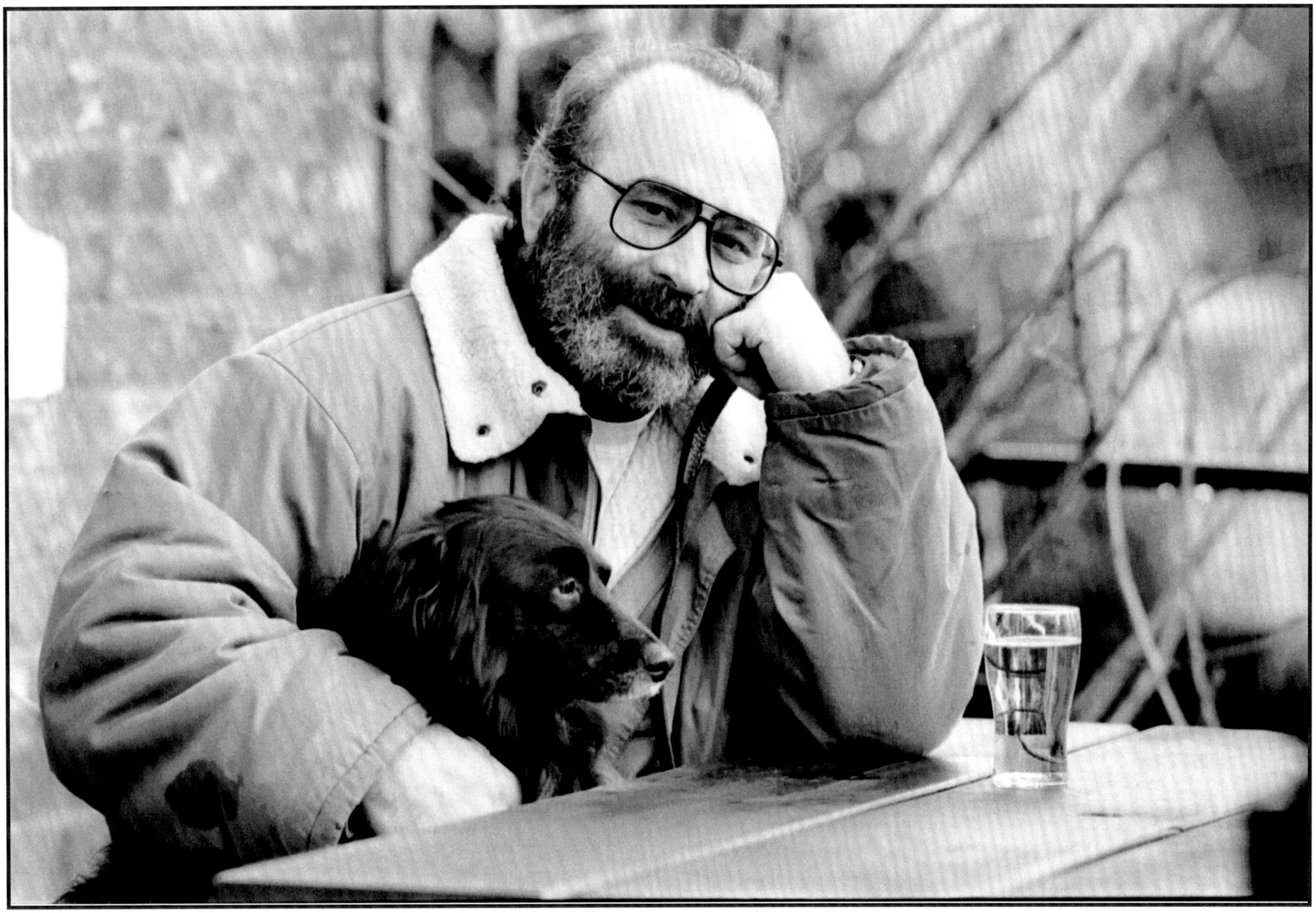

50.

Willie Whitelaw

1989, House of Lords

One of my favourite portraits. Demonstrating what a relaxed and patient nature he had, it was nominated by the Royal Photographic Society to be included in the collection at the National Portrait Gallery in London.

The RT. Hon. The Viscount Whitelaw, 1st Viscount Whitelaw, often known as Willie Whitelaw, was a British Conservative politician who served in a wide number of Cabinet positions, most notably as home secretary. He served Prime Minister Margaret Thatcher throughout her leadership of the Conservative Party as deputy party leader.

His loyalty was crucial to Margaret Thatcher during her early years in power - a fact acknowledged when she famously said: 'Every prime minister needs a Willie.'

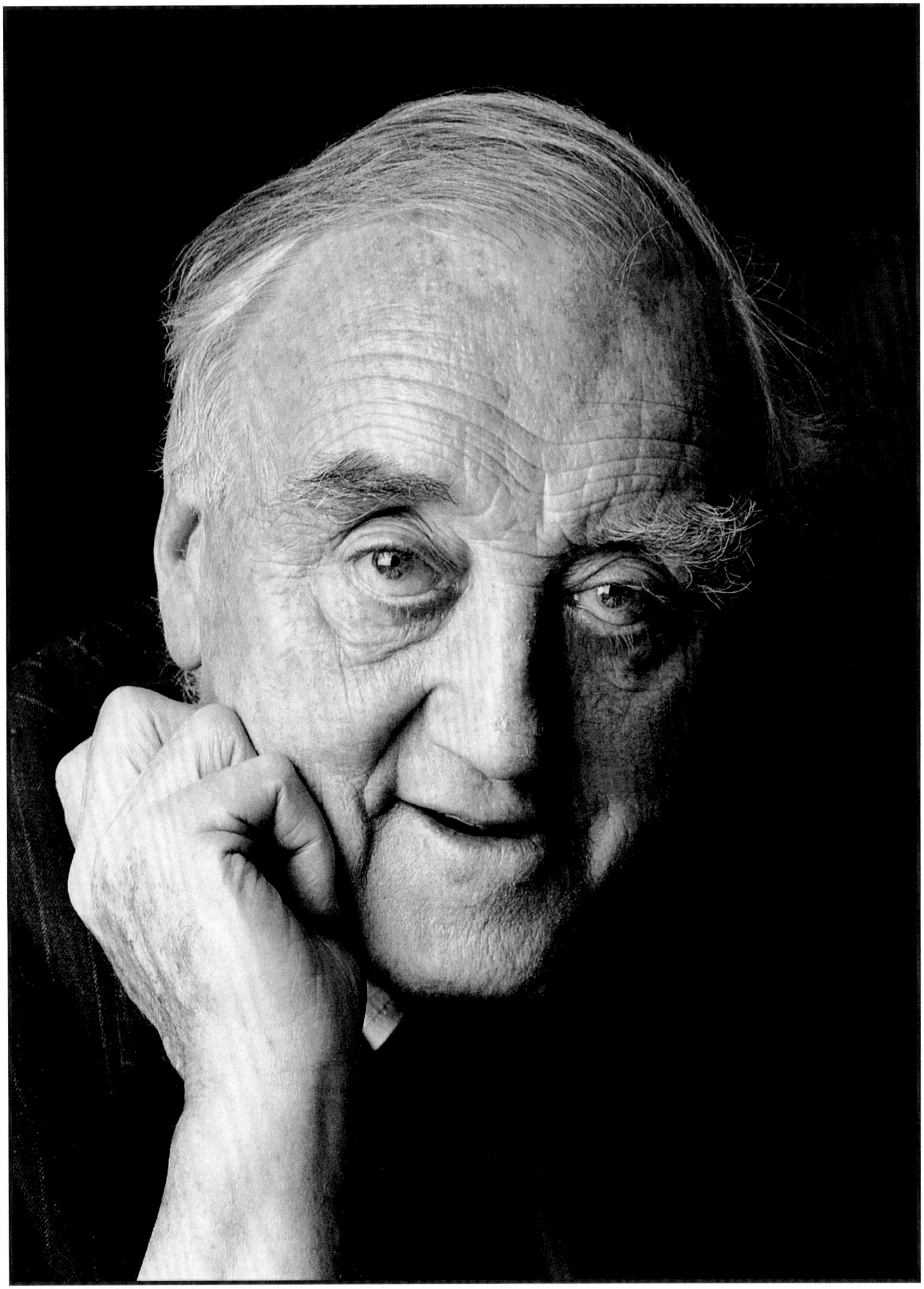

51.

His Highness Aga Khan

1990, France

Off Duty, in France this time, with H.H. Aga Khan. I spent an enjoyable day as his guest in his home near Chantilly. He is renowned in the horse racing world for his stable of champions, often bred by him at his studs in France and Ireland. Being a horse racing enthusiast myself was helpful when I interviewed him as we sat in beautiful surroundings with his dogs at his side. A very charming man who made a relaxed sitter for my portrait.

Imam and spiritual leader of the world's approximately 15 million Ismaili Muslims. His net worth has been estimated in excess of $13 billion.

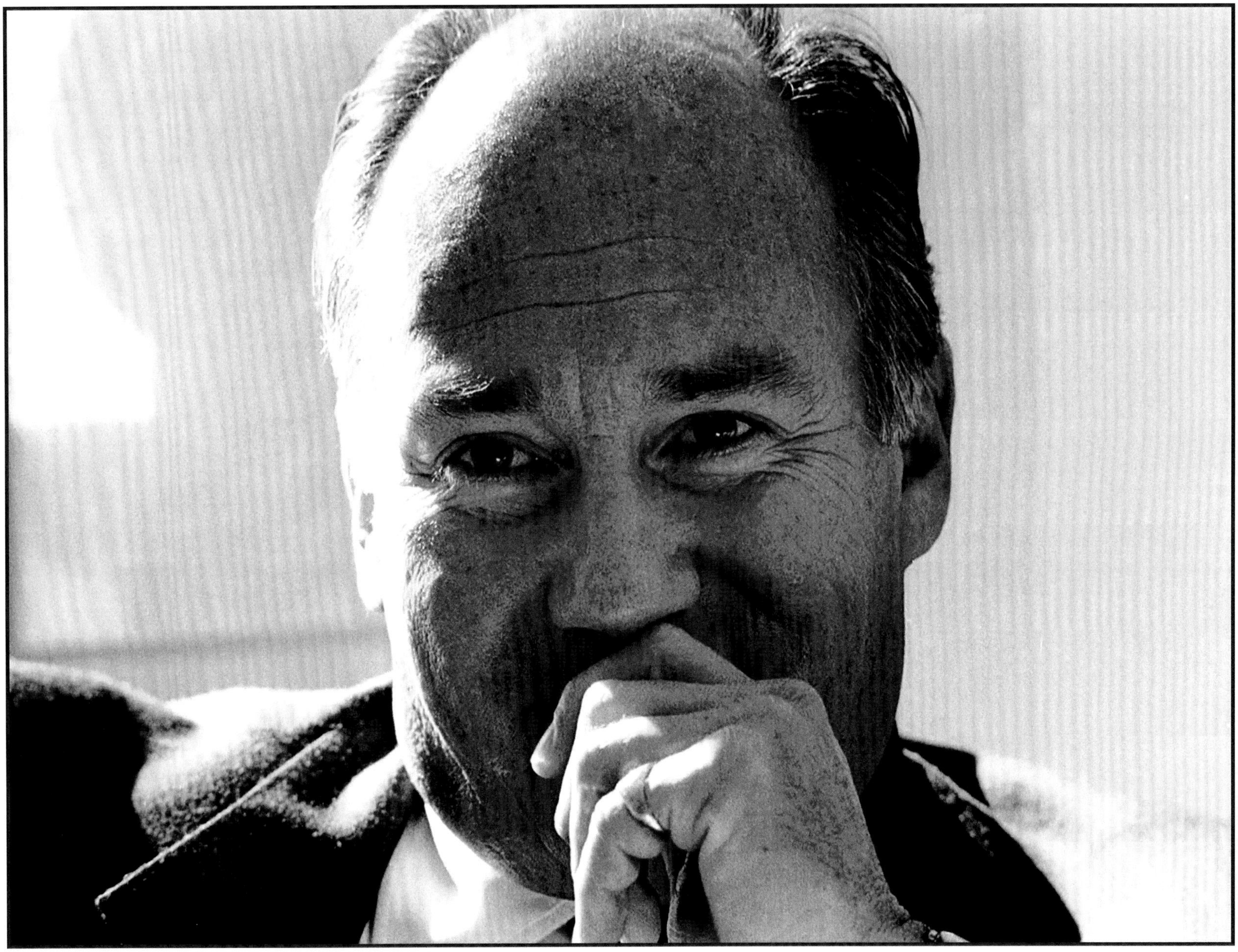

52.

Sheikh Mohammed bin Rashid Al Maktoum Ruler of the Emirate of Dubai.

1990, Dubai

I took this photograph of Sheikh Mohammed attending the Camel Derby in Dubai.

A keen equestrian, he is the founder of the Maktoum family-owned Godolphin stable which values its stallion interests in excess of $157 million, broodmares at $96 million, horses in training at $55 million, yearlings at $20 million and foals at $19 million.

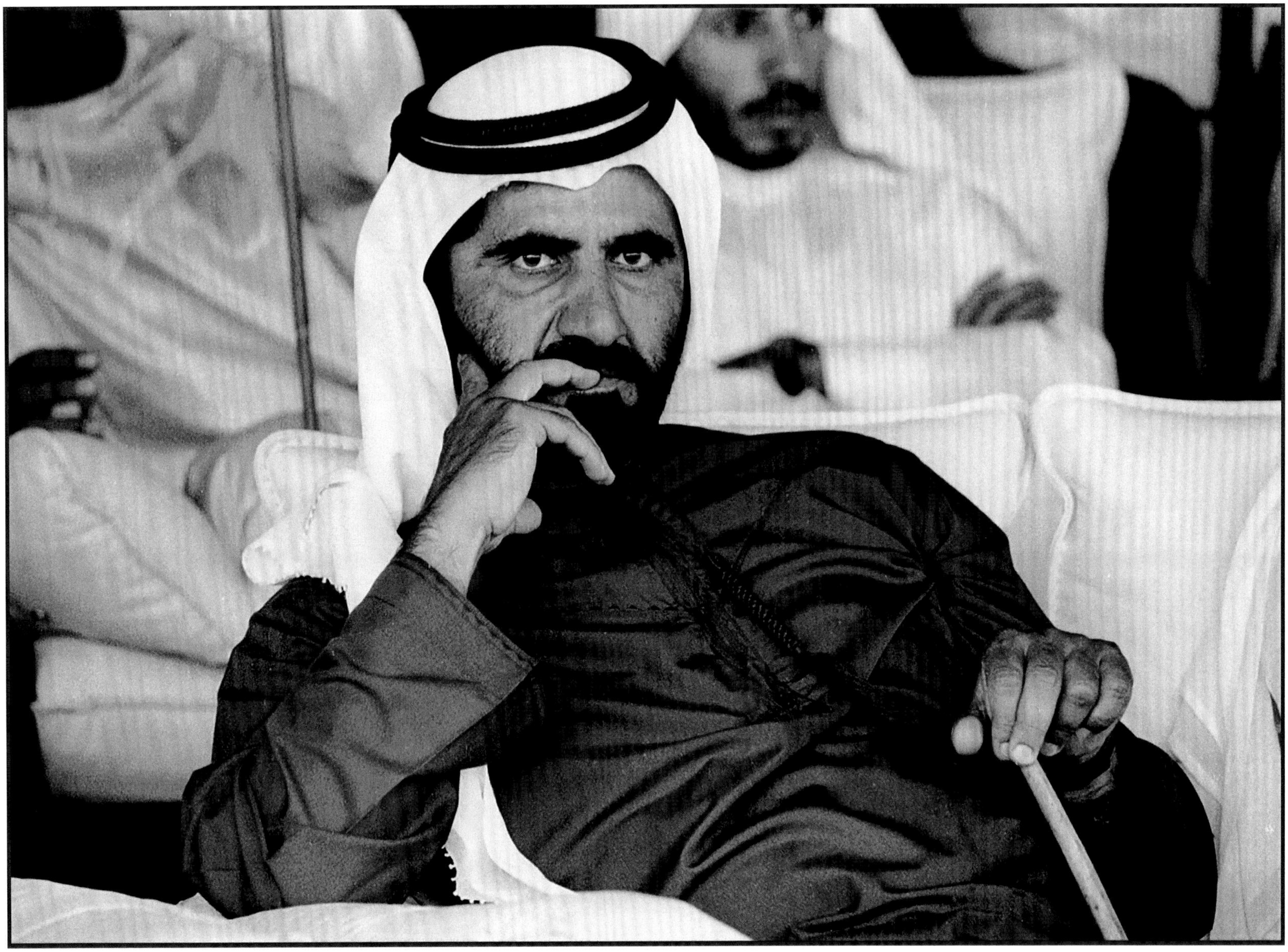

53.

Oscar Peterson

1990, London

Oscar Peterson was a Canadian jazz pianist, virtuoso and composer. He was called the 'Maharaja of the keyboard' by Duke Ellington.
One of Canada's most honoured musicians, he is widely regarded as one of the greatest jazz pianists of all time. He was renowned for his remarkable speed and dexterity, meticulous and ornate technique, and dazzling, swinging style.

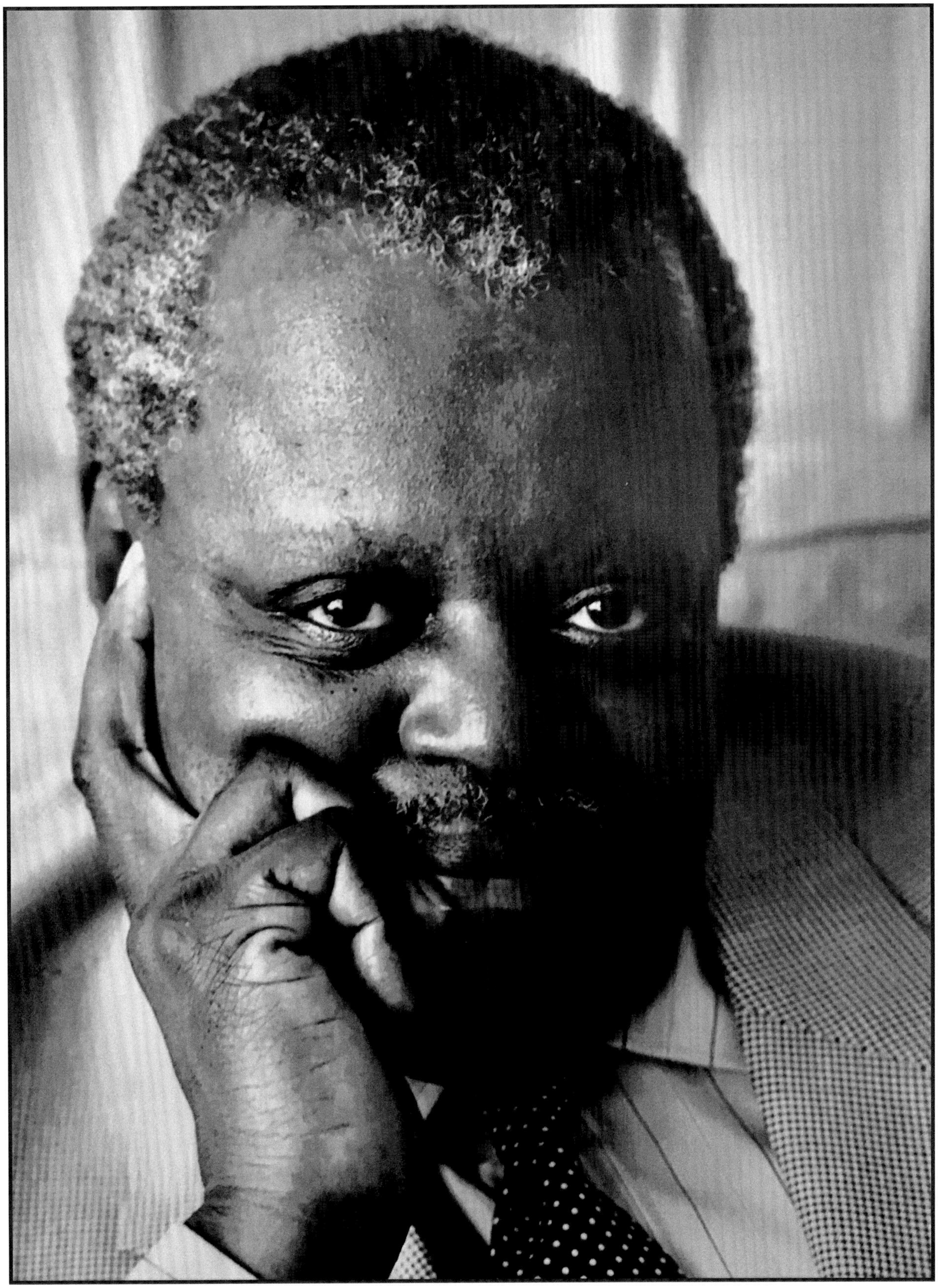

54.

Germaine Greer

1991, Cambridgeshire

Australian writer and public intellectual, regarded as one of the major voices of the radical feminist movement in the latter half of the 20th century.
On a visit to Warwick University where she was a lecturer, I once held a door open for her and she just stood there and glowered at me refusing to go through.
I won't do that again!

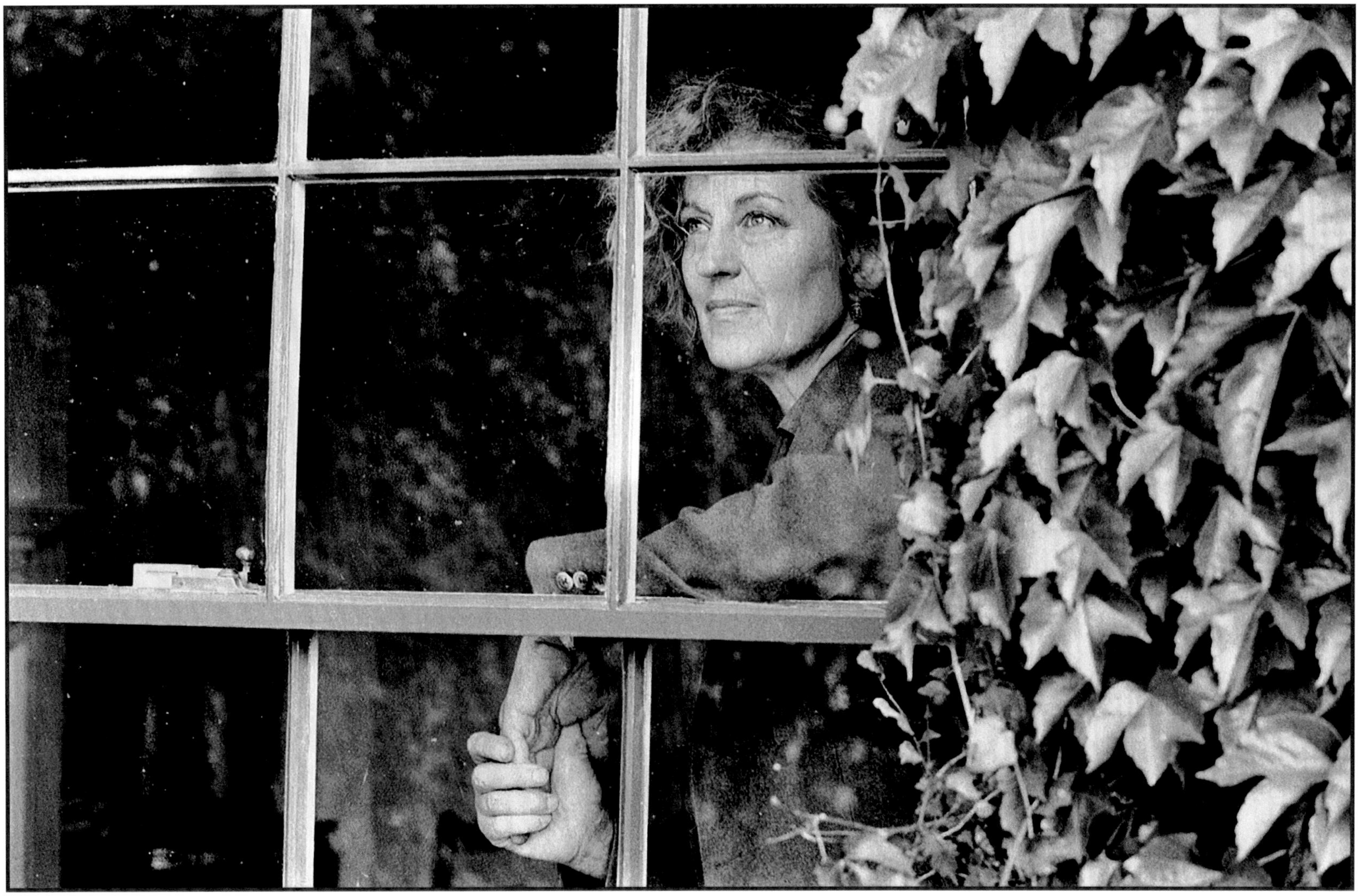

55.

Sir John Gielgud

1994, Buckinghamshire

It was a great honour to meet perhaps the greatest Shakespearian actor of his time, at his beautiful home in Buckinghamshire. He was a genial and easygoing host and delighted in showing me the stunning gardens, which were his pride and joy.

Gielgud had the rare distinction of winning an Oscar, an Emmy, a Grammy, and a Tony. He was famous from the start of his career for his voice and his mastery of Shakespearean verse.

There is a common feature I noticed about personalities in show business and people in the public eye. Few are self-conscious and when in front of the camera, they tend to look beyond which creates a relaxed and personal picture.

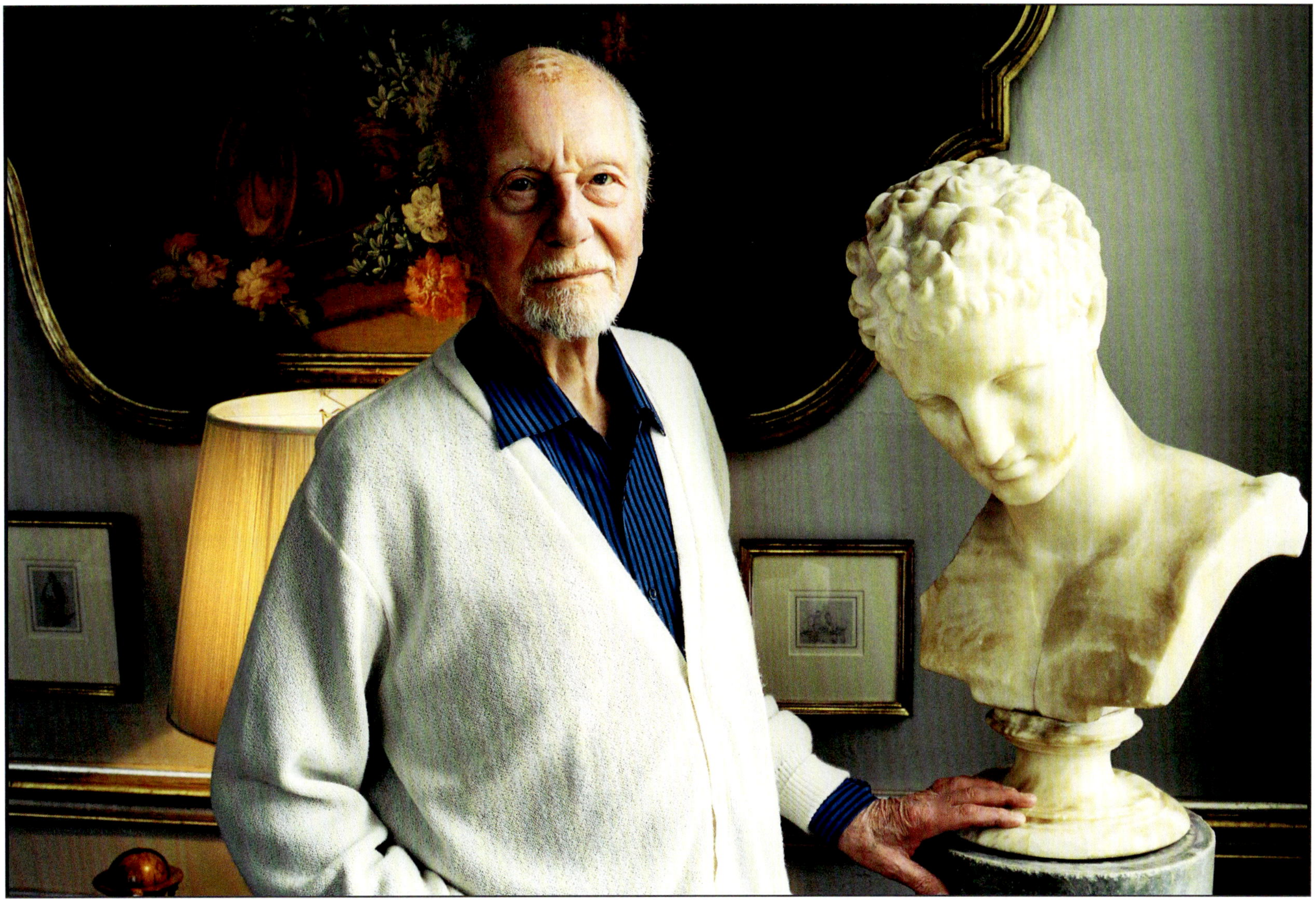

56.

David Herbert

1994, Tangier

Interior decorator, portraitist, international partygoer, cabaret singer, writer and aesthete, David Herbert was known as the 'Uncrowned Queen' of Tangier.

Tangier was reported by *The Times* as being a playground for the rich and nearly famous.

David Herbert was the second son of the 15th Earl of Pembroke and lived an elegant life in his pink palace high in the hills.

It was quite an experience meeting this wonderfully flamboyant and eccentric man.

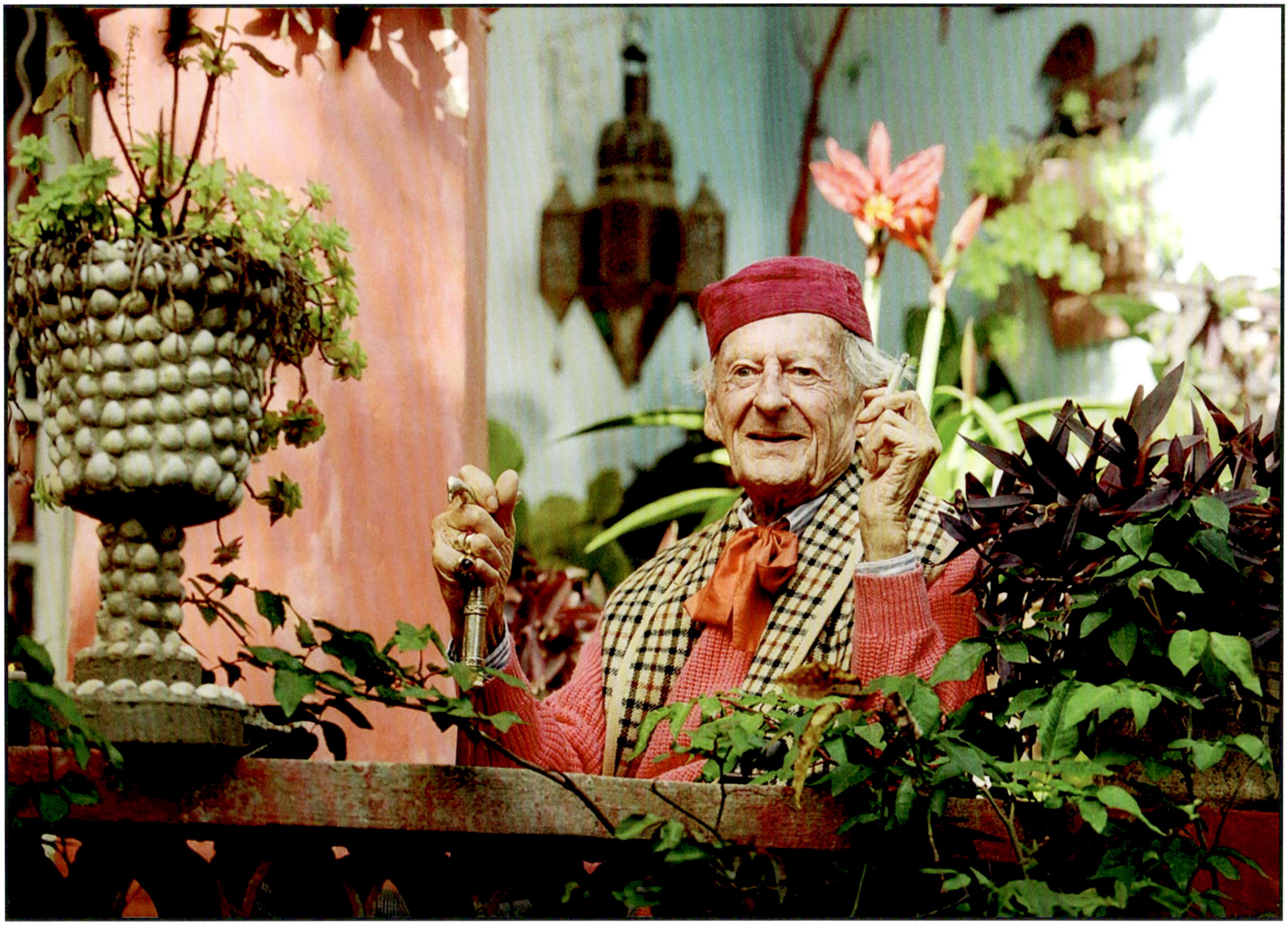

PART 4

THE TIMES TRAVEL PAGES

Covering news stories was naturally very exciting and often involved travel to far-flung places in the world. By the very nature of news, those assignments were sometimes dangerous, and always challenging.

Work for the travel section was far more relaxed without deadlines to meet. Seeing the world with an open-brief, looking for amusing or visually enticing shots provided welcome respite from the hurly-burly of hard news.

57.

Salmon Netting

1987, Scotland

As a keen fly fisherman, I was intrigued to be given an assignment to cover Salmon netting on the River Spey in the Highlands of Scotland. Being aware of the season when fish were likely to be running in that particular river, I thought it a strange time of year for netting to be carried out. Nevertheless, a large section of the river was 'swept' by the netsmen several times a day.

When I queried if there was any chance of getting any salmon at this time of year, they said 'Of course not'.

'So why on earth do you go to all the trouble?' I asked.

'Well, we work for the Crown and we wouldn't get paid if we didn't do it' came the reply!

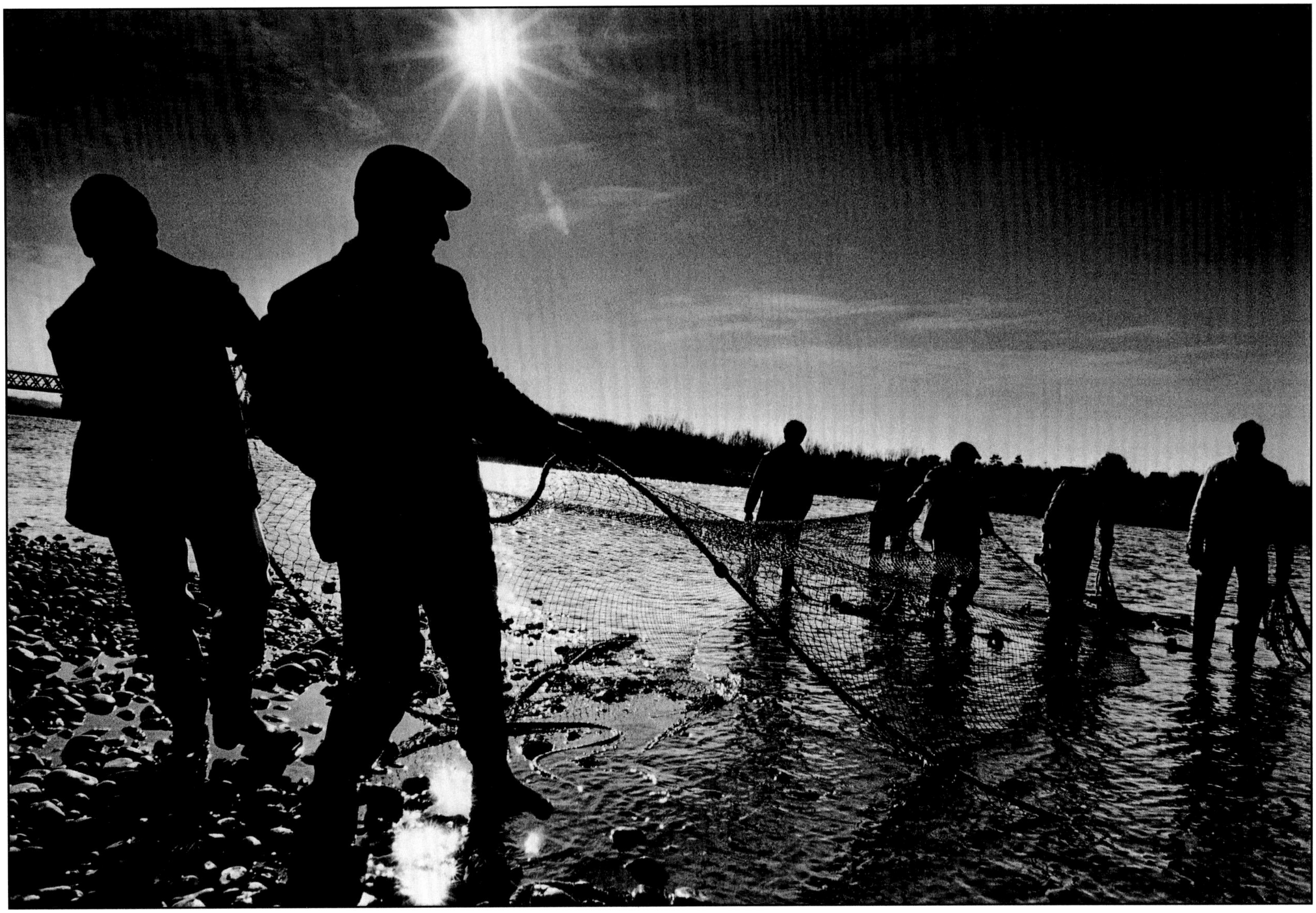

58.

Henry Cecil & Sheikh Mohammed

1988, Dubai

Sheikh Mohammed, one of the world's most powerful racehorse owners, took top UK racehorse trainer Henry Cecil for a camel ride at the start of a lavish party during the trainers annual visit to the UAE.
I had interviewed Henry Cecil as an *Off Duty* subject some time before and was delighted when he invited me to join him on his camel expedition in the desert. It was great fun.

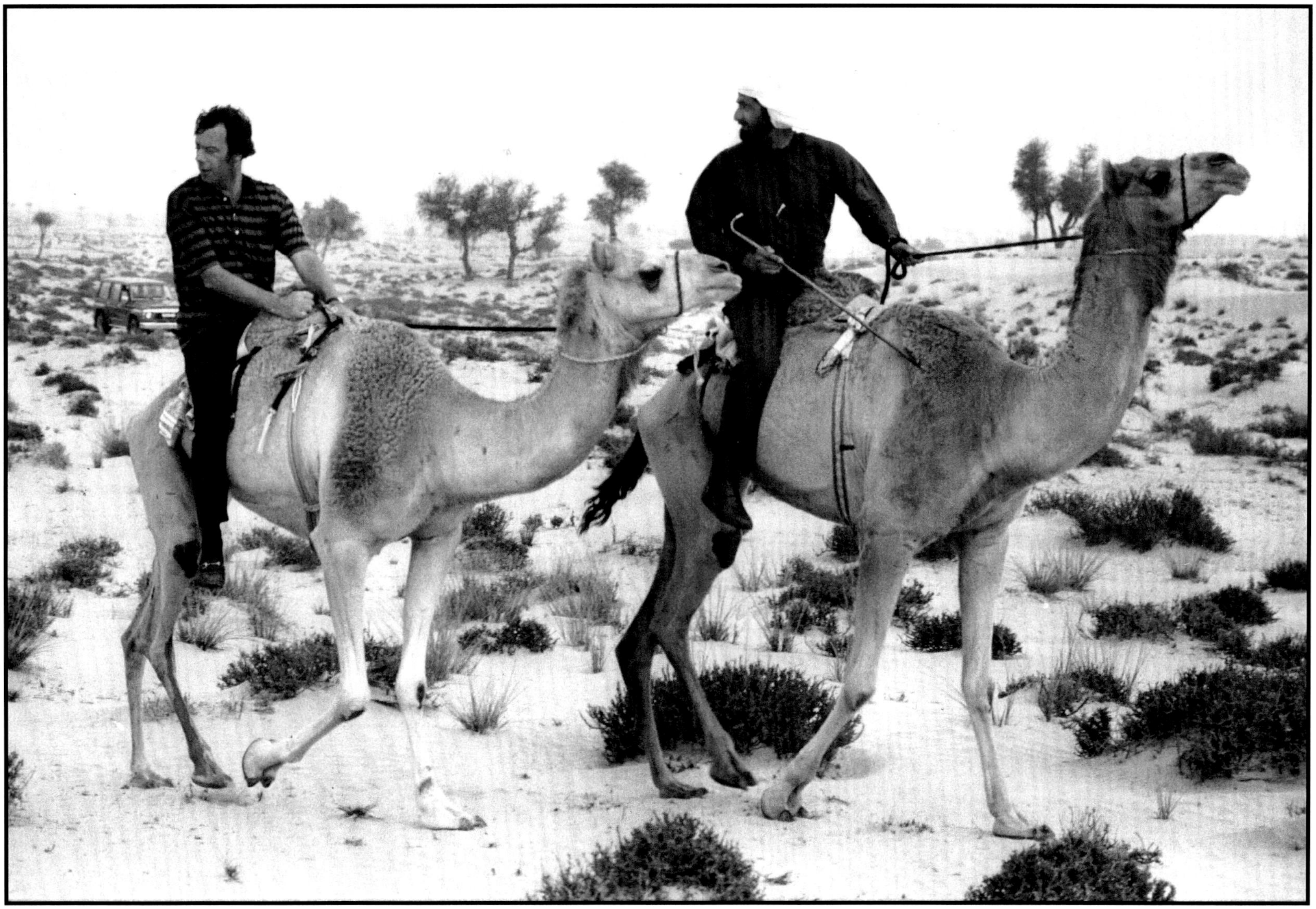

59.

Rhum Pony

1989, Inner Hebrides

The Isle of Rhum in the Inner Hebrides, off the west coast of Scotland, is the home of the famous Rhum pony. The terrain on the island is steep and these sturdy little ponies are used during the annual deer stalking season to bring the carcasses off the mountain, a picture that would be timeless.

I waited on the mountain top for two hours for this picture. The tail end of a hurricane had hit the island and high winds and torrential rain made taking pictures extremely challenging. I sheltered in a cave until eventually I caught sight of this girl leading a pony with a dead stag strapped to its back. In the short time I took to leave the cave to take pictures, I was soaked to the skin. I only managed to get two or three shots, but in those brief moments my camera also got a soaking.

Returning to *The Times* darkroom in London, I took the 35mm film cassette from the camera and, with the light off, tried to remove the film but heard the sickening noise of the emulsion ripping from the celluloid. Unbeknownst to me, the rain had not only penetrated my camera but also the cassette. I carried on with the developing process to discover that large pieces of emulsion had, indeed, ripped off. Photoshop didn't exist then. Heavy retouching by hand, a skill in itself, was necessary to disguise the missing pieces of the picture. A problem that would not be encountered in today's digital world.

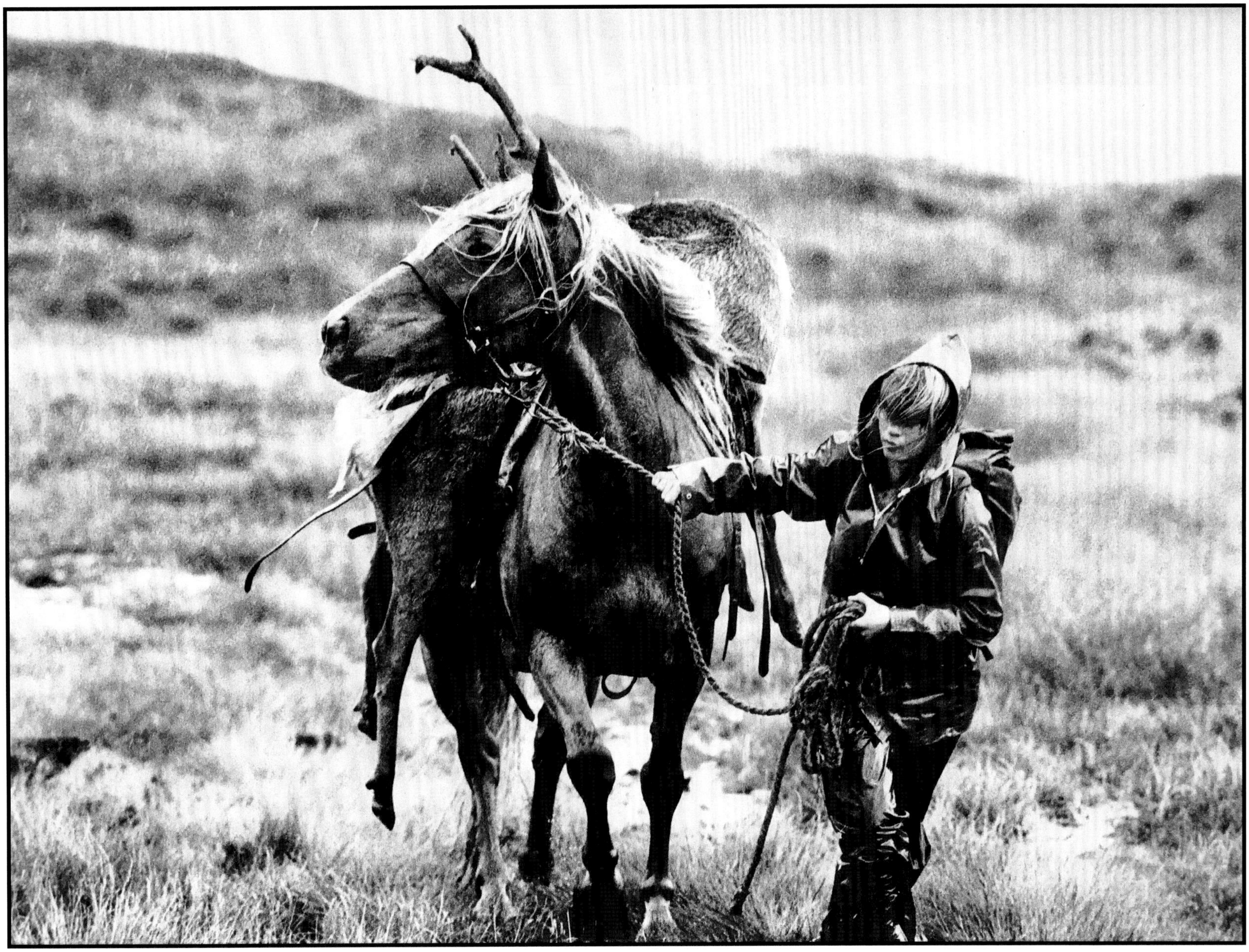

60.

Kruzenstern

1989, The Baltic

Working for *The Times*, I enjoyed some of the finest photographic opportunities imaginable. In 1989 the spectacular Tall Ships Race was going to be attended by one of the world's largest sailing ships. The famous four masted Russian windjammer 'Kruzenstern' was to compete in the race and I was to join them on their epic voyage to England, where they were to prepare for the race. Wow - what an incredible opportunity that was! The 376 ft.(114.5 m) ship was built in 1926, and I was absolutely overwhelmed by its size. With four masts, thirty one sails and and a crew of two hundred and fifty seven, it was spectacular.

As this was just three years after Glasnost and Perestroika, which led to the start of the break up of the Soviet Union in 1986, being allowed on this Russian Navy sail-training ship was indeed a unique experience. I approached the assignment with a degree of trepidation, but it took no time at all for me to relax and really enjoy the journey. The Captain and crew were incredibly welcoming. In fact it would be no exaggeration to say they gave me true VIP treatment. I was spoilt for choice with picture opportunities. The captain had given me complete freedom and assigned his officers to carry out all my wishes. If I wanted the ship in full sail, I only had to ask and the entire crew would spring into action. I was invited to dine at the Captain's table every night and I was bowled-over by the hospitality.

I still can't believe what happened as we sailed across the Baltic on our journey. One evening, over dinner, the Captain asked if I was happy with everything and if I was getting the photographs I wanted.

'Of course', I said, 'You have all been wonderful'. He then asked if there was anything more that I needed. 'Well', I said, 'The one picture I don't have of course, is the ship in sail taken from a distance'. 'We can fix that for you', he said. 'Be on the main deck at 9.00 o'clock in the morning'. Would you believe it, he slowed the ship down, instructed me to climb into one of the lifeboats, gave me a walkie-talkie and we were launched into the ocean! He had told me to radio him on the bridge and tell him exactly what I wanted - full sail, into the sun, against the sun... I have to be the only non-Russian ever to command a Russian Navy ship!

The weather was kind to us, and after I'd shot enough material, I could truly relax. A net was tied to the underside of the bowsprit of that majestic vessel. I suppose it was for one of the sails. I made that my 'nest' for the remainder of the journey. Lying there, sunbathing, ten or fifteen feet out from the ship, overhanging the ocean was an amazing experience. Looking back at 3,900 metres of sail billowing in the wind was breathtaking to say the least.

If all that wasn't enough, there was even more to come. Our first stop on our journey was a call into the Port of Liverpool. As we approached the centre of the city, I decided to climb high up one of the masts, and out onto one of the spits for a birds-eye view of events. We were enjoying a fabulous civic reception, and as we sailed slowly past the iconic Liver Building there was a brass band welcoming us.

What a great assignment, what a great memory!

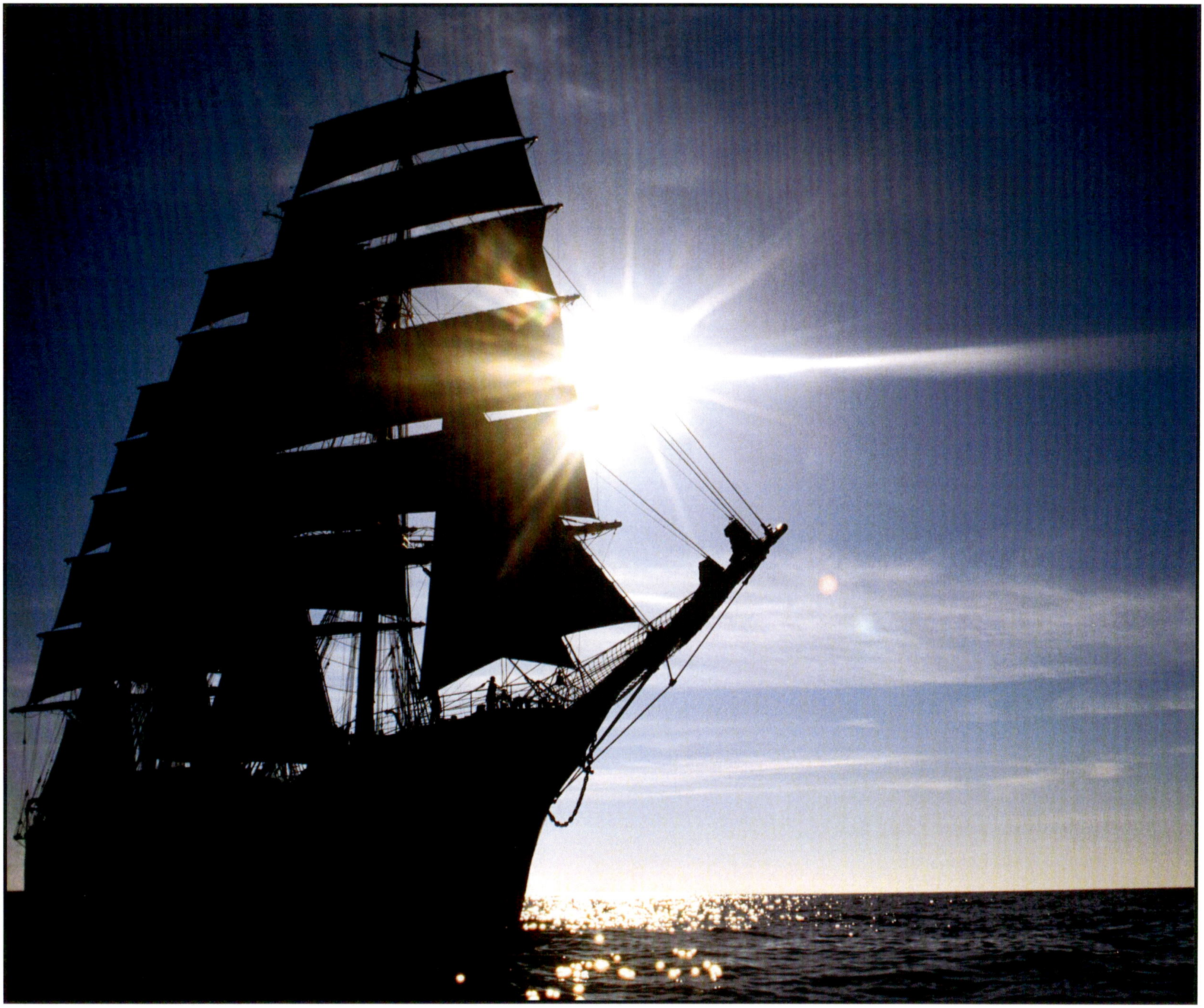

61.
Card Game
1990, Naples

Assignments for *The Times* travel section were very enjoyable, but sometimes challenging as well. I was working on a major Italian travel feature and spent a couple of days in Naples and I wanted to take some atmospheric shots in the back streets.
To my surprise, the Tourist Office insisted on arranging an armed guard for my protection whilst working there.

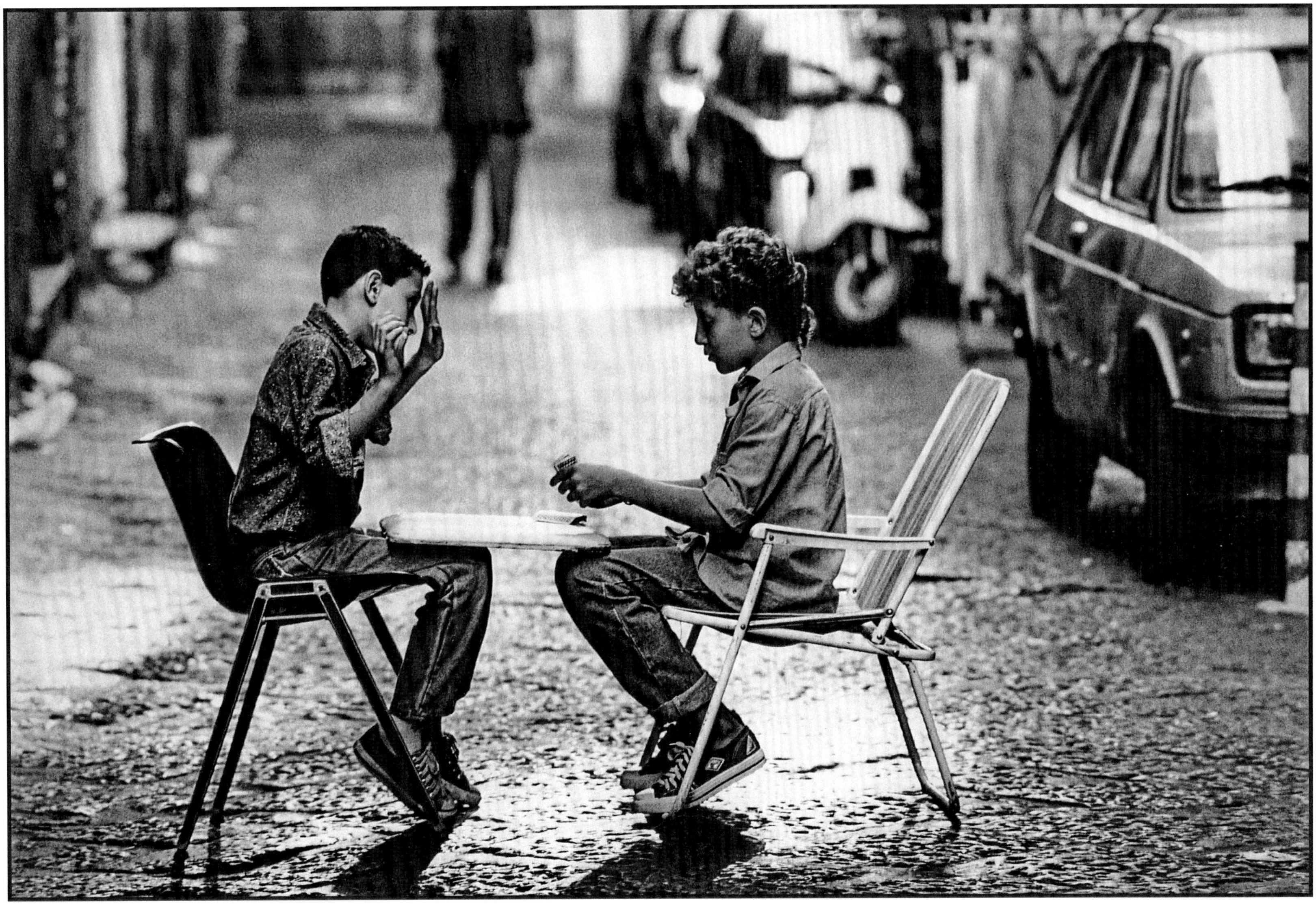

62.

Oxcart

1990, India - on the road to the Taj Mahal, Agra

So many picture opportunities in this wonderful country, I couldn't resist stopping my car for this shot.

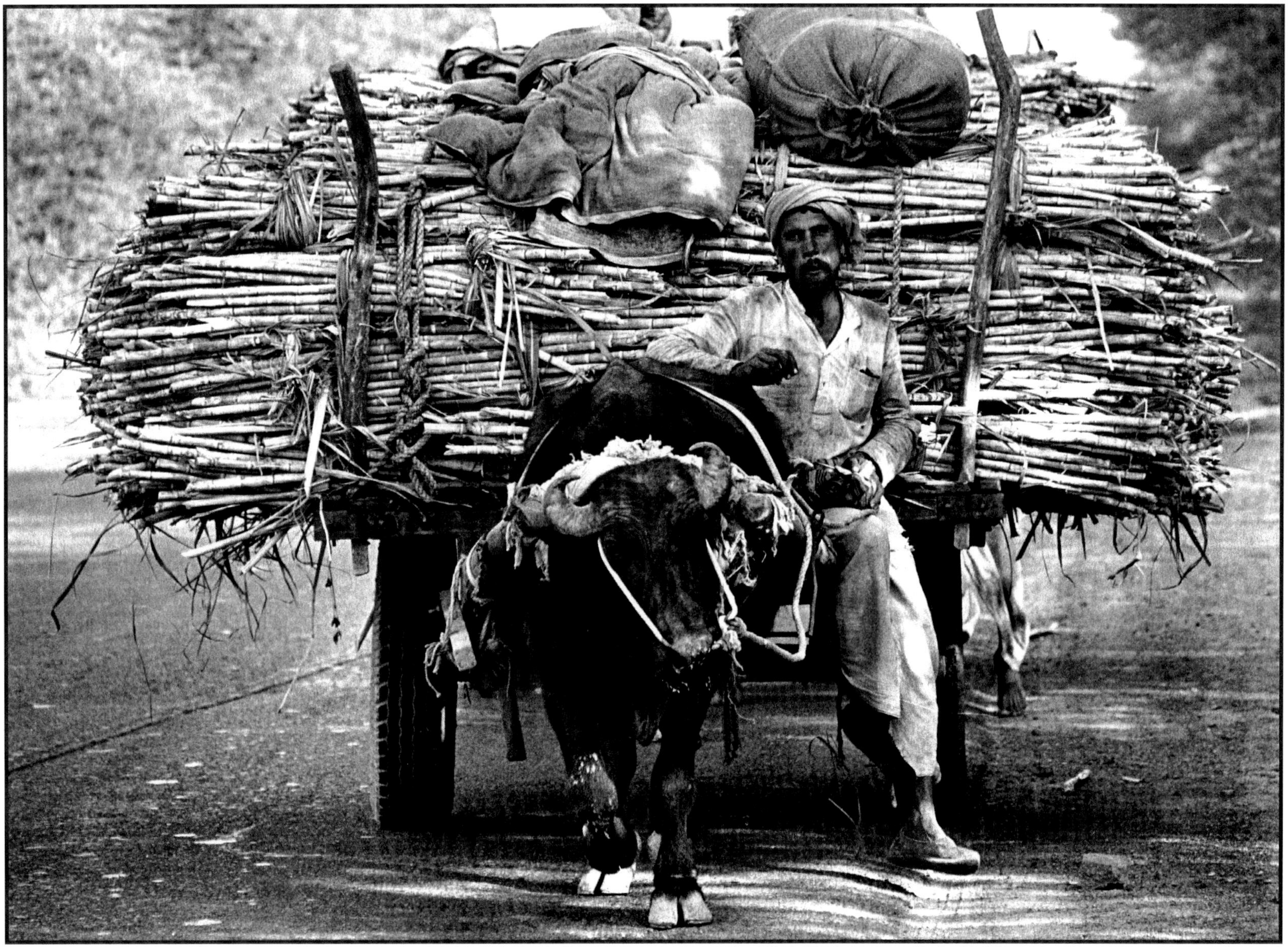

63.

Temple Woman

1990, Nepal

Major Hindu and Buddhist temples or their innermost sanctums are usually off-limits to non-believers, who are a possible cause of ritual pollution. I was allowed in and respectfully removed my shoes before entering. I left a few rupees in the donation box.

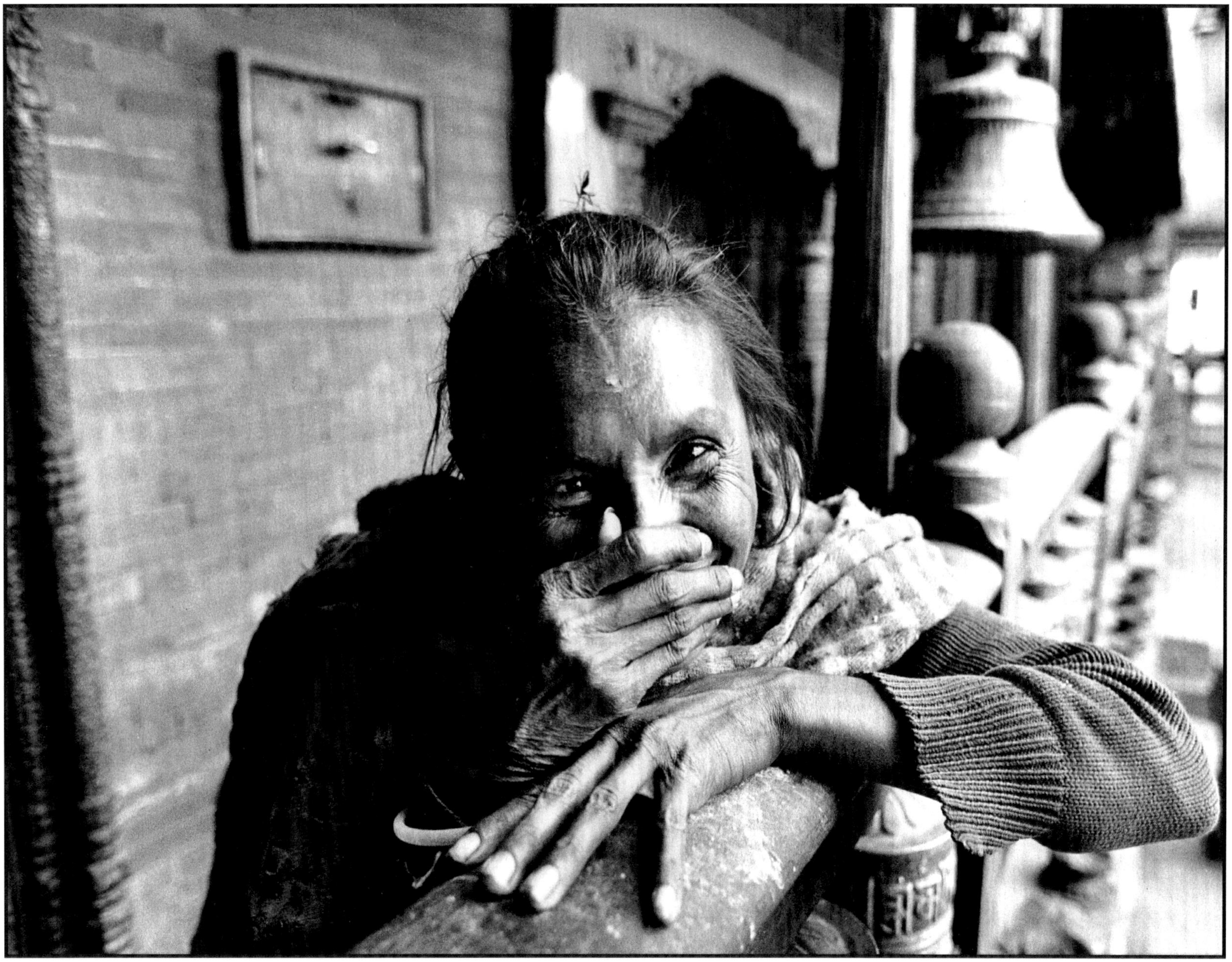

64.

Pipe Smoker

1990, Kathmandu, Nepal

I love this character portrait. The strong smell of his 'tobacco', which I was invited to try, left no secrets…

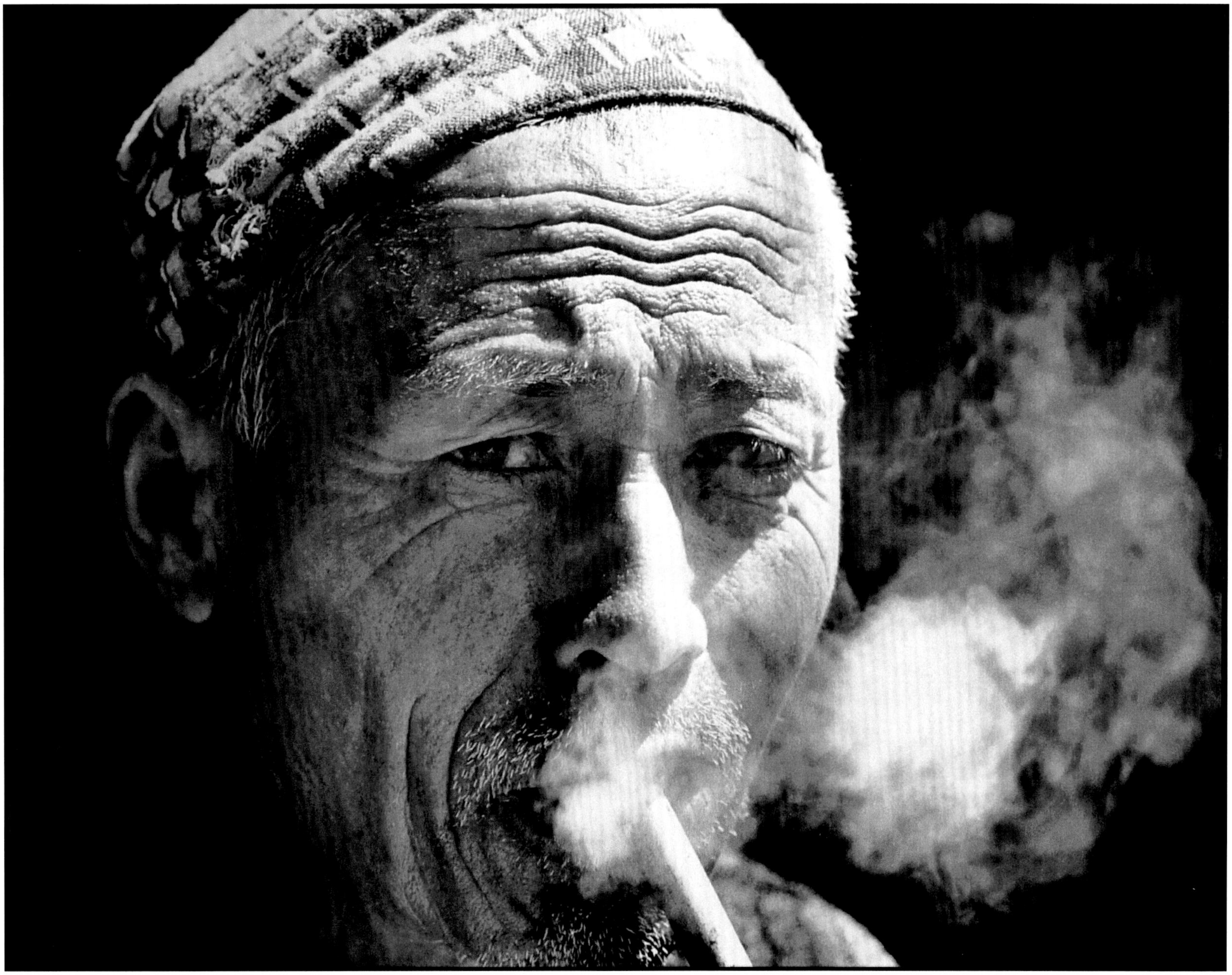

65.

Maintenance Man

1990, Bermuda Airport

Whilst on assignment in Bermuda for the travel pages I spotted this maintenance man complete with gold tooth and beret covered in cobwebs. What a wonderful smile!

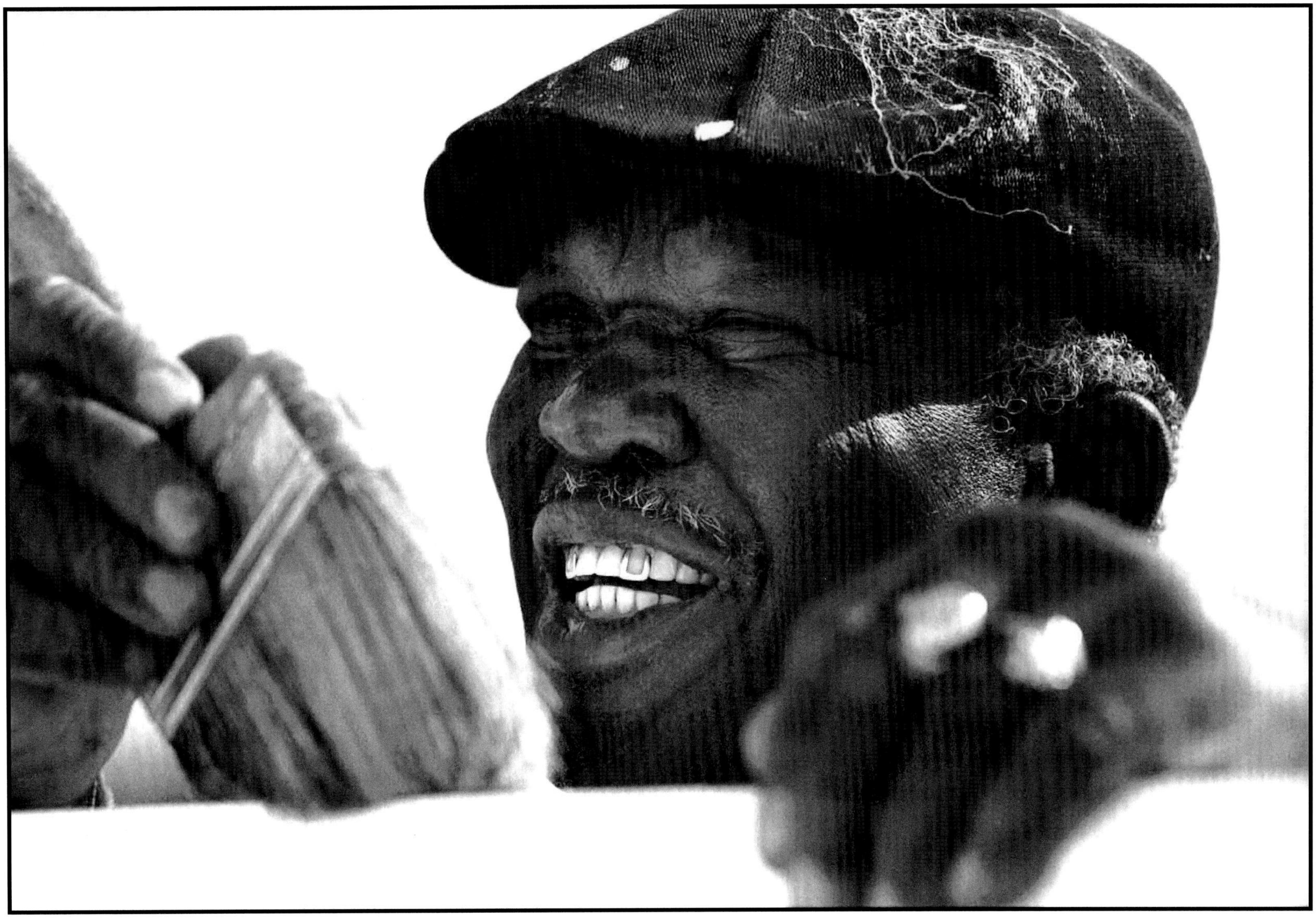

66.

Chicken in a Basket - Egyptian Style

1990, Cairo

Chicken in a basket was a popular bar snack in my local pub but quite different to this!

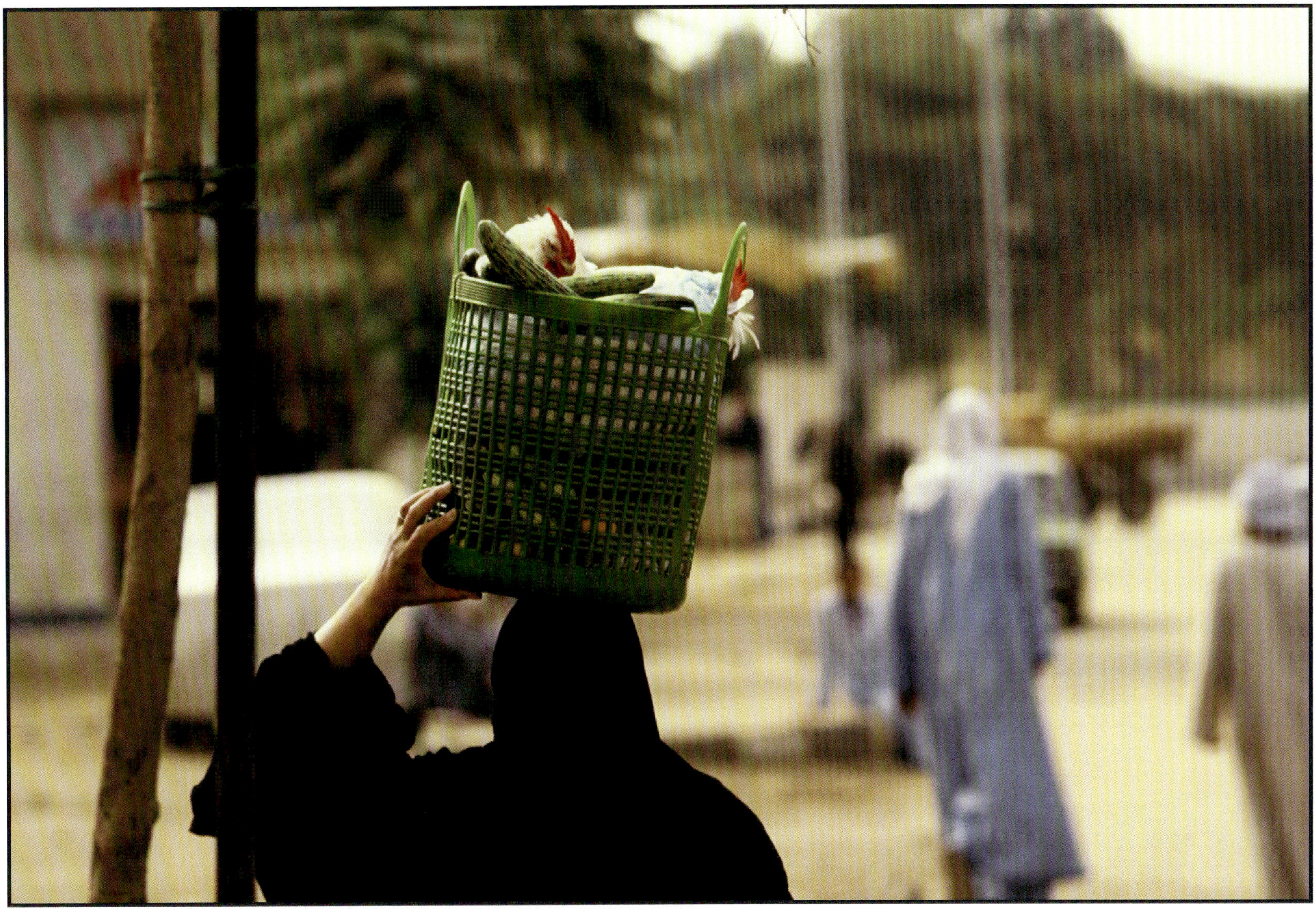

67.

Shoeshine Man

1990, Rome

Travel page pictures are not all about famous landmarks which don't convey any sense of local character. This unwilling subject gifted me an amusing shot.

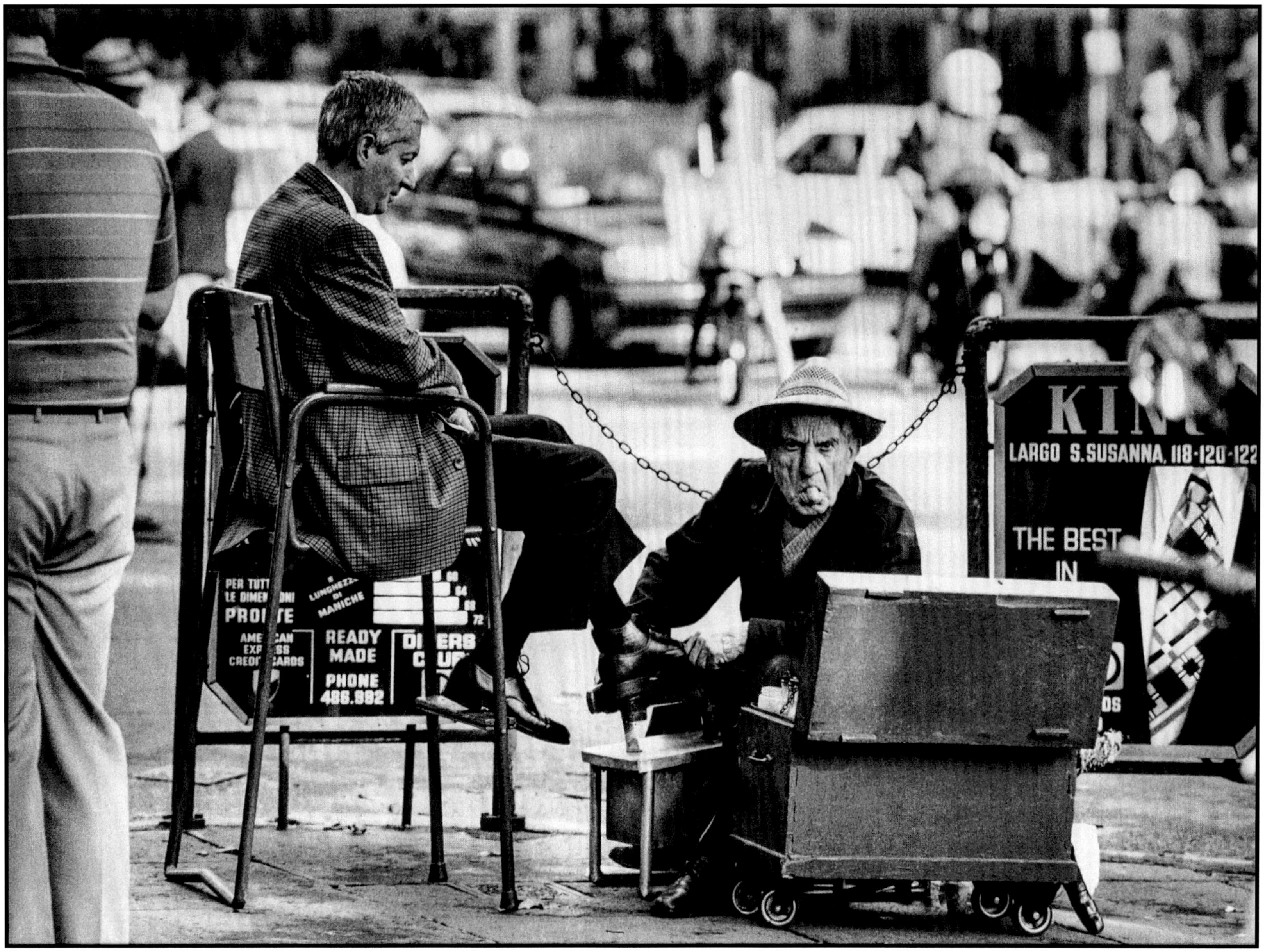
LARGO S.SUSANNA, 118-120-122
THE BEST
IN
READY
MADE
PHONE
486.992
MANICHE

68.

Balloon Man

1990, Barcelona

A grumpy face and colourful balloons don't seem to go together, but they produced a shot I couldn't resist!

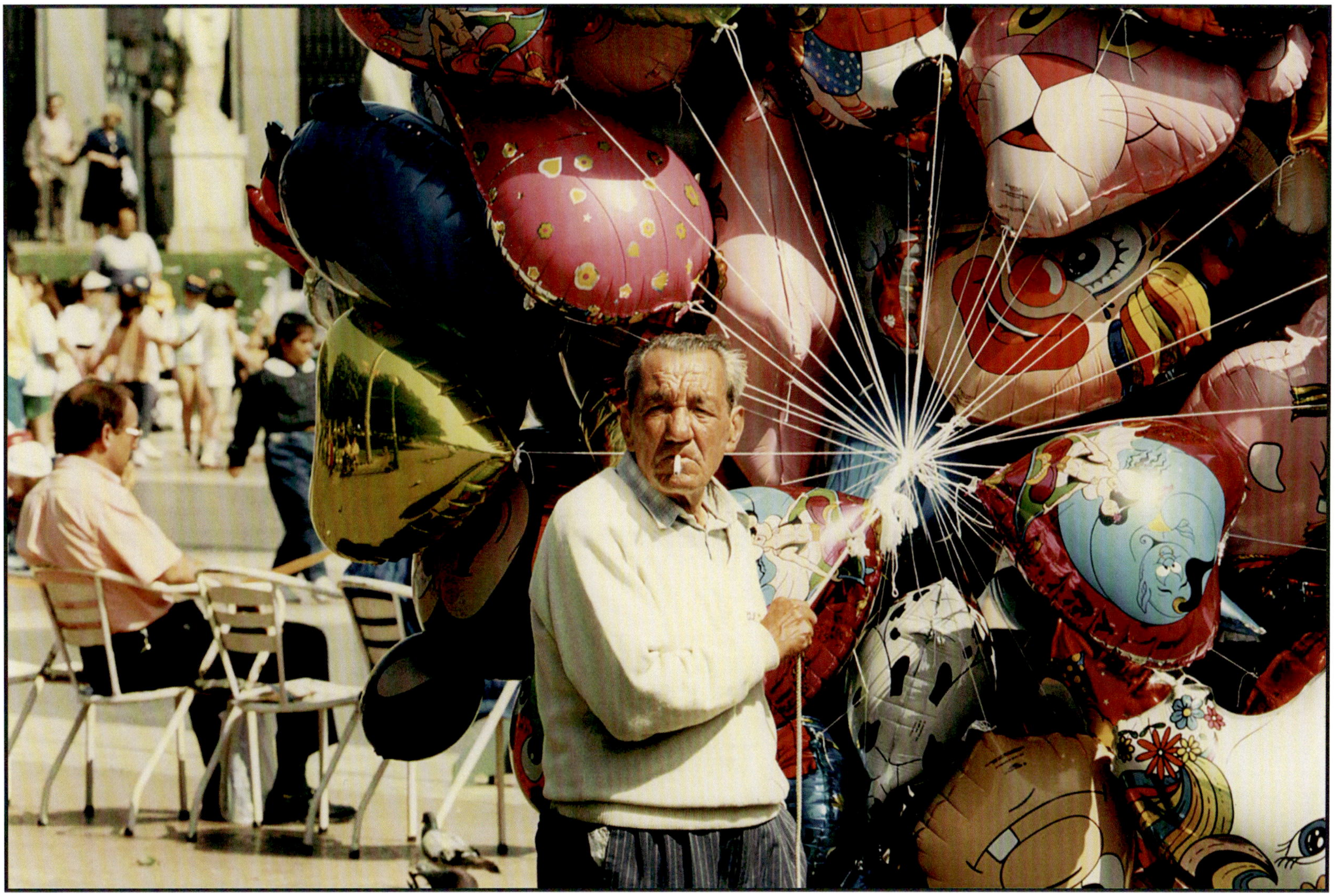

69.

Camel Jockey

1990, Dubai

Camel racing in the Middle-East is a popular sport.
I took this picture of a jockey with his steed at the Camel Derby in Dubai, UAE, where I was a guest of His Highness Sheikh Mohammed bin Rashid al Maktoum.
It seems to be an amazing talent to be able to stay aboard a camel when racing at speed, but the secret? Velcro patches on the saddle and the jockey's breeches!

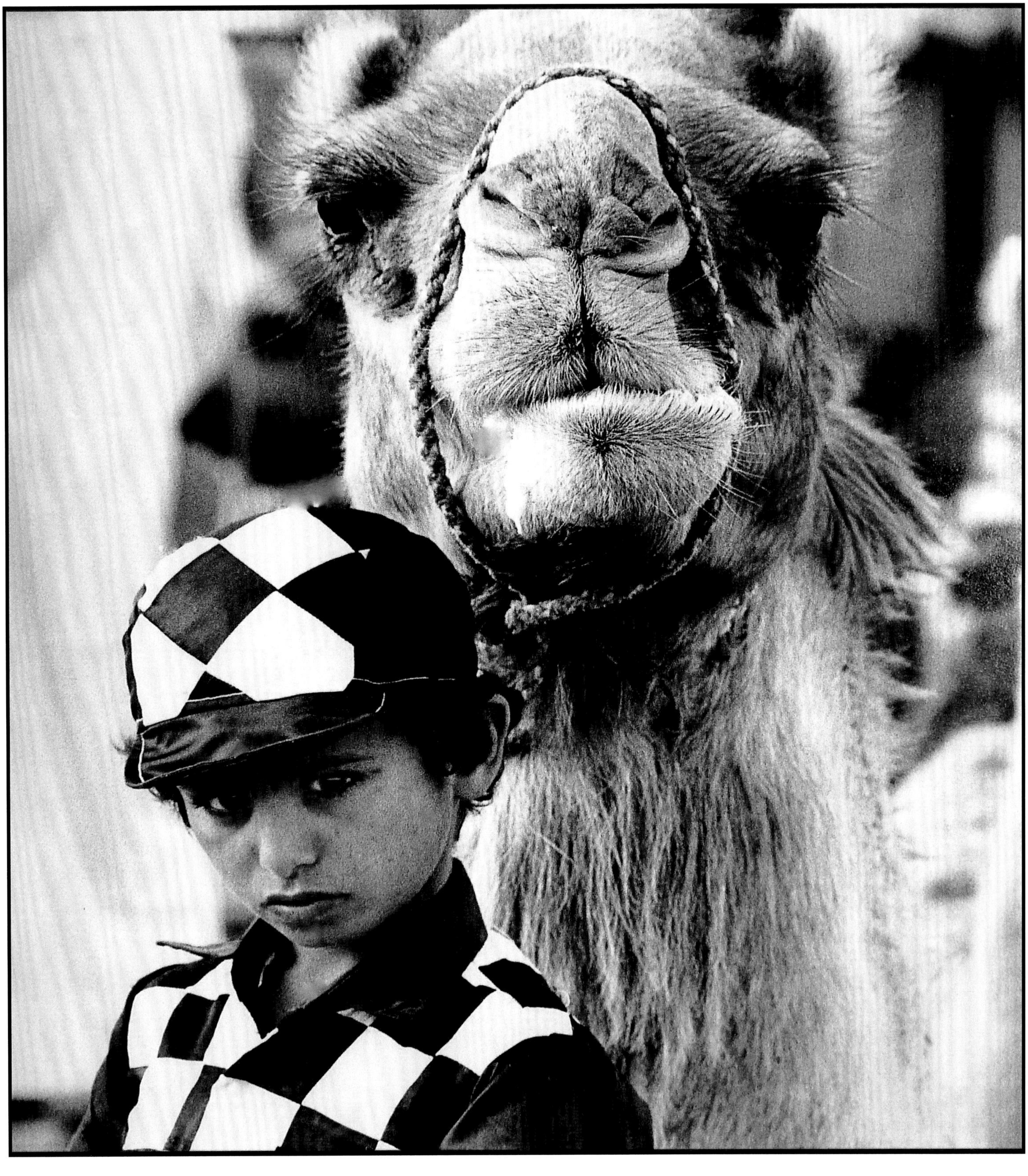

70.

Grouse Hawking

1991, Scottish Highlands

The ancient sport of using hawks to catch prey is not only still carried out in some Arab countries, but can also be found in the form of grouse hawking in the Highlands of Scotland.

I love country sports and was always interested in researching and photographing the action

Some phrases in common usage originate from this dramatic sport. The falconer is accompanied by a ghillie, who carries the hawks on a 'cage' suspended around his waist. The birds wear hoods to keep them calm. When the falconer wants a hawk he asks the ghillie to pass one from the 'cage', which is where the expression to 'cadge' something comes from. The sport involves using pointers, which are released onto the grouse moor to sniff out any birds. They are trained not to disturb them, but to go 'on point' signalling to the falconer that grouse have been found. The falconer 'cadges' a bird in readiness, removing the hood. (The remaining hawks keep their hoods on to avoid disruption if they see another hawk being flown. Hence the expression to 'hoodwink'). Using a dog whistle, the falconer signals to the hounds to move in and 'flush-out' the birds. The hawk is released and instinctively flies above the grouse then dives at amazing speed to catch one, killing it in mid-air. Spectacular!

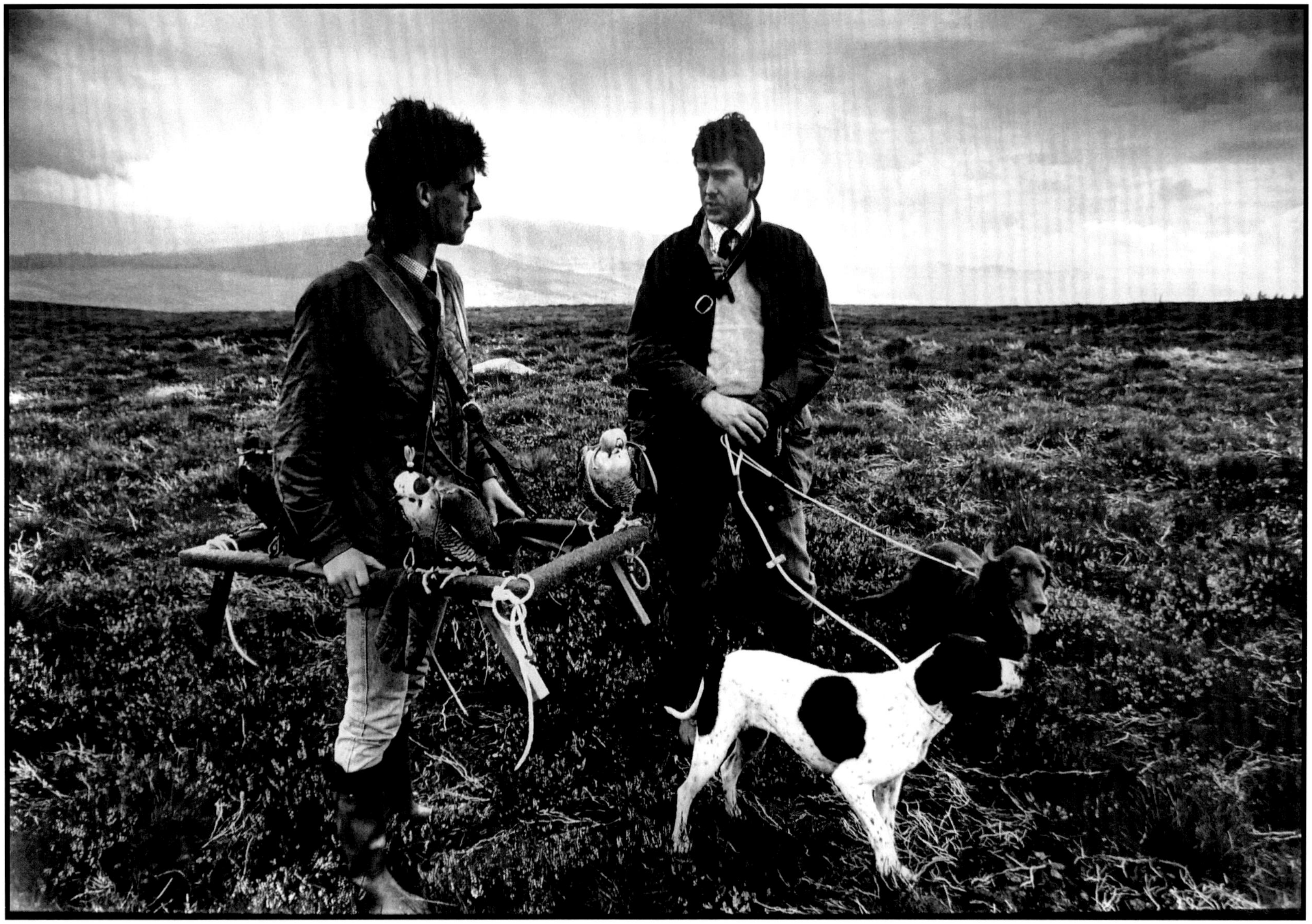

71.
Red Square
1991, Moscow

Not long after my epic adventure with the Russian Navy, I organised a trip to the USSR as there were some interesting stories I'd researched, particularly the aftermath of the nuclear disaster at Chernobyl. It wasn't going to be at all easy. In spite of the advent of Glasnost and Perestroika, the 'Iron Curtain' was still down and I would have to pad-out my itinerary to make it seem that tourism was the main focus, but I liked a challenge and so set my mind to organising what was to be quite an eventful trip.

During the Cold War it wasn't a question of just going to a travel agent and booking flights and hotels. The authorities would only allow travel to be applied for and organised by their own 'travel agency', Intourist, which I suspect was just a front for the KGB.

It was further complicated as I was not travelling direct from London but had arranged to enter the USSR through the satellite state of Estonia. I had made good friends with an Estonian State Television cameraman, Kristjan, who had also been on the the Kruzenstern trip, and planned to meet up with him in Tallin, and take some Christmas pictures of the city.

My next locations were in Russia. I had asked Intourist in London to book trains and a hotel in Leningrad for a few days, before going on to Moscow. At the last minute I needed to change my plans and go directly to the capital. In the normal course of events, you would think that it would be quite a simple matter to change travel and hotel bookings. Not in Russia in those days, particularly as a member of the foreign press.

In order to re-arrange my plans I had to go to the Intourist desk in my Tallin hotel. At first I was told it was not possible. I asked why, and the more I questioned, the more emphatic the Intourist agent became. I insisted, explaining that I needed to get to Moscow as soon as possible and no longer had time to include Leningrad in my itinerary. 'We can't guarantee a hotel at short notice' was the excuse. 'Why can't you telephone and ask?' I said. Then I was told the phone lines were down, the telex machines weren't working, and every reason under the sun. By this time it was a battle of wills. Realising that I wasn't going to be a push over, the girl spent the next half an hour making calls (on the telephone that didn't work), and eventually I was told that I could now go directly to Moscow.

Meanwhile, I needed to buy a new rail ticket. 'Which class would you like?' I was asked. 'I thought Russia was a classless society', I said. 'There are four classes of travel actually', came the reply. Tongue in cheek, I said I would take First Class, and blow me down if that isn't what she issued!

Kristjan took me to the station, well, more of a railway siding, with no platforms. I climbed up the steep iron steps of the train to find my sleeping cabin. Backwards and forwards I went, confused as I knew that I was in the right carriage, but it didn't seem right. Confused because my cabin had two beds. It transpired that 'First Class' meant sharing with just one other person, and the other classes with increasingly more!

I made myself reasonably comfortable, wondering who my travel companion would be. Not long before my trip, I had seen some great pictures Lord Snowdon had taken at a fashion shoot in Moscow using local models. Well, if I was lucky, it might be one of those as they were absolutely gorgeous. On the other hand, maybe I would get a 'Brunhilda' ... No prizes for guessing which one I got. She spoke quite good English and seemed pleasant enough, telling me that she was a travel agent.

Our bunks were side by side and we sat talking about not very much, until a steward announced that the dining car

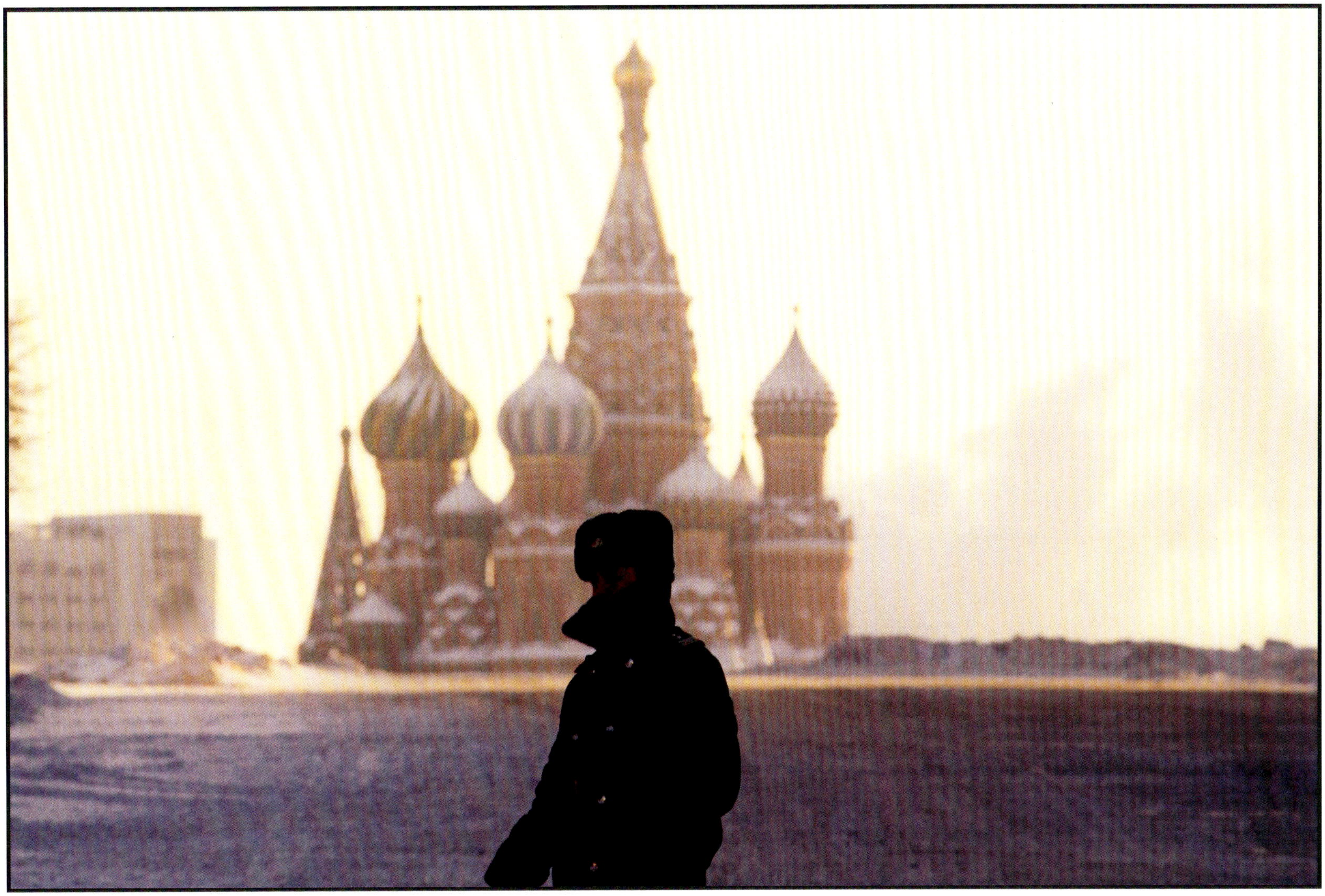

was open. I couldn't wait, I had ideas of 'Orient Express' style luxury dining with a nice bottle of wine. My cabin companion asked where I was going and tried very hard to dissuade me, producing a whole cooked chicken from a paper bag. I declined politely.

I made my way with great anticipation to the dining car. My naivety became clear, I suppose it could be likened to a refugee ship. It was crowded, and the wooden seats were very uncomfortable. There was no menu, you got what you were given (and it was awful), and there was no alcohol either, just a glass of water. I returned somewhat crest-fallen to my cabin, where I was greeted with a wry smile. My travel companion had saved me a chicken leg, for which I was more than grateful.

However, I was presented with an embarrassing scenario. She was lying in 'Rubensian' style on her bunk in her underwear, complete with an old fashioned pink corset. I wondered if she was trying to compromise me in some way. I went to bed with my clothes on!

The overnight sleeper arrived in Moscow, where the snow was falling heavily. I packed my things, collected my camera bag, and said farewell to my travel agent companion. I climbed down onto the platform and looked over my shoulder. She was talking to a man in a long black leather coat and jack boots. I saw her produce a piece of paper, which he signed, and she immediately got back on the train. It was then that the penny dropped - I was being 'signed' for! For 'travel agent', read KGB. All the fuss at the hotel had been because they had arranged for an agent to shadow me to Leningrad, which all had to be changed.

I started to walk down the platform when my new 'shadow' approached me. Calling my name, he asked me to follow him to his car. I declined, saying that I would get a taxi. It was then pointed out that there were about 50 people in the taxi queue, and he would rather I went with him anyway. In reality I had no choice, so I got into his chauffeur driven black Volga and left it all to fate.

The whole affair was like something from a James Bond film. They took me to my hotel and, by this time on alert, I found a listening device hidden in the radiator in my room. There was another in the door frame, and for sure the telephone was bugged too. I found it a bit intimidating, but on reflection it was all very crude.

The next day I was due to be shown around the city by a guide so that I could take pictures for the travel feature. By this time I didn't trust anyone. I met up with a young girl called Olga who said she was from the Tourist Office. It soon became clear that she was a KGB agent just like my 'companion' on the train. Olga was very pleasant but she never let me out of her sight. In different circumstances I may have been flattered by the attention, but it was clear that I was being shadowed very closely.

I was then scheduled to travel to Chernobyl, where there had been a catastrophic accident at the nuclear power plant in 1986, killing many workers and releasing a cloud of radiation with devastating effect. The disaster had crippled the Soviet economy and I wanted to take a look at how much had been done to secure the plant, and perhaps photograph any evidence of the fall-out. At short notice I was prevented from travelling there. I imagine the authorities were still very sensitive about the episode, and didn't want any further adverse publicity in the UK press. My visit was therefore cut short and I returned to England, without the pictures I went for but with quite a story to tell.

The Other Side of The Lens

1971, On Trend - Fleet Street

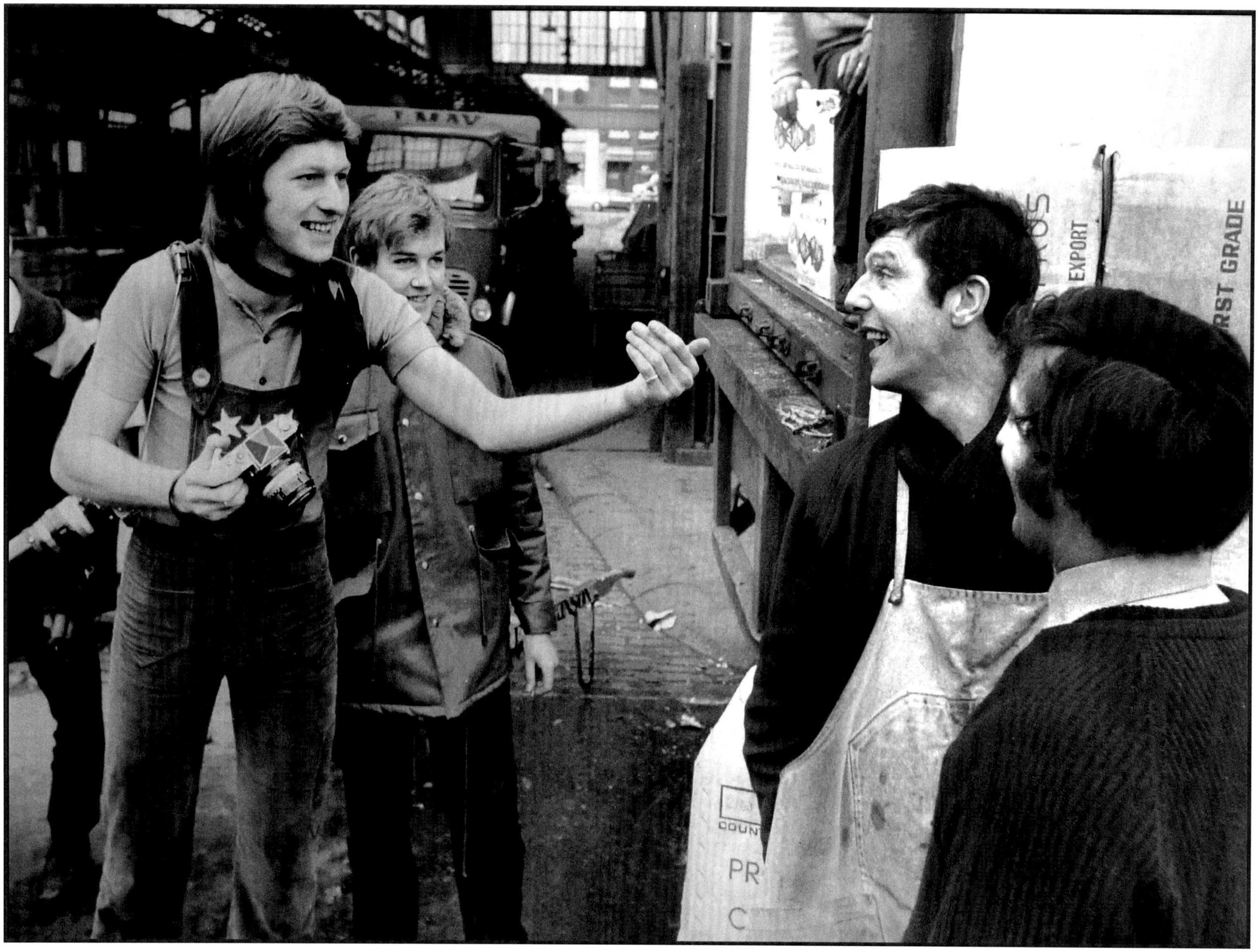

On one occasion I ended up on the 'wrong' side of the camera.
I turned up in the office wearing purple velvet dungarees with pink satin stars on the bib! I think they were a creation from designer Mr.Freedom. When the Fashion Editor Jean Rook saw me, she got very excited and commissioned another photographer to take pictures of me working on location. *The Sun* ran a spread on the fashion page proudly declaring how trendy their photographer was. My wife and children cringe when they see this shot of me!

1979, Nato Exercises in the Arctic Circle

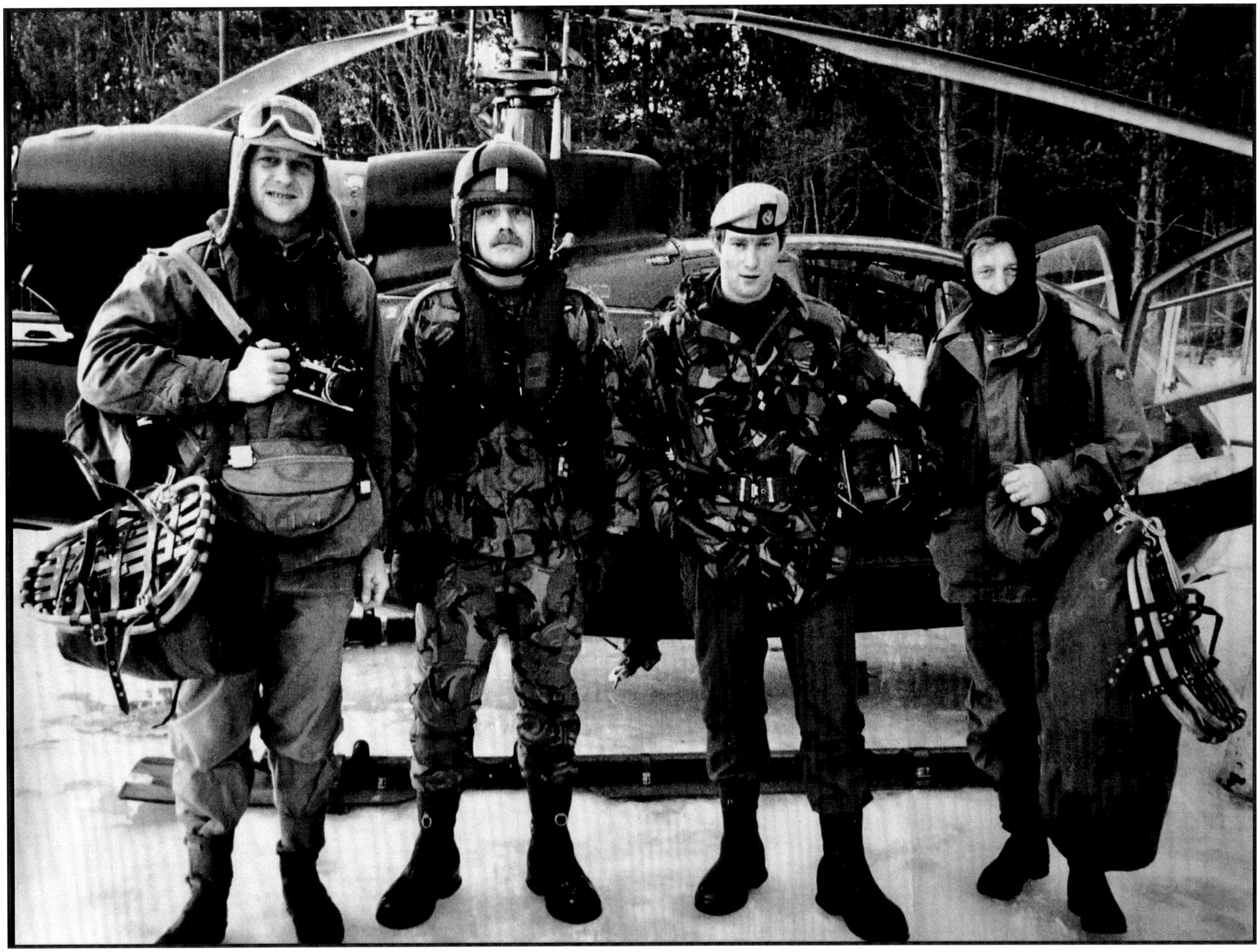

Occasionally, newspapers were invited to spend time with the military, and on one occasion I was sent to join NATO exercises in the Arctic. I equipped myself with some serious thermals to cope with temperatures of -40C. and my cameras were sent away to be 'winterised'. At one point whilst flying over the Hardangerjokulen glacier we spotted a lot of activity and landed to discover that *Star Wars-The Empire Strikes Back* was being filmed there. I took a few pictures but found myself surrounded by 'heavies' who tried to grab my camera. We had a fight in the snow before I managed to get back to the safety of the helicopter.

It's a Dog's Life

Sometimes a good picture is just a case of being in the right place at the right time!

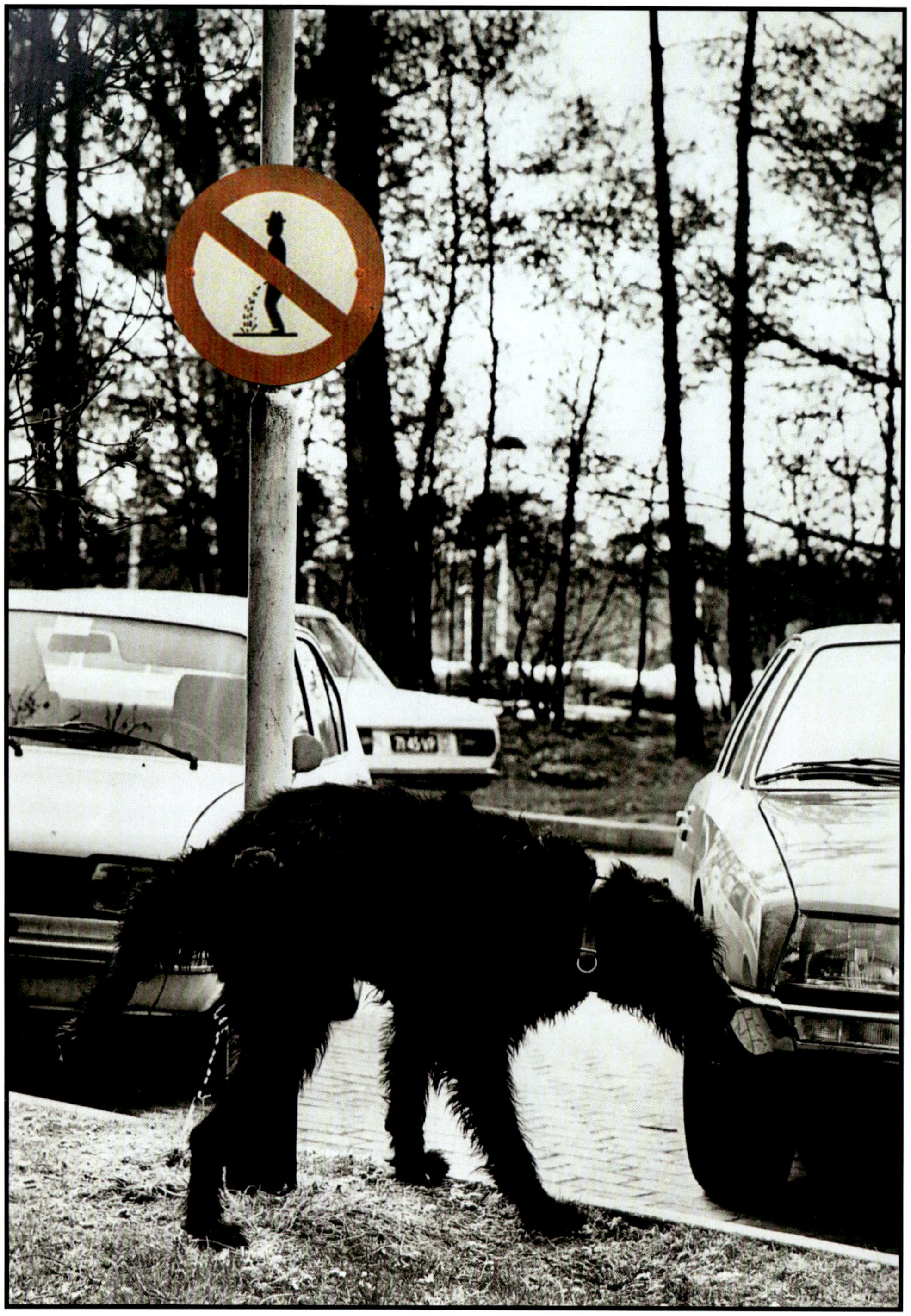

BV - #0056 - 021121 - C14 - 265/265/12 [14] - CB - 9781914424168 - Matt Lamination